CCAR Journal
The Reform Jewish Quarterly

Contents

CONTENTS

CONTENTS

Join the Conversation!

At the Gates — בשערים

In April 1953, under the aegis of Abraham J. Klausner, the CCAR produced the first issue of the Conference journal. Its stated purpose, in part, was to bring to Reform rabbis "reports and other information which will be of interest to you and, perhaps, of assistance in your daily ministrations." From the outset there was a noted tension between being a scholarly journal or a "trade journal." As mentioned in its preface, the actual issue represented a compromise between these two poles. The first issue focused on "The Sermon." Future issues were to (and did) investigate pastoral psychology, education, and prayer. Subscription for a year of issues was set at two dollars. In the winter of 2023 so much has changed, but the *Journal* continues to straddle between scholarly and practical rabbinics. It is hoped that the "reports and other information" we bring still will be of interest to you and, perhaps, of assistance in your daily rabbinates.

I am honored to be the new editor of the *CCAR Journal*, following a tremendous line of editors, editorial board members, contributors, and CCAR staff. This issue offers a few reflective essays in the current state of the Reform rabbinate from the point of view of the rabbis themselves, their experiences, challenges, hopes, and frustrations. (There are also several pieces published that were developed under the aegis of my amazing predecessor as editor of the *Journal*, Rabbi Elaine Rose Glickman. Her outstanding efforts have helped to refine the *Journal* as a tremendous resource for us.)

These past couple of years has challenged us in so many ways. Resilience has gone from being a nice attribute of character to a basic need in surviving. Maintaining our core purpose as rabbis, and keeping our integrity intact, while facing dramatically changed circumstances, should not have to be managed daily, and yet here we are.

Burnout, or its contemporary cousin, quiet quitting, is endemic to clergy. We are clergy because we want to meet the needs of others. But this also means that burnout is more likely. Especially for mid-career colleagues. Try taking the Maslach Burnout Inventory (MBI)—easy to find online—to see your level of burnout. These days clergy are not necessarily *needed* for anything, and for those of us who want to be needed, what does this mean? Also, how do we measure success? When we add helping people in their trauma, confidentiality, the multiple hats we wear, and the general intensity of our loves, how can we not be suffering?

Recent studies show that the biggest reason for work burnout are unmanageable work loads, lack of support from management, insufficient rewards, and lack of burnout recognition. There indeed is so much in our work beyond our control. But the question remains: What change in perspective will help us become more alive and thrive in this new and strange environment? What can we learn from the past and what shall we take into the future?

In this issue we begin with an essay from the current CCAR president, Lewis Kamrass, which is how the 1953 issue began. Lewis was asked to write not because of this precedent but because during his presidency he has put the health of the rabbi at the forefront of our Conference concerns. His eloquence evokes the timeless as well as the timeliness of our need for support and balance in our rabbinates. We feature an essay as well from Ellen Lewis on the inner workings of our desire for success, followed by personal accounts of colleagues on the meaning they have found in their long careers or short, second careers.

In the realm of scholarship, we offer selections on political insights from Esther, ancient Egypt, and interfaith dialogue, as well as the nature of repentance. Several book reviews are included as well, the majority of which focus on current issues faced by us and our people. Finally, some wonderful poems are included.

Please let me know what you think of our latest issue and any ideas for future ones. I am so grateful to those who have led the *Journal* before me, our editorial board, and the CCAR Press leadership, for the great assistance in providing for you this link in the chain of CCAR expression, from 1953 to today.

Correction

The correct attribution for the author of the "rope theory of Jewish history" in Rabbi Leigh Lerner's recent article, "Why Is the Jewish Family Complicated? Ask Jacob" (Fall, 2022) belongs to the Adolph S. Ochs Emeritus Professor of Jewish History at HUC-JIR, Michael A. Meyer, who brought forth the concept in the introduction to his book, *Ideas of Jewish History*.

Rabbi Edwin Goldberg, Editor

Articles

The Rabbinate as Career:
Challenges and Opportunities

Reflections of a Rabbinate

Rabbi Lewis Kamrass

One of the privileges of serving as president of the CCAR is the window I am afforded to better understand the lives of so many rabbis. I have benefited from a unique perspective of the rabbinate from the many individual conversations of both anguish and joy with colleagues. While each conversation is a zoom lens into the life of one rabbi, the larger tapestry of those many stories provides a wide-angle perspective that transcends the pain or the joy of each of us. Reflecting on our experiences, as well as our hopes and our anxieties for today and tomorrow, I can say that we all feel the uncertainties of a rapidly changing landscape and shifting sands beneath our feet. Whether we have been rabbis for five decades or for five years, the rabbinate today is significantly different from the one into which we entered.

And there is little doubt as to why! The world around us, and the Jewish world that we inhabit, has experienced rapid and dramatic changes. What was once certain and clear can no longer be relied upon. The trust that people once had in clergy, congregations, and institutions has eroded. Patterns of how people spend their time are ever shifting. We now work in an on-demand, customized culture where people want things done their way, and have little patience for when that may not be possible. Even more, Jewish life and the synagogue are often now seen as a consumer item to be "used" for what it provides to the individual, rather than viewed

RABBI LEWIS KAMRASS (C85) is the senior rabbi of the Isaac M. Wise Temple in Cincinnati, Ohio, and serves as the current president of the CCAR.

as a vessel of community to be supported and valued for its own sake. For rabbis who entered the rabbinate to bring people *toward* Judaism, we found ourselves consistently swimming against the current in a society that was increasingly detaching and moving *away from* institutional life and organized religion. Then came the diminished trust in clergy that was caused by the ethical lapses and abuse of a few clergy, yet making headlines, and eroding the credibility that previously served as the cornerstone of our work. And we dare not underestimate the pervasive influence of societal toxic polarization that permeated every corner of society in this last decade, a large barrier that inevitably swept into our congregations and institutions. All around us people feel free to make rash judgments of others, refusing to look beyond their own perspectives, unable to engage in civil conversations or productive disagreement. As rabbis, every day we heroically endeavor to bridge an ever-widening gulf between groups, trying to keep community stitched together as it was tearing itself at its seams, frustrated or discouraged when our efforts were unsuccessful.

Whatever major shifts had not been brought about by society, the pandemic came to accelerate the pace of changes and bring increased demands. Like many professionals, particularly those in organizations or small businesses, rabbis were confronted overnight with stretched resources and greater demands of daily work, including managing technology and complex logistics, even while the pastoral needs increased with so many people's heightened fears and vulnerability. We daily experience the burdens of care for others that are without boundaries of timeframe. Even physicians have days when they are off call, when their personal family life is not disrupted by emergencies or urgent needs. When does the rabbi find the time for self, for family, and for friends? It is the role of clergy to often absorb the pain of others—often late to awareness of what that does to us, and often not permitting ourselves to recognize the aching weariness of our own souls until we reach the point of depletion and even burnout.

So, if the rabbinic soul may be weary, why continue in this sacred but often demanding work? One answer would be that it is what we are trained for; we need to feel of service and to be needed, as we clearly are. Yet perhaps a deeper answer is that almost whispered calling that we glimpse when we make a deep connection with a student, or support and strengthen a family in grief, or

guide a person journeying through illness, loneliness, or vulnerability. When we help others find strength in what they receive
from our tradition, we are connected with what "called" us. We see
that glimpse in the note of gratitude we receive, the deep appreciation that cannot find adequate words, but that is expressed on the
face and in the eyes of someone, or when a person says, "Rabbi,
you [read: and my Judaism] were there for me when I most needed
help." That is more than feeling needed or fulfilled; it is indeed an
echo of that whispered calling.

And while we live in unique times, the essential challenges are
not new. Over two thousand years ago, the Sages of the Mishnah
understood the delicate balance required to serve and to lead, to
nourish one's soul while tending to the needs of others. In our own
day, we rabbis strive for that same sense of balance, between deep-
est fulfillment and the burdens of responsibility, between limitless
human needs and the limits of our abilities. It is a timeless question
for any human, but certainly even more important for those of us
dedicated to serving and leading, who challenge the shortcomings
of our society, yet tend to the wounds and pain of the individual.

הוּא הָיָה אוֹמֵר, אִם אֵין אֲנִי לִי, מִי לִי. וּכְשֶׁאֲנִי לְעַצְמִי, מָה אֲנִי.
וְאִם לֹא עַכְשָׁו, אֵימָתַי

He [Hillel] used to say: If I am not for myself, who is for me? But
if I am for my own self [only], what am I? And if not now, when?
(*Pirkei Avot* 1:14)

To change the sequence of this wisdom: *If I am only for myself, what am I?* We entered the rabbinate to make a difference,
to nurture others, to lead, to serve, and to care for the needs of
the community. This is what drives us in our work, in our desire
to create sacred community, to touch lives, to lead communities,
and to teach Torah. We come to our tasks with deep hearts and
for most of us, on most days, we truly know the deep sense of
reward that the rabbinate uniquely brings. Most of us could not
imagine a more fulfilling career! We are blessed with the anchor
of tradition, the creativity we bring to the needs of today, the care
we provide to others, the intellectual and spiritual stimulation
of our study with which we are nourished. At our core, we want
to teach, to serve, to lead, to guide, and to stand with those in
need. Most jobs are far less satisfying, and even most professions

cannot provide the variety and sense of reward that we rabbis are fortunate to enjoy. Even as every day presents potentially destabilizing challenges, our rabbinates, in whatever role we serve, helps us to know that our sacred work has great meaning and that our lives are about so much more than the narrow confines of being only for ourselves.

The Sages guide us: *If I am not for myself, who is for me?* Navigating our present challenges is not easy, nor is the path easily discerned. With the challenges that accompany the rewards and fulfillment of the rabbinate, shaping a "resilient rabbinate" is the significant question for our time and indeed, for our souls. Who cares for the rabbi? I believe that our institutions and congregations need to critically view themselves and the manner in which the rabbi and other Jewish professionals are treated. If rabbis are to remain in service to Jewish communities and congregations, those bodies need to more clearly see the strains and the stresses, and respond with changed expectations, and a deeper sense of care. If that is to happen, that is a cultural shift that will take some years. But with the need pressing as it is now, I would suggest that even if we are fortunate to work within a collaborative professional team, or know the support of understanding lay leaders, ultimately it is the care for ourselves that most sustains us. While we ought to seek available help from many corners, rabbinic resilience and care begins primarily in our own hands.

While there is no one universal answer for us all, and there are likely generational differences as to what properly constitutes self-care, we have an obligation to consider our self-care as essential resilience. Indeed, self-care is not self-serving. Nourishing ourselves as the resilient rabbi is not only for one's self-interest, not only for the sake of what we can bring to our organizations or congregations, but it is essential even for the benefit of the rabbinate itself, already facing a potential shortage of rabbis. Even more, if Jewish life can flourish only with healthy rabbinic leadership, then more than ever, we need experienced, engaged, and fulfilled rabbis in their work.

And while none of us masters each of these areas of focus at any one time, we would all do well to strengthen the rabbinate and to enrich Jewish life by a deep measure of self-reflection that includes honestly examining where we need work, how we can achieve better balance, and what we must better cultivate to plant deeper roots of resilience. Here are a few areas of introspection and resolve for our consideration:

We need to be genuinely honest with ourselves. Self-awareness does not fall like manna from heaven. It requires much tending in our days and through the years. We need to be more aware of where we are failing, when we are struggling, and where we feel most vulnerable in our rabbinate. None of us can flourish at all that is asked of us, to be sure. But we need to know what is most difficult for us, to identify what personal and professional areas need our attention. We need to seek out ways to build the skills we are lacking, to grow not with mastery or perfection as our goal, but nevertheless, to grow into what we are capable of becoming. Therapists can help us discern what may allow to be hidden from ourselves, and to support us with the fortitude to move beyond today. So too, we need to be the kind of honest friends to one another, who uniquely understand one another's experience, friends, and colleagues who will push us to see what we may not allow ourselves to clearly see.

We need to be more vulnerable in settings of trust. Like Moses, too many of us confuse success with being able to do it all ourselves. It was only when Moses could confide in Jethro, his father-in-law, did he learn to chart a different path, bringing in others to help with tasks too demanding for one person. With those we trust, we need to recognize that seeking help is not a lack of strength, but a deep virtue of leadership. We all could benefit from the courage to be vulnerable in circles of trust, finding that none of us is as unique or as alone as we might think.

Beyond nurturing the soul of others, we need to nourish our own souls. Rabban Gamliel cautioned us in his teaching "do not say: 'when I shall have leisure I shall study'; perhaps you will not have leisure" (*Pirkei Avot* 2:4). In this warning, perhaps he foreshadowed the sometimes-overwhelming demands of the rabbinate that serve to undermine even our most heartfelt or inspired intentions. Finding a *chavruta* partner for regular study is not only a blessing, but a lifeline for continued learning and growth. Exploring the boundaries of one's own spiritual growth is equally important. We cannot coast or get buy on yesterday's knowledge or on spiritual grounding that is not well-tended over changing times and an ever-changing self. We must follow Gamliel's instruction to make this first in our schedules rather than what is left over for the precious spare time that may not appear.

We need to have focus for fulfilling our vision. Most of us end each day having done that which appeared on our calendar for that day; we respond to demands raised, react to issues, and we meet the challenges that arose during that day that had not been anticipated. What often is lost is the importance of our own focus for what we believe to be the priorities for our congregations or organizations. As rabbis who respond to the urgencies of the moment, we must still act upon the importance of what we believe our leadership calls us to do. We need to sift through the urgent needs of the day and to lift up and safeguard the imperatives we know matter. Urgent matters will always get our attention, but the vision and the plans that we can address with our leadership should not be delayed or forgotten. To lose sight of that focus is to distract our direction, and thereby, to diminish our needed sense of fulfillment as leaders.

We need to carve out time for self. Exercise, meditation, and hobbies are not merely activities; days off and vacation time are not merely days on the calendar. Together, these comprise the way we balance the important or urgent demands we feel with the need for self-care. Our tradition gave the gift to the world of Shabbat, a means of seeing time for renewal or pause, not only as utilitarian, but as sacred and prized. Our momentary retreat from our to-do list, from the great needs of so many that we serve, is not to diminish their importance, but to nurture ourselves to better respond to those needs.

We need to always remember that of all the families we serve, our family needs us the most and in the most fundamentally human ways. As much as we rabbis try to be fully present for families in times of need or celebration, so too, we must challenge ourselves to be fully present for the needs of our own family. Most professionals have weekends or evenings for time with their families, so we must find other times and different ways of being known not for our absence, but for our presence, for our care, and for our joy that we share. Our families should have us not when we are tired or depleted, but when we are whole and filled with joy, and a giving spirit of love for them. And we should hold those simple moments of family as sacred as any responsibility we know.

None of us have ever mastered this list! Perhaps we manage to do better with some ingredients of resilience than we did last month or last year. At times what we once mastered has slipped away as we face new demands or circumstances. Balancing is seldom graceful or even sustained over long periods of time. Soul-care and self-care are a thing of the moment. Yet resilience means we always have one eye on our needed focus for today, the balance that we need in this moment, and hoping to achieve in other areas in the future. The resilient rabbi does not get every aspect of balance right, yet such a person is working consistently to embrace one area of balance now, and another area for the future. The resilient rabbi is not simply the rabbi who stumbles and learns to stand again, as all of us will do. Nor is the resilient rabbi the persistent faith leader who refuses to acknowledge the challenges of our day. The resilient rabbi is the one who is ever balancing so many challenges with the deep sense of fulfillment unique to our calling, the one who embraces both the difficulties and the great satisfaction of our work. The resilient rabbi is the one who considers the areas where she/he/they may have stumbled and who stands more confidently, because that rabbi seeks to balance thoughtfully, and to resolutely refine one's habits. The resilient rabbi grows and shapes his/her/their future in the rabbinate, not only in a moment of crisis, but each day, in the way we live our days. We owe that to ourselves, to our family, to our work, and to our calling. And we owe that to one another.

וְאִם לֹא עַכְשָׁיו, אֵימָתַי?

And, if not now, when?

Getting What You Wish For: Jewish Professionals and the Emotional Meaning of Money[1]

Rabbi Ellen Lewis

In 1985, five years after I had been ordained, I moved from Dallas back to my home state of New Jersey. They had done things differently down there in Texas, so I tried to get myself oriented in my new place. When there was a regional meeting of Reform rabbis, I figured that was a good place to begin. I asked what I thought was a simple question, "What do people charge for weddings?" My question was greeted with an uncomfortable silence. Finally, someone bravely made a recommendation: "What if we anonymously write down what we charge on pieces of paper and pass the paper up to Don at the front of the room and he can read out the amounts?" And that's what we did.

When I repeated this story to another colleague, he immediately said, "They are afraid they are undercharging." The other possibility, I thought, is that they are afraid they are overcharging. Whether the conflict manifests itself as insecurity or grandiosity, the need to keep the fees a secret seems to reflect a conflict. What is this about, I wondered, the unwillingness to name themselves and say the figures aloud in front of colleagues? Is it about competitiveness? Is it about shame? Whatever it is, it doesn't have anything to do with money. That doesn't mean that money isn't real, and it doesn't mean that money isn't relevant in the lives of Jewish professionals. But it does mean that we have a lot to talk about before we ever get

RABBI ELLEN LEWIS (C80) is a certified and licensed modern psychoanalyst in private practice in Bernardsville, New Jersey, and New York City. After her ordination at HUC-JIR, she spent over thirty years serving congregations in Dallas, Texas; Summit, New Jersey (named rabbi honorata); and Washington, New Jersey (named rabbi emerita). She now practices full-time as a therapist, supervisor, pastoral counselor, and professional coach.

to the tachlis issue of salaries and negotiation. And what we must talk about is in the emotional realm, especially for those of us who have chosen to earn our livelihood by teaching Torah, whether in the rabbinate, the cantorate, Jewish education, communal service, or academia.

Being paid to teach Torah has always been an emotional issue in our tradition. We have inherited conflicting attitudes. It isn't that we don't believe other Jews deserve to earn a living. The Talmud tells us that over and again.[2] We just aren't sure how teachers of Torah are included in that divine plan. For instance, how should we interpret these oft-quoted words from *Pirkei Avot:* "Do not make the Torah into a crown with which to adorn yourself or a spade with which to dig."[3] Maimonides' commentary on this Mishnah is legendary:

> One who decides that instead of working he will occupy himself with Torah study and live from charity, profanes God's name, disgraces the Torah, extinguishes the light of the law, brings harm upon himself, and removes himself from the World to Come, for it is forbidden to derive benefit from the Torah in this world. Hence the Sages teach: whoever derives benefit from his Torah knowledge removes himself from the world.[4]

Maimonides does make a few exceptions, most notably the following:

> If it is local custom to receive a salary for teaching children, he may receive a salary. This applies only to the teachings of scripture. As for the Oral Law, it is forbidden to teach it for pay, as it is written, 'See I have taught you statutes and judgments as the Lord as commanded me, etc.' Just as I Moses learned gratis from God, so did you learn gratis from me. Thus, in future generations, teach gratis as you learned from me.[5]

The Rambam cites Rav, who says that the payment to teachers is not for teaching Torah per se but for childcare, and Rabbi Yochanan, who says that the payment is for the teaching of cantillation, which again is not teaching Torah per se. To be fair, Maimonides does allow for other benefits that might assist a Torah scholar in earning a living: certain specific tax exemptions, preferential treatment in the marketplace, and investment management.[6]

Maimonides' position was widely accepted although not by everyone. The Rashbatz says that our Mishnah "applies to one who studies Torah for the sake of receiving honor and reward. He who has earned the reputation of a Torah scholar, however, is permitted to receive honor from the community. If he is a public servant he may receive a salary . . . if a high priest is permitted to accept wealth from his fellow priests, how much more so may a Torah scholar, who is considered of higher stature than a high priest, be allowed to receive financial support."[7] Since then, many respected scholars have added their arguments to the discussion and most agree that times have changed. If we want Torah taught, our teachers must be paid or we might end up without, particularly in America. In a letter dated July 16, 1920, to M. B. Friedman, one of the leaders of Cleveland's Jewish community, Cyrus Adler wrote:

> The scarcity of rabbis is part of the general scarcity of teachers and professors. Men have drifted away from these professions because they feared they would not have the chance to live in them. The tenure of the rabbi is also very uncertain. Of course, you in Cleveland have large congregations who pay good salaries . . . but when it comes to the smaller town where men are offered $1800 or $2000 a year, are asked to preach in English and Yiddish, superintend and teach a school and in some cases to even act as hazzan, you can readily see that the men get discouraged.[8]

The Jewish community in which we live and work has inherited these attitudes. We may have unknowingly internalized these attitudes. To add to the conflict, these attitudes from the tradition might match personal conflicts we already possess. Those conflicts generally lie in the area of self-worth. Parker Palmer, who writes about the nexus of leadership and spirituality, says: "One of the biggest shadows inside a lot of leaders is deep insecurity about their own identity, their own worth. That insecurity is hard to see in extroverted people. But the extroversion is often there precisely because we are insecure about who we are and are trying to prove ourselves in the external world rather than wrestling with our inner identity."[9] You might ask; if you feel insecure, why would you possibly put yourself in such a vulnerable position? It may not seem logical, but it makes sense emotionally. We human beings often put ourselves in a position where we are forced to confront a part of ourselves that challenges us. I sometimes laugh when I see that pattern in myself. When I left the salaried world of the full-time pulpit, where there was almost no such thing as fee for service, I entered the world of private practice, where every appointment is linked to a fee and has to be negotiated. And yet I feel more comfortable confronting my discomfort this way. It is no accident when an historical conflict matches your personal conflict. If you feel conflicted about your own self-worth, consciously or unconsciously, those conflicts will be reflected in how you relate to money.

If you don't recognize these issues in yourself, it doesn't mean that these issues have been resolved; it just means that you have chosen to live with them, ignore them, fight them, or merely complain about them. Presumably, you believe you should be paid for being a Jewish professional, although you are aware that there are pitfalls, both the inherited ones cited by Maimonides and the Rashbatz and others new to our time. But how do you determine how much you should be paid? Who decides how much the job is worth? How much do you want? How much do you need? How do you know how much is enough? What is the relationship between how much you are paid and your professional satisfaction? What is the relationship between your salary and how valued you feel?

I confess that I asked none of these questions in 1980 when I applied for my first rabbinic job, or to be more specific, when I applied for a terrible job that everyone warned me not to take. And I mean everyone, from the placement director on down. The congregation had two senior rabbis who hated each other and made no pretense of hiding it. The previous assistant rabbi had gotten caught in the middle and, I was told, had been eaten alive. So what possessed me to apply? If you had asked me at the time, I think I would have answered pragmatically: I was a woman, I was a mother, and I was married to another rabbi who also needed to find a job and already had a possibility in Dallas. When you ask what being a woman had to do with it, you have to remember that this was 1980. No one was beating a path to our doors to hire us. By the time I got to the Dallas interview, I had already had my fill of interviews in which the senior rabbis said things like, "I would feel very bad if I had to ask you to go out at night and leave your baby" and "I would feel bad calling you at 2 in the morning" and (my favorite) "What we have here is the case of the proverbial female rabbi with the three-month-old." As far as I know, I was at the time the only female rabbi with a three-month-old. I'm not sure who was considered more of a liability, my baby or me. I walked into the Dallas interview expecting more of the same. Instead, the first question out of the mouth of the search committee chair was, "I see you have a young baby. How could we help you and your family be happy in Dallas?" I took that job.

When I look back, I think of that moment as the moment I realized—if only unconsciously—that it wasn't about the money. Three years later, I learned that lesson again, but this time it was painful. My job had originally included running the school and being on the pulpit each Shabbat but only preaching every six weeks or so. I had asked not to be on call for life-cycle events like funerals and weddings because I wanted a manageable schedule. While I worked hard, I was home for dinner every night and tucked my baby in. Then I had another baby. When I returned to work after my maternity leave, things between my two seniors had reached a crisis point. By July, one was gone. In August, the other one went on vacation. And there I was, running this 2,200-family congregation by myself for the month, officiating at three funerals a week, preaching Friday night and Shabbat morning, hiring the teachers, etc. I would never want to do it again, but I confess I was pretty proud of myself. I had proven that I could do it, although you might wonder what I was proving and to whom. Then, one Friday afternoon, the president and a member of the executive committee asked if they could pay me a visit. I remember having the fantasy that they were going to say thank you for a job well done. Instead, this is what they said: In the next year, we plan to hire in a new senior rabbi and he deserves to have a clean slate. You can stay for the next year and a half, but that will be the end of your tenure here.

So much for fantasies. But by the end of the following week, in that confusing and unpredictable way in which Jewish institutions seem to work, the whole situation had reversed itself. It seems that the original decision to let me go had been an attempt to appease the remaining senior rabbi but they had subsequently changed their minds about that. The co-chairs of the search committee came to see me and told me that the first thing they were saying to the senior rabbi applicants was, "We have a great associate rabbi and we plan to keep her." They had changed their minds, but the damage to me had been done. Sometime later, when they realized I was close to taking another position, I was invited to a past-president's house. In my four years in Dallas, I had never before been invited to this house. I can still picture looking around the room and wondering idly if the Chagall and the Picasso were real. They served wine and cheese. Then a select group of people offered me anything I wanted if I would stay. I admit that now and then it crosses my mind to think about how much money I might have now had I taken their offer, but at the time I wasn't even tempted. While I couldn't have verbalized my reason then, I know now that I had to leave that job once I stopped feeling valued.

I tell you the story of Dallas because it was there that I learned three important lessons: what it feels like to be valued, what it feels like not to be valued, and how neither experience had anything to do with money. Or maybe I should say: what we think money is about is not what money is really about. What is it about? In order to answer that question, I want to start with an assumption. I believe that people have drives of which they are largely unconscious. Freud thought of them as the aggressive drive and the libidinal drive; the Rabbis called them the yetzer hara and the yetzer hatov. Everyone likes to think that their yetzer hatov is more powerful than their yetzer hara—in fact, many teachers of Torah would prefer to think that they have no yetzer hara at all—but as many of you know, the Rabbis have told us that were it not for the yetzer hara, no one would marry, build a house, have children, or engage in business.[10] The alternative, then, lies in the arena of accepting both your yetzer hatov and your yetzer hara and getting to know yourself in a more profound way. It is only in the context of knowing yourself that you will ever figure out what money means to you emotionally. When you figure that out, you will either be a happier person and more satisfied with your career choice or you will understand that you need to make a different choice.

Because money is all about emotion; it is about wanting; it is about human appetites. And human appetites have their root in childhood. Children are born wanting and it obviously isn't money that they want. It isn't hard to guess what young children want because they make their needs known so unselfconsciously. Children want to play, eat, and sleep. They want to be loved and held. They want their every need responded to immediately and unconditionally. Parents may want their children to feel loved and attended to

and they may even enjoy how uninhibited children are in expressing their needs, but parents also want children to be able to live
in the world. That means children have to learn that they can't
have everything they want all the time. Parents spend a lot of time
civilizing children so that they sublimate or repress those wants,
and those appetites may go underground, but those appetites are
still there. What happens to those appetites when children grow
up? They become wishes. Those childhood wishes live on inside
you, but they reside in your unconscious. Freud says, "We [adults]
are only really happy . . . when we satisfy a childhood wish." And
Adam Phillips adds, sometimes we use money to wish with.[11]
If that is the case, then you won't be happy with any amount of
money unless you figure out what your wishes are.

No adult remembers those wishes. Since we all have childhood
amnesia, all of us have to work in deliberate ways to become more
aware of our buried adult wishes. This work, however, presents a
particular challenge to those of us who have chosen to earn our living as Jewish professionals. What makes the awareness of wishes
a direct challenge to teachers of Torah is that we are people who
tend to be more attuned to the needs of others than to our own. We
are by and large giving people and we are people with a mission.
We may want to make the world a better place, we may want to
make the Jewish community a better place, we may want to make
a Jewish organization a better place, we may want to inspire, we
may want to help others find spiritual wholeness, we may want
to teach children to love God, we may simply want to increase
Torah study *lishmah*—but our focus tends to be more external than
internal. All this is admirable but at root it is not entirely altruistic.
Behind the desire to love others lurks the wish to be loved; behind
the desire to care for others lies buried the wish to be taken care
of; behind the desire to be everything to everybody is hidden the
yearning to be recognized for who you truly are. And behind the
desire to bring change into the world lies the wish to change the
people who brought you into the world. Henri Nouwen calls us
wounded healers, "the one who must look after his or her wounds
and at the same time be prepared to heal the wounds of others."[12]

What does being a wounded healer have to do with money in
this Jewish nonprofit world you have chosen to enter? Forget for
the moment the financial desires of which you are conscious, like
being paid enough to live in the community, being paid enough to

cover day school tuition, and being paid enough to cover health care for your family. Think instead about bringing to the negotiating table your unconscious desires to be loved, to be recognized, and to be cared for. The only contract that feels "right" from an emotional standpoint will be the one that slakes those thirsts; and no contract is going to do that. Let your employer offer you less and you will see what I mean. The simple emotional equation is this: less money equals less love and more money equals more love. Instead of seeing the process of negotiation as a business transaction, Jewish professionals are particularly prone to personalize the process. Rabbi Arnold Sher, the former director of placement for the CCAR, described the conflict when he said to me that, "Some rabbis define themselves successfully by how much they are getting paid; they judge their self-worth by what they are bringing home. On the other side of the equation, rabbis don't know how to put a value on money vis-à-vis their time."[13] These two statements may seem contradictory, but they share an unconscious link. If you work tirelessly and devotedly, if you put no limits on your own time, then the wish is that you will be loved and admired and will be paid as unconditionally as you share your time. And if you are not sure how much you are really worth, you had better work hard so that no one can criticize your value. There is a link between how you feel about your salary and your own self-worth. That might explain the vignette with which I began. Asking the question, "How do I decide how much I should be paid?" is really asking, "How much am I worth?"

To complicate this emotional scenario further, of course, you are not the only one sitting at that negotiating table. "No wonder many clergy find the money side of ministry distasteful!" wrote Dan Hotchkiss of the Alban Institute: "It is the arena in which it is clearest how much we depend on those we are supposed to lead. It is the locus where sexism, racism, bias against homosexuals, social competition, and sheer anticlerical hostility walk most nearly naked through the church. It is where people express most unambiguously their true evaluation of the place of faith in the 'real' (that is the economic) world."[14] Those people on whom you depend are also the people you are supposed to lead and they, too, have an unconscious. They, too, are probably unaware of how they transfer their personal feelings onto you as an object of their wishes.

Children expect to receive from their parents; they don't want to give. They certainly don't want to pay for love and neither do those people upon whom you depend for your salary unless they are aware of how their own childhood appetites live on in their psyches. I once took a position in a synagogue located in a wealthy community; my predecessor had been there for thirty-five years. They told me that he never negotiated a contract; they just came to him every year and told him, "This is what we are going to give you this year." He retired making such a low salary that the congregation had to supplement his retirement. In his final years, he had two heart attacks. During my first year following him in that pulpit, a representative appointed by the board came to me and wanted to discuss my next contract. This man was a very successful Manhattan attorney, at least by economic standards. I was happy to begin the conversation and mentioned that another member of the synagogue would be helping me with the negotiations. To my surprise, this man reacted angrily and said, "We do not negotiate; only blue-collar workers negotiate. We will tell you what we are going to give you." I can look back now and tell you that in that moment, I represented someone else in that man's emotional life. I was an object upon which he transferred some old childhood feelings. His anger was clearly inappropriate and disproportionate to the situation. But I didn't know that at the time. My response was to take it personally; I experienced his anger as a narcissistic wound. Hadn't I worked hard enough? Hadn't I met their needs? Shouldn't they be showing their appreciation?

The greatest danger in discussing money occurs when you find sitting at the table two children thinly disguised as adults, both operating out of those early unconscious appetites, both "using money to wish with." Hindsight tells me that in that negotiation I just mentioned, we both would have been better off if he had reacted with less yetzer hara and I had responded with more access to my own. Negotiations for money always involve a combination of aggression and appreciation, yetzer hara and yetzer hatov, so we are back to those fundamental drives of which Freud spoke. Freud calls this the "psychopathology of everyday life" because we all have those drives. But those of us who are wounded healers tend not to be so good at using our yetzer hara appropriately. Our discomfort with aggressive feelings can lead us to repress them, suppress them, or, at the other extreme, indulge them. I once had a conversation with a colleague who described himself as a very aggressive negotiator. He told me that he negotiated his own contracts so effectively that he always got what he wanted, but the victory was a Pyrrhic one. His board left the table feeling resentful and angry. Eventually he decided to have someone else represent him in contract negotiations. I don't know if he received less money as a result, but I know he came to value a good working relationship more than winning everything he could.

Earlier I mentioned that this conflict over money can manifest itself as insecurity or grandiosity. So far, I've focused on insecurity; let me say a few words about grandiosity. If you were to define grandiosity, you might call it simply an "unrealistic notion of superiority."[15] But the roots of that apparent superiority lie in the same childhood place as the roots of insecurity. Both lie in those lingering childhood yearnings for love and admiration. Grandiosity is just a different attempt at compensating for what you didn't get. Instead of saying to yourself, "I am defective," you compensate by saying to yourself, "I am perfect."[16] I first noticed this grandiosity in action about twenty years ago, when the interfaith clergy association in my community decided to sponsor a fundraiser. They arranged to bring in a team called the Harlem Wizards. They were like the Harlem Globetrotters, professional ballplayers who performed all kinds of antics on the court. We the clergy were to play them in a basketball game. I naively signed up, only to arrive at the first practice and discover that I would be the only player out of forty using the girls' locker room. Having gone to HUC in the 1970s, I was used to that by then. What I wasn't used to was being ignored by my own teammates; even in practice, they wouldn't pass to me. Instead of our being able to practice together and develop a sense of camaraderie and teamwork, these mild-mannered ministers had become competitive monsters. They played against these professionals as if they actually thought they could win. They were so viciously competitive during the game that the Wizards left the court, took them aside and told them to lighten up. Despite my team's grandiose hopes, we lost, of course. I was the only one to score a basket because the opposing team passed me the ball, guarded me from my own teammates, and waited patiently for me to shoot—and they gave me ten points for my basket. I admit to feeling a little grandiose satisfaction when I recall that story.

The way that grandiosity manifests itself when you get to the negotiating table is that you expect too much. That is a perception held by senior colleagues and laypeople about recent graduates: "When I graduated, I didn't even have a contract, but these new graduates want everything spelled out." I don't advocate returning to the days of no written contracts, no days off, no parental leave, inadequate pensions, and being underpaid, but there is also a danger in being too specific if that desire comes from the grandiose part of you. The best results in salary negotiations occur when they are conducted in the context of a respectful relationship, not when you are seen as demanding and they feel they are responding to those demands. There has to be some amount of trust in the beginning of the professional relationships you will have. Even if an initial contract doesn't include everything you want, that doesn't mean that the next contract won't. It helps to have patience and remember that developing a professional relationship takes time. And frankly, as a lawyer-friend once told me, those contracts aren't worth the paper they are written on when it comes to holding up in court, not that you would want to take an issue to court. When you negotiate, it will help to remember that grandiosity like insecurity stems from a sense of childhood deprivation. Even an extravagant contract won't satisfy that childhood wish.

No matter how much money you make, most of us are going to work in communities where we make less money than the people who decide on your salary. That can be an emotional trap if you measure your self-worth by what you make. I once read a magazine article about happiness that said, "Although many economists agree that money doesn't make people happy, disparities in income make people miserable, according to most happiness literature. Happiness, in other words, 'is less a function of absolute income than of comparative income,' as [Harvard professor Daniel] Gilbert puts it. 'Now, if you live in Hallelujah, Arkansas . . . the odds are good that most of the people you know do something like you do and earn something like you earn and live in houses something like yours. New York, on the other hand, is the most varied most heterogeneous place on earth. No matter how hard you try, you really can't avoid walking by restaurants where people drop your monthly rent on a bottle of wine and store windows where shoes sit like museum pieces on gold pedestals. You can't help but feel trumped. As it were.'"[17] Being less satisfied because your neighbor has more hearkens back to that old bane of child-hood existence, sibling rivalry. What children want to share their parents' love?

None of us will be paid what we are worth if we measure in dollars. I have a friend who is a financial manager at a major financial institution. She says that people never think they have enough money. When couples sit in her office to discuss their money, often one of them storms out of the office before they are through. She says it's only the people who have their personal act together who don't act out around money; the more secure they are, the less they act out. The rabbinate was once a vehicle for upward mobility. It was a way of making a good salary, a better salary than your parents and your constituents, as well as a way of garnering instant respect. Now, instead, you find yourself interfacing with board members who are wealthy beyond your wildest dreams. My friend the financial manager and I were discussing the recent articles about the size of the famous bonuses given out at Goldman Sachs. Since this particular friend has also been the president of a synagogue and has raised millions of dollars to renovate their building, she has insight from both angles. She says it is important to remember, "These people might be your congregants or constituents. They may be jerks. But you have to come to terms with what they make vs. what you make."[18]

In other words, none of this is fair. It is also not fair that how much you are paid may be influenced by your gender, sexual orientation, where you live, or whether you are older and in a second career. But think for a minute about what it means emotionally to feel that something is not fair. It's something adults may think, but children say out loud. "Why did you give him the bigger piece? How come she gets to stay up late and I don't?" Again, it is all about that unquenched childhood thirst called, "Why do you love him more? Why can't I get all the love I need?" There are a number of healthy responses to the unfair distribution of money in our society. One is to try to change the system. That is admirable; isn't it what the prophets tried to do? We do believe in speaking truth to power. Our basic goal is the pursuit of justice. Admirable though it might be, however, beware the emotional pitfalls if your motivation falls under the heading called, "Marry the man to change him." If trying to change the system for you is a repetition of trying to change your parents, it will be frustrating and unhealthy.

If it is about achieving justice as an act separate from yourself, it will be a satisfying challenge. Another response is to distinguish between your sense of personal injustice and what we might call social injustice. In other words, it isn't fair on a societal level that teachers are paid so little, but the injustice isn't personally directed any more than substandard wages are personally directed at third world workers. Perhaps the most important way of responding is to be aware that you have made a choice. When you become a Jewish professional, you give up the possibility of the million-dollar bonus.

And speaking of fairness, let's note that Jewish professional choices are not the same for women as for men even though we have made progress in the years since I was ordained. I want to say a word about gender and money. We know that women in our society are paid less than men. We know that where there are no unions, female teachers may be paid less than men. We know that female rabbis in the Conservative Movement are paid less than men; we know it in the Reform Movement, too.[19] The reality of financial inequity struck my female classmates early on. As we entered the placement process almost three decades ago, I recall my male classmates reassuring us, "Don't worry, you're smart, you're good, you will get hired." When you sit by the phone and wait for the call that doesn't come, you learn the painful way that it doesn't matter how smart or how good you are. We weren't even guaranteed a job. We certainly weren't guaranteed a salary commensurate with those of our male colleagues nor did we even think about it. The financial plot thickens when it comes to women for reasons that are complex. First, we women take actions that often reflect our sense of inadequacy. My impression is that women are too quick to give up salary and benefits in exchange for working fewer hours and feeling less guilt, but then work harder in those hours to compensate. Second, women continue to be viewed differently by lay leaders, whether in the rabbinate, the cantorate, as the executive director of the Federation or as a member of the university faculty. I used to joke with a rabbi in my community that when his congregants ran into him in the supermarket, they walked out thinking, "What a terrific husband and father!" But if he had been a woman, they would have walked out thinking, "What's she doing at the store instead of being at the synagogue?" People feel deprived if they think the rabbi loves someone else more, even if that someone else is your own family, but they seem to feel more deprived if the rabbi is a woman. My male classmates were well intended but wrong; it doesn't always matter how smart you are or how good you are. Financial negotiations are still more complicated for women.

You may have noticed in all this discussion that I haven't mentioned the relationship between money and how smart you are. That's because it doesn't matter. In fact, being smart can sometimes be a disadvantage. I don't mean just because you might be smarter or have a better education than your constituents. I mean that you can use being smart to defend against your feelings. And money is all about feelings. The key is to become emotionally smart and have access to those feelings. You might ask; how do I do that? One important insight: You can't talk too much to colleagues. Talking demythologizes many taboos including the sacred cow of money. I also recommend that you talk in supervision and you talk in therapy and that you do that for your entire career. What you want to work on all the time is being aware of your choices, broadening your options and thinking creatively so that your responses don't emanate from some remote childhood fantasy. There is no such thing as knowing yourself once and for all because you will change and your needs will change. And even if you feel like you are in touch with those childhood wishes, it doesn't mean those wishes will disappear. But if you continually prepare yourself for that fact, then when you feel a twinge you will understand why and will have the choice of deciding how you want to respond.

In short, I want to encourage us to do the emotional work necessary to make us feel happy with our choices. I am suggesting that in order to feel comfortable with money, you rethink how you relate to your work. Marshall Breger observes that at one point in time "traditional Jews never invested significant meaning in their jobs. Such meaning came from activities completely outside of work: Religious study, charity, and family life. The relevant question about a job was whether it provided enough to support one's family and afforded one the time to study. Work was a means, not an end. It was a part of the journey, not the entire journey. One was not, therefore, defined by one's job."[20] We have an opportunity not to be defined by our job, our employers, our salary or our unconscious wishes if we are prepared to do the emotional work. Remember, too, that this endeavor is a sacred one. As Rabbi Yishmael counsels, "One who wishes to acquire wisdom should study the way money works, for there is no greater area of Torah-study than this."[21]

Notes

1. This article is adapted from a keynote presentation to the Wexner Foundation Wexner Graduate Fellowship, Winter Institute, 2007.
2. "The divine plan makes it necessary to devote time to providing for one's own material needs." BT *B'rachot* 35b.
3. *Pirkei Avot* 4:5.
4. Maimonides, *Mishneh Torah*, Laws of Torah Study, 3:10.
5. Maimonides, *Mishneh Torah*, Laws of Torah Study, 1:7.
6. Maimonides, *Mishneh Torah*, Laws of Vows 4:3. Quoted in Reuven Grodner, "Maimonides' View of Receiving Compensation for the Teaching and Studying of Torah," in *Chidushei-Torah*, 44.
7. R. Shimon ben Tzemach Duran (1361–1444, Spain, Algiers). *Magen Avot* (commentary on *Pirkei Avot*). Quoted in Grodner, 45.
8. Quoted in Kimmy Kaplan, "In God we Trust: Salaries and Income of American Orthodox Rabbi, 1881–1934," *American Jewish History* 86, no. 1 (March 1998): 77–106.
9. Parker Palmer, "Leading from Within: Reflections on Spirituality and Leadership," in *Let Your Life Speak: Listening for the Voice of Vocation* (John Wiley and Sons, 1999), chap. 5.
10. *B'reishit Rabbah* 9:7.
11. Adam Phillips, *Going Sane: Maps of Happiness* (HarperCollins Publishers, 2005), 160.
12. Henri Nouwen, *The Wounded Healer* (Random House, 1979).
13. Rabbi Arnold Sher, private communication, December 19, 2006.
14. Dan Hotchkiss, "Salary Anxiety," *Congregations Magazine*, September/October 2002, 20.
15. Nancy McWilliams, *Psychoanalytic Diagnosis* (Guilford Press, 1994), 158.
16. H. Kohut, *The Analysis of the Self* (New York: International Universities Press, 1971), 27.
17. Jennifer Senior, "Dark Thoughts on Happiness, " *New York Magazine*, July 17, 2006, 32.
18. Private communication, December 17, 2006.
19. In the years since this presentation was written, we have seen progress in understanding the relationship between female-identified rabbis and income. The CCAR published *The Sacred Calling: Four Decades of Women in the Rabbinate*, a volume that explores the trajectory and impact of women in the rabbinate. The CCAR also established

the Task Force on the Experience of Women in the Rabbinate, which developed materials including Implicit Bias Resources, Tools (including awareness-raising program, compensation study, staff training, and assessments), Research and Resources, all of which are made available on the CCAR website for colleagues to use "for their own professional growth as well as the overall advancement of their communities." The WRN has raised the issue of pay equity and structural inequality as one of its main focuses of the last few years. The Handbook of Placement Procedures has added the following important information to equalize pay:

Base Compensation

In 2018, the Rabbinical Placement Commission adopted the policy that all search applications must provide a stated range for proposed base compensation (the sum of salary and parsonage). The RPC made this decision after engaging in learning and discussion about the ways in which publication of salary ranges impacts positively on congregations' successful completions of their rabbinic searches and on narrowing the gender pay gap.

Implicit Bias Training

In 2020, the RPC adopted a policy requiring that all search applications include the responses to several questions related to implicit bias training. Implicit bias training is strongly encouraged, and the CCAR has produced training materials that are provided free of charge to all congregations in search.

The training currently is also offered online in conjunction with the ACC and the URJ REDI (race, equity, diversity, and inclusion) team. An upcoming compensation will also shed light on the discrepancies.

20. Quoted in Jeffrey K. Salkin, *Being God's Partner: How to Find the Hidden Link Between Spirituality and Your Work* (Jewish Lights Publishing, 1994), 45.
21. BT *Bava Batra* 175b.

Fifty Years with One Congregation: A Memoir of Sorts

Rabbi Peter H. Grumbacher

A "charmed" rabbinate is what my wife, Suzy, called the fifty years in the Wilmington, Delaware, congregation I served. I was there for thirty-seven years before I retired. Over the past thirteen years I remained involved with the congregants on many levels, always aware that I was now emeritus, understanding the limitations but having to stress to many who were with me for a long time that I no longer was the rabbi.

Truly it has been a rewarding half-century. I was able to pursue my interests in the pastoral aspects of the rabbinate because of a very encouraging—and generous—Board. They allowed me the time to travel weekly to New York where at the Post-Graduate Center for Mental Health I received certification in pastoral counseling; and a decade later at Yeshiva University's Wurzweiler School of Social Work, I received my MSW.

My focus has always been on the pastoral side of the rabbinate. In retirement I worked for a while counseling clients at our Jewish Family Services, but my training came in most handy in my role as interim rabbi in one of the three congregations I served. Sure, there was the need to counsel congregants in the other two, but the most challenging period of time—far beyond anything I experienced before—were the two years during the pandemic. Who among us ever thought we'd live through such an event! We members of the clergy had to deal with emotions—our own and those of congregants—often so dramatic that sometimes getting through one day seemed miraculous. How much the more so the elderly and the youth, and of course their families, who lived with

RABBI PETER H. GRUMBACHER (C72) served Congregation Beth Emeth, Wilmington, Delaware, since ordination in 1972. He has served as interim rabbi in three congregations along I-81 in Virginia.

uncertainties without the pandemic but now had its added burdens and heartaches.

What could I best offer these people? Needed for sure was a renewed sense of community. So many were accustomed not only to regular worship, but a variety of programs and social events associated especially with small congregations. Now there was a closed building and their own isolation. Understand please that all these interim positions were not only part-time, but I also commuted from home, a minimum of three hours from each of the synagogues I served. Could I offer a rabbinic connection that I felt was so vital for people, young and old, healthy and infirm, who, quite frankly, were fearful? All over the country there were family members unable to be with loved ones who were hospitalized, even ill at home. I was one of the lucky ones who spent a week in the hospital with COVID-19 but walked out on my own. Thankfully, no one—neither congregant nor their family members—died in this period. But, regardless, all too often they were alone; and even with a family under their roof, there were so many moments of anxiety and tension.

We know that a trip to the supermarket, an afternoon at a movie theater, a weekend in the mountains, can work wonders, can give you a sense of renewal. When, however, we can barely drive to the convenience store for a quart of milk because of the specter of COVID-19, the dynamics under a roof dramatically change, let alone the inner turmoil, which is felt when we cannot connect with others. Feeling some of that myself, I felt it a major mitzvah to be in touch with congregants.

I made regular telephone calls and often congregants who needed to talk would reach out. There was more. I also wrote daily articles dealing with all kinds of topics; and I confess that I ended all three hundred or so articles with a joke. People rarely commented on my writing but, wow, did they have things to say about my jokes! When someone commented how "enfolded" they felt when they received my emails, I thanked them but also stated that this exercise was for me as well. At the very least it gave me something to do each day, but it also made me feel that much closer to people beyond my own family members. And, of course, we all need more than a dash of humor at times like that.

How well we know that colleagues and congregants became very familiar with Zoom. Yet is there one of us who did not hear,

"Oh, Zooming is fine, but soon we'll be able to shake hands, hug, and talk face-to-face with each other"? It hasn't been soon enough. As I told my congregation not once but often, "We might not like to Zoom, but we must understand that it's here to stay. If we assume everything will return to normal in a short time, if we believe the virtual *Oneg Shabbat* is a here today–gone tomorrow phenomenon, if we don't put our collective imaginations together on all levels of congregational life to employ Zoom creatively, then we are in great danger of becoming irrelevant as a religious institution. I, too, would rather have all of you gathered together on Shabbat, but right now gathering together via Zoom is the best we can do. Let's take advantage of it."

The opportunities Zoom has placed on our plates seem endless. We can bemoan its impact on the future of affiliation, the future of the synagogue in general, and there's plenty to bemoan. But embrace today and make the technology work for you! At our virtual community seder we had a family from Italy join their American cousins. Would they ever have been able to celebrate a family Pesach like this one without Zoom? Perhaps, but probably not.

The elephant in the room, I came to realize, is the phenomenon of livestreaming. It brings an entirely different perspective on worship attendance. While it allowed us to be with our congregants, there was one consequence yet to be fully evaluated: you literally can spend Shabbat around the world, participating in worship in a multitude of congregations from sunset to sunset, even earlier and later, but will our people come back to our Shabbat celebrations? I've read that over eighty countries are represented each Friday evening tuning into New York's Central Synagogue. My wife and I have Shabbat dinner worshiping with Central, but then I "switch channels" and worship at my former congregation and then the one in which my cantor is now the *chazan*. Far too many of my congregants are doing the same, and while some are three- and four-generation members, they are questioning the need to maintain their affiliation. "After all," one said, "we come only on the High Holy Days anyway, and you don't need a ticket when you watch over livestream." As I wrote earlier, there is plenty to bemoan, and many challenges we are going to face post-pandemic.

For ten years I served as associate rabbi to Herbert Drooz. Known to his peers and others as the Gentleman Rabbi, they hit the nail on the head. Several colleagues seemed to covet my position; they often told me the tribulations they had with their seniors. Not only was Herb a wonderful guy, but his wife Florence was a hoot, very supportive of me but also my wife, Suzy. She often told her, "Be yourself." It's not that she had to be told, mind you, but it's very affirming to have the wife of your husband's boss affirm your efforts in your profession and in the life of the congregation.

He was so kind, and he was deeply religious. My goal was to be able to pray like he did, especially those selections we read at *N'ilah*. When I succeeded him, Suzy would say to me at the Break-the-Fast, "Pretty good, Peter; close but no cigar." I knew in my heart that as hard as I tried my efforts didn't reach the *Ribono shel olam* like his did!

Rabbi Drooz was a type 1 diabetic. It was a miracle that he lived into his eighties, but it was Florence who kept him as healthy as he was. Despite that, I had (and still have) stories about him related to times when he had diabetic reactions. Florence and he would tell us a whole host of incidents, some of them truly hysterical. Easy to say inasmuch as he lived to tell about them. But there were some only I experienced. Just as he prayed fervently, he blessed fervently as well. On the occasion of his final Confirmation as he was in the midst of blessing the kids, I could tell there was a problem. How? He didn't stop the blessing of one of them. I quickly ran to his office and took an English toffee candy he would pop in his mouth when such an issue occurred. "Now," I wondered, "how am I going to do this?" I pulled the next confirmand from the line—the poor kid didn't know what was happening to her—and when he began blessing me, I waited until his mouth was wide open and plopped the candy in. Moving quickly, I left the line, pushed the girl back into her place, and no one was the wiser. Indeed, that little bit of sugar took effect immediately and he continued to bless the confirmands.

I can say without question that in those ten years we had only one disagreement. He was virulently anti–bat mitzvah. He often said, "Then the girls will drop out before confirmation like the boys do." No matter how many times I showed him the figures, he couldn't believe that very, very few of our boys dropped out after bar mitzvah! Oh, well, only one argument in ten years isn't bad, but he wasn't happy that my first congregational vote when I succeeded him was to initiate bat mitzvah. We had only one negative vote that day. Not even his wife voted against it.

Earlier I wrote how supportive my Board had been across the decades. Colleagues have a hard time believing that our most trusted friends have been the presidents and their spouses. In fact, those friendships have continued to become stronger across the years.

I enjoyed going to Board meetings. The dynamics were always fascinating, and thankfully there was rarely any *rishus*. Purposefully, I never sat around the table but always on the perimeter. One of my associates remarked, "Now I understand the secret of your success." When I wondered out loud what that secret might be, the answer was, "You say very little at Board meetings, so when you do chime in, they know you mean business!" That was correct. I recall vividly when Sylvan Schwartzman told us, "If your Sisterhood president asks what side of the kitchen the new refrigerator should go, tell her any side she'd like!" I thought his was a perfect MO for a rabbi to have in all facets of congregational life, and it worked well for me. When there was an ethical or moral issue, or when I felt they could be a little looser with their finances, I spoke up. On one occasion we were the recipients of a large gift following the death of a wealthy congregant. I sensed confusion as to what to do with the money; all kinds of options were discussed, none of which I found to be the best for the congregation in the situation we were in at the moment. I offered one sentence: "Don't let this gift be an albatross around the congregation's neck." While one finance-oriented Board member was furious with me, the rest of the members allowed my warning to sink in. I'm so glad I said it (and, by the way, that guy was one of the few with whom I didn't get along).

After twenty-five years in Wilmington, one of my classmates asked me, "What are the good and the bad aspects of being with the same congregation for all these years." My answer was the same for the bad as it was for the good, namely, getting to know all the people. After fifty years that much more so!

Do we get desensitized to death when we must officiate at the funerals of those we met the very first day of our rabbinate, people who were young, whose children were running up and down the hallways of our religious school, who looked forward to all the rites of passage ahead? I cannot answer for others, but I know that if there isn't some desensitization it can be overwhelming. I grew up in a family that couldn't be defined as "emotional" (an understatement), but I never realized how helpful that actually was in our "business." I suppose there's more than a bit of self-revelation in that comment, but truly I have been able to hold it back even when I sat and grieved with the widow(er) of a beloved friend of mine whose involvement in the temple was inspirational to so many others, myself included.

In my seventeenth year I officiated at four funerals in a period of two days. Each one of them was a person who became a family friend. Maintaining professionalism combined with compassion is the necessary component whether a rabbi has served a year or a half-century in a congregation. It was that last funeral I'll never forget; that was the one in which I lost it.

Just for the sake of sharing a unique personality with you, let me mention a few things about her. She was the matriarch of her family. Her husband had died many years before. Her elderly brother lived with her. Her sons—one extremely successful and one not—lived far away. There wasn't a member of the *lamed vavniks* among them. So when I use "matriarch," she was, in fact, the Queen of Denial.

She had taught in our religious school. She scared the bejeebers out of everyone for no other reason than she reeked of garlic. She was, however, a good teacher, a very good one especially as she grew older. She often needed to talk to someone. I was that someone. While she did inquire from the front desk if anyone was with me in my office, it was probably only luck that never was someone sitting across from me when my friend came up the stairs. I'd hear her; the footsteps from her hard shoes told me exactly what mood she was in, and how long to expect her visit to last.

But what was so unusual about those visits was that she'd enter, sit down, and begin speaking. Sometimes she spoke for five minutes, usually more, and occasionally for up to an hour. The one thing I knew for sure was to keep my mouth shut. It was a nonstop monologue. Not one word emanated from my mouth.

She never asked anything of me; she just had to get things off her chest. When she felt better, she would rise, saying only, "Thank you, Rebbenyu," and exit exactly as she entered. I did have to leave my office for the rest of the day, however; the space had to be fumigated from the garlic as best as possible. Interestingly, as I recalled our unique relationship, every visit came flooding into my mind when I stood on that bimah and began my eulogy. For me to even choke up (to become *verklempt*, as it were) is unusual; to shed a tear as I did, unheard of.

I retired at sixty-two. I honestly never wanted anyone to ask, "When's he going to retire?" but in truth there were things I wanted to do with the rest of my life. An Orthodox rabbi who was also one of my professors in Wurzweiler, found out I was a rabbi. When I told him about six hundred families were affiliated with the congregation, and that I had three young children at home, he looked at me in disbelief and said, "I had a tiny congregation when I was ordained. I stayed a year because they drove me crazy and then pursued a Ph.D. In Psychology. Why are you doing this, Peter?" I replied, "First of all, my flock isn't driving me crazy; but most importantly I'm looking ahead. In my retirement I won't do woodworking." And so I worked for a few years for JFS as I mentioned earlier.

I also felt the need to tell my father's story, a mission that turned into an obsession. He was interred in Dachau on Kristallnacht, the Night of Shattered Glass, November 9, 1938. When he left (yes, he walked out; that's part of the story) and he and my mom came to this country, he enlisted in the army. His heroism was highlighted in a newspaper article. So many survivors never spoke about their experiences; my father was one of them. I decided to learn as much as possible about his experiences—not an easy task, and it took a long time—and share them with whatever audience invited me. I call it, "Sharing the Silence: The Son of a Survivor Tells His Father's Story."

I had already toured the country during one of my sabbaticals speaking to a variety of audiences, but with the number of survivors and veterans of World War II dying, unable or unwilling to witness, I believe a member of the second generation had the responsibility to do so at every possible opportunity. I am one of that generation, so I wanted my retirement to include these talks. I was so pleased that there was a positive response from the folks I addressed. And I was told my congregants lapped up my weekly descriptions of the places and people I encountered in the previous seven days in a series of articles that I wrote for our newsletter. I called the series "On the Road"—not original, but it made the point.

Delaware is a small state, the second smallest after Rhode Island. We know our members of Congress just as we know so many in state politics. And, yes, I did have an encounter with Joe Biden while he was campaigning. A short while before the death of one of our congregants, the former vice president called her, promising her he would be at her funeral and offer some words. She and her husband had been major supporters of Biden as a twenty-nine-year-old who was running for the United States Senate and maintained a relationship with him across the years.

This woman had asked me to offer the eulogy. Following that there were six speakers, Biden being the last. He told the thousand or so gathered in the sanctuary and auditorium how grateful he was for all that the couple had done for him. "She even got me a rabbi to officiate at the wedding of my daughter to a nice Jewish doctor." Then he turned, looked at me and said, "Because you wouldn't!" Nor despite the invitation to participate in the funeral of his son, Beau, would I do so on Shabbat. It's not at all that I'm *shomer Shabbat*. I believe, though, that I would be representing the Jewish community. A more traditional colleague chose to participate. So it goes.

Snippets of my rabbinate with its challenges and opportunities abound. I often say, "When I write my book . . . " and then hear my kids and others say, "Yeah, yeah, write it already." But when I do so (no snickering please) you can believe I'll do my best to bring to mind more of the moments of my life. I can't wait to read it. Yeah, yeah!

Joys of Being a Second-Career Rabbi

Rabbi Sanford Olshansky

Whatever a Jewish person's first career may have been, a second career as a rabbi can be very meaningful and fulfilling. For some that will be serving in a congregational pulpit. For others it may require defining a different path and navigating unfamiliar territory. There are professional and spiritual rewards to be found, although there are also no guarantees of professional success.

20/20 Hindsight

In 1977 or '78, when I was in my late twenties, my primary-care doctor, with no prompting from me, said, "Being a rabbi is no job for a nice Jewish boy." (There were few female rabbis then.) He added, "If you have five hundred congregants, you have five hundred bosses." That is one distinction between a career in the rabbinate and a career in business. During my thirty-five-year business career, I worked for six companies. In each there were owners and customers, who were *different* people. In synagogue life, the owners and customers are the *same* people. (The same is often true in church life also.)

With 20/20 hindsight, I'm glad I didn't try, as a young man, to "make my way in the world," as a rabbi. I probably would have failed. I'm grateful to the men and women who chose to serve as rabbis in their twenties and thirties. Judaism and the Jewish people needed you! (A Christian co-worker in business once told me that he believed all faiths should have their clergy begin to serve at age 40, so they would have a lot of life experience. While this makes

RABBI SANFORD OLSHANSKY (AJR11); MA in Jewish Studies (Gratz College, 2011); CCAR (2013), lives in Brevard County, Florida, about a half hour southwest of Kennedy Space Center, with his wife of fifty years, Marilyn Olshansky, a retired attorney. They have a son, daughter-in-law, and two grandsons, ages eight and four. They love to travel domestically by car and often cruise internationally sense in theory, it's not practical. I applaud the Jewish movements and Christian denominations that have meaningful mentoring programs for younger clergy.)

Why would I, or anyone, choose to pursue a second career in the rabbinate? I've met several second-career Christian ministers who speak of their roles as a "calling." That may apply to some rabbis also. In my own case, I became emotionally engaged in synagogue ritual at a stage in life when I was ready for a change. Later I found meaning in making a difference in the lives of others—Jewish people and, in many cases, their non-Jewish family members. I've often used the term *keruv*, bringing Jews closer to Jewish tradition and belief, which could evoke Chabad, with their "mitzvah mobiles." For me, the rabbinate came to be about serving people Jewishly, in accordance with a teaching quoted in the old Hertz/Soncino *Chumash* that one way to "love Adonai your God," per Deuteronomy 6:5, is to love people and treat them in godly ways.

Initial Inspiration

In my twenties in the Detroit area, I met an Orthodox rabbi who had been a submarine commander in the US Navy! He performed a funeral service for one of my father's siblings. We talked a bit, though I can't recall what were his motivations. My first real encounter with a second-career rabbi came when my son enrolled at Dartmouth College, in 2000, and we met Rabbi Ed Boraz (HUC-JIR '93), who served the campus Hillel and the local Jewish community. Previously, he had been an attorney in the Chicago area. However effective he may have been as a lawyer, I found him to be a sensitive, caring rabbi. Moreover, he was making a difference in a dual role: as a spiritual leader and pastor for the students and for the area's nonstudent Jewish population.

My ultimate inspiration to pursue a second career in the rabbinate came later that year when my wife and I joined an independent, trans-denominational or hybrid synagogue in Westchester County, New York, and met Rabbi Mark Sameth (HUC-JIR '98). He had been a songwriter and arranger in Nashville until age forty and was that young congregation's first rabbi. With his musical talent and experience performing in the "house band" at B'nai Jeshurun, in Manhattan, Rabbi Sameth led large parts of the Shabbat and holiday services from an electronic keyboard. He is also an engaging and charismatic preacher and teacher. My wife and I connected with Rabbi Sameth and with some of the members of this previously lay-led congregation.

Because the congregation was lay led before hiring Rabbi Sameth in 1998, it remained very participatory. Before long they had me reading Torah, chanting *haftarot* when there was no bar/bat mitzvah student, and serving as a *gabbai*, *b'nei mitzvah* coach, and occasional substitute religious school teacher. I started giving short *haftarah d'rashot* to complement the weekly *d'var Torah*. Rabbi Sameth encouraged me in all of this. After a few years I asked him if I was too old, at age fifty-seven, to do what he did at age forty. Rabbi Sameth said I wasn't too old and referred me to the pluralistic, trans-denominational Academy for Jewish Religion (AJR), which trains rabbis and cantors without requiring a year of residence in Israel.

Rabbinic Education

Although AJR's rabbinic training is officially a five-year program (seventy courses plus a thesis), it also differs from HUC-JIR and JTS by allowing students to progress at their own pace, rather than move with their class. This is important to someone making a transition from another career. Many of AJR's faculty were teaching concurrently at JTS and some had taught previously at HUC-JIR. Some of my AJR teachers were well-known Reform rabbis who have written articles for this journal.

One of AJR's most important educational requirements is practical rabbinic experience. In this, I was very fortunate to have been placed with Rabbi Ken Emert (HUC '77) at Temple Beth Rishon (TBR), in Wyckoff, New Jersey. In addition to being a great mentor, Rabbi Emert pushed me to take on a great variety of duties, giving me a wealth of practical experience. He allowed me considerable "freedom of the pulpit" on occasions when it was my turn to preach, even though we differ substantially about US politics. Rabbi Emert encouraged me to *enjoy* leading services, consistent with AJR teacher Rabbi David Ingber's suggestion that helping others to pray could be part of one's own spiritual practice.

One of my favorite experiences at TBR was serving as director of its supplementary religious school. In the tradition of Rabbi Adin Steinsaltz, *z"l*, I challenged TBR's elementary school students to "make your teachers' lives miserable" by asking the toughest Jewish questions they could think of. I visited classes regularly to answer questions that the teachers couldn't answer, such as "Who created God?" "Why is there evil in the world?" and "Why doesn't God show God's self to us?" This gave me opportunities to discuss profound spiritual matters often lacking in Jewish supplementary education. I rewarded such questions with dollar-store trinkets, which went home in sealed envelopes with certificates that said the student had asked a great question. I also enjoyed reading expressively to TBR's kindergarten, first, and second grade students seated on the bimah on Sunday mornings from *God's Mailbox*, by Rabbi Marc Gellman (HUC '72).

I benefited greatly from the diverse and creative musical offerings of TBR's amazing cantor, Chazan Ilan Mamber, *z"l*. His repertory ranged from Sol Zim and Shlomo Carlebach to Danny Maseng and Craig Taubman to Tsvika Pik and Meir Finkelstein, and of course Debbie Friedman. Chazan Mamber was a master at engaging people, regardless of their beliefs and religiosity, or lack of it, with the music and ambiance of the synagogue. He was also a master, as is Rabbi Emert, in engaging young people and interacting with them at their level. I gained almost as much from his mentorship as from Rabbi Emert's, though in different aspects of Jewish life.

Long before I arrived, Rabbi Emert and Chazan Mamber began holding a "family service" on one Friday evening every month, each featuring a different religious school grade. It became my job to tell or act out a story, often interacting with members of the featured grade seated on the bimah. On several occasions I decorated the custodian's six-foot ladder with cardboard angels and "slept" on the pulpit steps to teach, per Jacob's dream, that God can be found anywhere. My favorite family service moment came when I asked one group the name of the man who led the Israelites out of Egypt. Without waiting to be called on, one eager student yelled out "Mozart!"

Finding My Place

Although I grew up Conservative and was trained to be either a Conservative or Reform rabbi, I decided, just before my 2011 ordination, that I preferred Reform so that I could marry interfaith

couples. Unfortunately, due to historical "baggage" and other issues between HUC-JIR and AJR, it took me over two years to be
admitted to the CCAR, in November 2013. When I decided, in the
fall of 2012, at age sixty-two, to seek my own pulpit, no Reform
congregation would interview me—though it may have been as
much due to "ageism" as my lack of CCAR membership. After
auditioning at several Conservative synagogues, which weren't a
good fit, my wife and I decided to move to Florida's "Space Coast,"
where friends from New York were enjoying a very laid-back life.

On Rabbi Emert's advice, I reached out to several colleges and
universities and found that the University of Central Florida
(UCF), in Orlando, needed to replace a Judaic Studies teacher. I
began teaching introductory Hebrew there in early 2014. Soon af-
terward, one of my faculty colleagues told me that his Reform synagogue, which had been served for many years by Rabbi Howard
Simon (HUC-JIR '63), had a falling out with Rabbi Simon's successor. I led Shabbat and holiday services there for three years, during a transition to smaller locations and to being led by a talented
unordained cantor who had grown up in the congregation and is a
trained opera singer. While I found my part-time pulpit meaningful, I was ready to give it up.

Although I've remained close with Rabbi Emert and visited him
in his new home in California, I had the benefit of being mentored
officially, for three years, as a condition of my admission to the
CCAR, by Rabbi Phil Kranz (HUC-JIR '71). While I have yet to
meet him in person, I found Rabbi Kranz's advice invaluable in
dealing with challenging situations that arose in connection with
my part-time pulpit and the inevitable pastoral role that accompanied it. Although I visited Jewish patients in a Christian hospital
almost weekly for five years, while serving at TBR, and performed
many funerals, situations arose in Florida for which I was unpre-
pared by my past experiences. It was both helpful and comforting
to be able to call Rabbi Kranz for his insights and wise advice.

Destination and Theme Park Weddings

One important role that a second-career rabbi can play, other than
pulpit work, is officiating at weddings, especially because many
congregations don't allow their clergy to perform "outside" life-
cycle events. In my case, in Central Florida, only 20 percent of the

Jewish population are synagogue members. Most of them are Conservative or Chabad/Orthodox. Accordingly, there are few Reform rabbis *available* to perform weddings of interfaith couples—the majority of non-Orthodox weddings today. Performing such weddings, including "destination weddings," fulfills part of my mission of *keruv*, especially as I don't co-officiate with Christian clergy.

Having performed 114 weddings through July 2022, mostly of interfaith couples, I believe I'm qualified to share some general observations:

1. Most Jews, even if they're not very religious, don't want to be married by a pastor or priest because of the "baggage"—the history of persecution. There is almost a "gut" reaction.
2. Most of the couples I've married have been living together for several years, often long enough to be considered "common law" spouses in some US states. They were all going to be married by somebody, so is this necessarily putting a *kashrut hechsher* on *t'reif*? I don't think so, especially because I don't co-officiate with Christian clergy.
3. A large percentage of my couples have told me, voluntarily, that they intend to raise their children as Jewish. (I don't ask, lest they feel obliged to lie.) This is consistent with surveys that show a high likelihood of children being raised Jewishly when the parents' wedding was performed by a sole Jewish officiant.
4. Many Christian parents and grandparents are grateful that their child or grandchild in an interfaith relationship chose to be married by a rabbi rather than a secular officiant. In their minds it was still a religious ceremony and God was still present —more so if they understand the extent to which Christianity grew out of Judaism. Many Christian guests have told me, in the cocktail hour, "I've never attended a Jewish wedding before. It was really beautiful."

In addition to the satisfaction of serving couples and their families, I find wedding officiation interesting because of its creative aspects. Every couple is different and, accordingly, every ceremony should be different. All my wedding ceremonies are customized and personalized. I assign every couple "homework," which includes watching two or three movies, reading one or two books on relationships, and answering three questions, which become the basis of my personal remarks to them and about them, often with a touch of good-natured humor: "What does each of you *especially* love about the other?" (multiple things) "When and how did each of you *decide* that the other is 'the one?'" and "What will *change* now that you're getting married?" Couples have told me that they read my remarks to each other on an anniversary. What a compliment!

Fulfillment—Today and Beyond

At the age of seventy-two, and as a seven-year prostate cancer survivor, I'm glad not to be tied to the schedule of a physical pulpit. I still teach in the Judaic Studies Program at UCF, but only online courses: Jewish History, Hebrew Bible as Literature, and Religion and Science, one of my chief academic interests, which I also teach in an interfaith adult education setting. I've served as a cruise ship rabbi—for High Holy Days, Chanukah, and Passover. I've found this interesting and meaningful, especially on a 2021 Caribbean cruise when I was asked to conduct an interfaith 9/11 memorial service, which was attended by many passengers who probably had never met a rabbi.

Given the dearth of rabbis in Central Florida, due to the low level of Jewish engagement and affiliation, I'm frequently called on for funerals and hospital visits, on the "Space Coast" and in the Orlando area, where there is a fine community rabbi, Rabbi Arnold Segal (HUC-JIR '72), who simply can't be everywhere. I've also been contacted, primarily through 18 Doors (formerly Interfaith Family) to engage with an increasing number of potential conversion students. While I always make them aware of the option of in-person Introduction to Judaism courses, many have chosen to study with me on an individual basis. I also find this work interesting and meaningful.

While none of us knows what the future holds, I look forward to continuing to perform weddings and my other rabbinical functions for many years to come, including theme park "destination" *b'nei mitzvah*, and baby namings—especially for couples whose weddings I performed. While I send all wedding couples a one-month, one-year, and five-year anniversary message, being able to reconnect with them for a baby naming, when they live in the area, is a special treat.

In conclusion, I'm glad that I became a rabbi and I'm glad that I became a Reform rabbi. There are many meaningful roles, other than serving as the spiritual leader of a congregation, for a second-career rabbi to perform. I hope that others who are considering a second career as a rabbi will seek pulpit roles. I've read, in one of Rabbi Lewis Kamrass's CCAR newsletter articles, that there is a shortage of new students enrolling in HUC-JIR. That could ultimately lead to many Reform synagogues lacking rabbis. Jewish people, although they have become less Jewishly engaged in my lifetime for various reasons, need rabbis. I'm glad to be one who is currently serving them.

"That's No Job for a Jewish Boy": In Honor of Those Who Guided Me in My Rabbinate

Rabbi Philip Bentley

When I told my grandfather I had applied to rabbinic school, he said, "Rabbi? That's no job for a Jewish boy." He was joking but also serious. He continued, "You'll have 350 bosses." Family members had been mentoring me in the ways of business all my life. Now I had chosen a profession unique in my mostly secular family. What I did not know then that I know now is that my understanding of business would be an asset in my chosen calling.

Mid-career I considered alternatives to the pulpit, perhaps working for an NGO, one involved in *tikkun olam* or serving the Jewish people. With that in mind, I took courses leading to a certificate in labor-management studies. That included courses on negotiation, conflict resolution, human resources, and labor law. However, a man plans, and God laughs; I served pulpits for the remainder of my career.

I realized having some business skills was a significant asset in dealing with the pulpit as a workplace. Rabbis are not hired as employees but elected as independent contractors. It is easy to forget that serving at a pulpit is a job. In doing that job we have to perform many functions that require organizational and interpersonal skills.

I developed my pulpit skills at my student pulpit, where I served for three years. My faculty supervisor was one of my favorite professors, but he did not really have pulpit experience. When I had

RABBI PHILIP BENTLEY (NY73) retired after a career serving pulpits in New Bedford, Massachusetts; Curaçao; Jericho, New York; Floral Park, New York; Chicago; and Hendersonville, North Carolina. He is the author of many articles and papers on *tikkun olam* issues, including environmental ethics. He lives in Hendersonville, North Carolina, with Phyllis, his wife of fifty-four years.

questions I went to the only full-time faculty member who had had significant pulpit experience, Leonard Kravitz. From him I learned a lot and got practical advice on difficult situations I encountered.

What follows is an account of some of my experiences on the pulpit as a workplace.

The Congregation as an Organization

Edwin Friedman, z"l, used to say that some congregations are pickles and others are plums. He said this to clergy about being clergy. He explained that congregations, like other organizations, have personalities. Some will always be good to their clergy—the plums—and some will not—the pickles. Organizations, like people, develop personalities and engage in repeated behaviors. They tend to be resistant to change.

In trying to make needed changes, the rabbi must seek the support of lay leaders, the members, and staff members. I think a big part of the difference between pickles and plums is willingness to work with the rabbi in making changes.

The two congregations I served the longest were both pickles. Both of them were hard on their rabbis and one, up until my time there, had fired every rabbi and cantor they ever had. I also served congregations where I enjoyed the support of the Board and the membership. These were the plums.

As much as we might want to be considered *mara d'atra* (master of a locality), we are no such thing, certainly not in the eyes of most of the people in the congregation. We serve our congregations. However, we are also expected to lead. This can be difficult—to both serve and lead. The best advice I can offer is to make others— staff, lay leaders, and members—partners in bringing new ideas and improvements to the organization.

I remember asking Karl Wiener, the rabbi of my family congregation, about bringing a new program to my student pulpit. In my last year of college I had met with him to talk about my going to HUC-JIR. He spent a good hour telling me all the downsides of being a rabbi in a congregation. He wanted me to be certain I wanted to be a rabbi despite the challenges I would face. So now, a few years later, I went to him as a congregational rabbi with a problem. He gave me very good advice. Seek a Board member who liked the idea I wanted to present and have them present it. Indeed, my experience since taught me the wisdom of that advice. Avoid making yourself the issue.

This works not just with lay leaders, but with staff and members. For example, at one of my congregations, women were barred from ascending the bimah in slacks. They were required to wear a skirt or dress. This was the 1990s. These policies were set by the ritual committee, which consisted of older congregants. I had just started a school committee and a parents' group, which they did not have before (at least not in my time there). I spoke with some of the women in those groups and suggested, since they wanted that rule dropped, to attend a ritual committee meeting and present their case. A few women showed up for the meeting wearing very nice slack suits. They said, "What's wrong with this outfit?" That was the end of that rule.

Never fail to give laypeople or others on staff credit for their work and let them take the credit for achievements, even if you think the rabbi deserves the credit.

I was very close to Zalman Schachter-Shalomi and was a member of his *chavurah* in the mid-1960s. After graduating college, I spent a year in Winnipeg to learn with him both as part of his *chavurah* and at the University of Manitoba, where he chaired the Department of Jewish Studies. At that time, I had abandoned the idea of being a rabbi—too establishment. But Zalman believed that this was the right path for me. One day he said to me, "Phil, you'll go to rabbinic school and jump through all their hoops and then you'll be a rabbi and you can do that any way you want." In later years Zalman gave me good advice on being at the pulpit, but, of course, it is not true that a rabbi can do pulpit any way they want.

Are we to try to coax people to change from where they are or do we try to lead them to something better by moving ahead saying, "Follow me!" I am assuming here that people who become rabbis have ideas about better ways to practice our traditions. This tension can be eased by giving in and just doing what is comfortable for the congregants. But I think that does not really ease the tension between our "is" and our "ought. That tension can lead to professional burnout.

A rabbi who wants to move things forward means facing opposition from those who do not want change. Sy Dresner, *z"l*, commented about being an outspoken rabbi, "If you are not being criticized, you are probably not doing anything exceptional."

Sometimes the rabbi is going to be the issue. Deciding which issues are worth the agita is the question.

My role models in the rabbinate were and are social activists. That adds to this stress. How does a rabbi stay at a pulpit despite saying and doing things that make some in the congregation really unhappy? I suspect there was not a single year of my career someone was not seeking my ouster.

What saved me from year to year was being very attentive to my pastoral role. If the rabbi helps a family through a difficult time, they will find you to be a good rabbi. Once my Board wanted me gone and I demanded a congregational meeting about this (actually required in the State of New York). I delivered my case and got a standing ovation. I left the room for the discussion to follow and was later told that several people rose to comment on how I had helped them and no one from the Board had anything much to say. I won over two-thirds of the vote.

At my last congregation I was blessed with a member who styled herself TKOR ("The Keeper of Rabbi"). She made it her role to keep up with who was in need of contact from the rabbi and each week gave me a list of who to contact and why. I think every rabbi needs a TKOR.

The Rabbi as Negotiator

One of the most essential skills a rabbi can possess is the ability to negotiate. I am not referring only to negotiating one's own contract with the congregation. In fact, I recommend that a rabbi should avoid negotiating their own contract. When the time to negotiate a contract comes, the rabbi should realize that those they negotiate with are usually professionals who possess negotiation skills. What is also true is that they are congregants. Based on my experiences, the rabbi should seek people, preferably congregants, who have professional negotiation skills, such as lawyers. The laypeople doing the negotiations can be made to understand that the rabbi is humbly avoiding the give-and-take of a contract negotiation. They may even respect the rabbi's wisdom in not doing their own negotiating.

Whether or not the rabbi does their own negotiating, the manner of negotiations can be determined from the outset. There are two basic models that can be followed: competitive and collaborative.

Competitive negotiations are those where the two sides each try to get the best of the other. In a rabbinic contract negotiation that means the rabbi is trying to get as much as possible in salary and benefits, while the congregation is trying to give as little as possible. Collaborative negotiations are those where both sides work to get the best deal for the rabbi with the least impact on the congregation. These two modes can be considered in any instance of negotiation.

Those appointed to negotiate with the rabbi are not likely familiar or comfortable with any mode of negotiation except competitive. The congregation's negotiators agreed to a collaborative approach only once in my career. This is a reason for my advice to recruit someone to negotiate on the rabbi's behalf. Both modes can lead to an agreement that both sides are happy with. I have included in the bibliography a book that I think is the best guide to negotiating. It is called *Getting to Yes*.

To illustrate my ideas about using negotiating skills in other situations, here is a small one and a large one.

One year my confirmation class complained about the idea of wearing robes for their service. I told them the reason is that it is usual for all the confirmands to appear similarly dressed. I suggested an alternative. Boys would wear white shirts and black slacks and girls would wear black skirts and white blouses. That created an uproar as they wanted to be dressed as for a party for the *Oneg* celebration after the service. My response was that, if they wore robes, they could wear whatever they liked underneath the robes. It was just a matter of finding out what they really wanted. That is always a key in negotiations.

During my time on Long Island one year, I was told some in the congregation wanted twilight *b'nei mitzvah*. At that congregation then there were over seventy *b'nei mitzvah* a year and, so, many were doubles. I had two problems with this request. One was that this would require me to conduct three major services in one twenty-four-hour period. The other was that I knew realistically that these requests came from the more affluent members of the congregation. They would be coming dressed for an evening reception and I knew that the minds of those attending would be focused on that reception and not so much the service.

I felt that I had to put up some barriers to make these requests for a twilight service rarer than they would be otherwise. I really did not want to do such services at all. I told my Board and ritual committee that, as I saw it, I should be paid extra for the extra service, but that this fee should be paid directly by the family and not the congregation. Then I told them that the service would be a *Minchah/Maariv* with a *Havdalah* and would take place at the appropriate hour. I was then very much a *davar yom b'yomo* rabbi and also a *shaah b'shaato* rabbi. In other words, the service would be just as long as the morning service and it might take place at an hour that would be inconvenient with caterers in mind. I should note that in practice, I was willing in May and June to finesse the time of the service with the caterer in mind. On Long Island, the caterer was sovereign.

After some give and take, the congregation agreed with me on all of this. That meant I was able to restrict those twilights to a few per year. The families were not at all opposed to the small extra fee. And I was able to be "generous" on such matters as the time of the service. Everyone got what they wanted—the families, the congregation, and the rabbi and cantor. Again, the key was figuring out what everyone really wanted.

Three Rules

Over the decades of my career, I have formulated three rules to remember working at a pulpit. Actually, I think these rules apply in most workplaces. Here they are:

1. Never accept responsibility without getting authority.
2. Get everything in writing.
3. Never be afraid to say no.

In dealing with members, especially lay leaders, always remember that your pulpit must always be a place of trust. But, as Ronald Reagan put it, "Trust but verify."

Never Accept Responsibility without Getting Authority

To illustrate this, I refer to one of my non-pulpit experiences, the one when I saw this must be a rule for me. During my time as a Hillel director, I did not earn enough to really support my family, which included two small children. I therefore accepted a job as director of a JCC camp. This included several months of work preparing for the summer, as well as two months at the camp. I was hired by the executive director of the JCC that owns the camp.

I was chosen, because, as a rabbi, I was expected to strengthen the Jewish aspect of the camp's programs. I had done this before in Chicago, when I worked at a JCC there. Part of my job was to bring some Jewishness to the JCCs, which were, not just secular, but secularist.

Now I was again hired to do a similar job at a summer camp that brought in campers from several states. The problem was that most of the staff were not on board with this. I had not met them, let alone hired them. That was done by the JCC. This was a ranch camp whose focus was on horses and, with one exception, none of the wranglers was Jewish. The counselors were, but several of them were essentially college-age campers. When one counselor was fired, a sixteen-year-old was put in charge of that cabin. I saw this as a serious mistake, but I was over-ruled by my bosses who asserted that I had no authority over work assignments. I had taken a job and was not given the authority to do it right.

Many years later, I worked at a congregation where my job included being the principal of its school. In this case, I was given full authority including human resources and budget. That meant that I could make the necessary decisions to run the school, which flourished in my time there. No one tried to tell me how to do my job.

The only problem was a conflict of roles (maybe another rule should come out of this). As principal I sometimes had to discipline children whose acting out disrupted class lessons. That meant dealing with the parents, some of whom simply said it was my problem. I lost a few families over that kind of thing trying to be both principal and rabbi. In this case, my authority as principal conflicted with my role as pastor.

There are some roles for pulpit clergy that get in the way of being a pastoral figure. I recommend that a rabbi should not oversee the school, if that can be avoided. I also recommend that one's congregation should expect a rabbi to be a pastoral counselor, but not a therapist. Even if one has the chops to be a therapist, some congregants are not comfortable with clergy who know too much about them. Be warned. Refer congregants who need more than counseling to therapists outside the congregation.

Get Everything in Writing

A great many cases in business law in the Talmud are about agreements that have no written record. Without that, these cases become a matter of the word of one against the word of the other. I strongly urge colleagues to make it a matter of standard practice to get agreements about work conditions and practices in writing. We must deal with lay leaders who might change their minds or with new leaders.

I first learned this lesson the hard way. My understanding with the lay leaders at my congregation told me that I did not have to officiate at weddings and funerals for family members who were not in the temple member's household. This was important, because in those days, early in my career, I was not really paid enough to live in the community I was serving and part of my deal with them was living in the parsonage next door to the synagogue. They told me I could freelance doing funerals and weddings outside the congregation. But what about the extended family of congregants?

I was asked by a congregant to officiate at the funeral of their parent. Nothing was said about payment for the service. I officiated and made the terrible mistake of asking about payment after the service. I don't blame my congregant for being offended. I was utterly new to this and made a mistake. There was nothing written in my contract about such services. After some negotiations, my temple president agreed I was entitled to be paid for services to a nonmember, even if a close relative of a temple member, but I was not to ask for payment. In practice, most of the time, the family would ask me how much I should be paid, but not always. Looking back, I should have gotten this matter noted in writing as temple policy.

Where issues like this arise, it is better all around to have the conversation and the agreement, but, in the end, it is best put into writing and passed by the Board.

Never Be Afraid to Say No

From time to time, anyone working at a job might be asked or told to do something that is either not possible or is objectionable for whatever reason. Clergy is no exception.

Before the Reform Movement ordained women as rabbis in sufficient numbers to affect policy of congregations and of the

Movement itself, rabbis were not always thought of as husbands and fathers. That the rabbi is a parent and spouse was not considered in making demands of the rabbi's time. I still hear from my wife about times when I was prevented from participating in a family occasion. The one that has always stuck out was when a couple demanded that I perform a renewal of their wedding vows on Mothers' Day. I should have said "no." The influence of our female colleagues made it clear that family must be considered in what is asked of the rabbi.

One reality for synagogues is that families often join a temple when their oldest reaches the age, usually fourth grade, which represents the minimum of Hebrew school required for *b'nei mitzvah*. They quit in the year that their youngest celebrates *b'nei mitzvah*. That is just a fact of life for synagogue membership on Long Island (and I suppose elsewhere as well). My Board asked me to call members who were quitting to try to talk them about not quitting. Most of those leaving had planned to quit all along.

I tried to do that the year they asked and had a lot of awkward and unproductive phone calls. It took some effort to tell the Board I would not be doing that again, and eventually they gave that task to the membership committee. If I had not said no, I would have been stuck with a very uncomfortable waste of my time.

It is important that, when clergy says "yes," that this means the rabbi will do their best to do as promised. By the same token, it is essential that the rabbi says "no" when there is a problem with "yes." This is a matter of credibility. Saying "yes" while thinking "no" will lead to trouble.

One More Thing

I could go on at book length with my ideas about using business skills in pulpit work and other organizational work a rabbi might do. In fact, my idea was originally to write such a book. However, I will conclude with one more subject: the training of rabbis for being in the pulpit as a workplace.

Before rabbinic school, one should be taking undergraduate classes and workshops on business skills. The skills courses offered at the College-Institute should be taken and taken seriously. Throughout their career the rabbi should continue to take courses and workshops on these skills. Which skills? Here is a brief list:

- *Organizational Behavior*. Here is a good definition of this subject:

  All businesses have an internal culture that is unique to their company. Each employee contributes not only a certain skill set but also a personality with inherent values and beliefs, and those values and beliefs will determine how they will interact in work groups, with other employees, and toward management. Organizational Behavior (OB) is the multidisciplinary study of the employee interactions and the organizational processes that seek to create more efficient and cohesive organizations.[1]

  I tend to wince whenever a Board member says, "we are a business," because that often means something like, "Let's be cheap." Nonetheless, this field applies to a congregation as much as it does to a business organization.

- *Rabbi as Executive*. This includes skills like time management, grant writing, event planning, human resources, conflict resolution, negotiating, marketing, conducting interviews—and this list is not exhaustive.

- *Rabbi as Fiscal Management*. This includes budgeting, fundraising, and other functions involving funds.

What follows is a short list of books that I found useful and helpful. There are plenty of other books and now streaming courses, etc., on these subjects. I hope this article will be helpful to my colleagues.

Recommended Books

Here is a list of some of the books I have found to be useful in succeeded in the job aspects of the pulpit. The list is intentionally not in alphabetic order, but as I see their subjects:

- Norman Shawchuck and Roger Hauser. *Leading the Congregation: Caring for Yourself While Serving Others*. Nashville: Abingdon Press, 1993.

- Norman Shawchuck et al. *Marketing for Congregations: Choosing to Serve People More Effectively.* Nashville: Abingdon Press, 1992.
- Roger Fisher and William Ury. *Getting to Yes: Negotiating Agreement without Giving In.* New York: Penguin Books, 1981.
- Leil Lowndes. *How to Talk to Anyone.* Contemporary Books, 2003.
- Edwin H. Friedman. *Generation to Generation: Family Process in Church and Synagogue.* New York: The Guilford Press, 1985.
- Carolyn Schrok-Shenk and Lawrence Ressler, eds. *Making Peace with Conflict: Practical Skills for Conflict Transformation.* Scottsdale, PA: Herald Press, 1999.
- Peter L. Steinke. *Healthy Congregations: A Systems Approach.* Alban Institute, 1993.
- Bill Easum. *Sacred Cows Make Gourmet Burgers: Ministry Anytime, Anywhere, by Anyone.* Nashville: Abingdon Press, 2011.
- Herbert Tarr. *Heaven Help Us.* New York: Random House, 1968.

Note

1. https://online.usi.edu/degrees/business/mba/human-resources/what-is-organizational-behavior/.

Making the Circuit

Rabbi Jordan Parr

I do not live in the city where I serve. I travel from Dallas to Odessa, Texas, roughly once per month to be with my tiny congregation of thirty-five families.

I had learned about itinerant rabbis traveling through the Deep South in generations past but I thought they had gone the way of the traveling peddler, a time when Jewish immigrants traveled from town to town, struggling to find a permanent home where they could establish the "Jew Store," usually a dry goods or garment shop, in a town that grudgingly opened its door to these exotic (but still white) people with foreign accents and a foreign religion. My itinerant rabbinic forebears wandered with these immigrants, themselves settling in small, Southern towns when there were enough Jews congregated to form a synagogue. Stories of itinerant rabbis in the Deep South go back to the nineteenth century, when German and later Eastern European Jews left the port cities of New York and especially Galveston, Texas, in search of a new life.

But my story did not begin this way.

I began my rabbinic career like so many rabbis: Assistantship at a large temple, becoming the associate rabbi, serving four years in all, and then serving two small congregations for the next eighteen years, one in Georgia and then another in suburban Dallas. After twenty years, I thought I was on the typical smaller-congregation rabbinic career track: I'd end my rabbinic career in Dallas, with love and tears abounding. I truly thought this was the last stop on my professional journey.

But it didn't happen that way. I left my suburban Dallas pulpit, one that I had shepherded from a suite of rented spaces in a strip

RABBI JORDAN PARR (C86) is the rabbi of Temple Beth El, Odessa, Texas, where he has served for over eight years. He is also the creator and host of Torah for Christians, a podcast devoted to teaching the beauty of Judaism to a larger audience.

mall to a permanent space where we could worship en masse and where we could end our triple sessions on Sunday morning. Leaving was not my choice. My Board and I had frequent clashes; they eventually decided to take the congregation in a different direction. That was their prerogative, although the process of separation was unnecessarily divisive and painful for all, especially for my family.

Bitter and exhausted, it was time to try something new. For many years, my wife and I had planned that I might leave the pulpit after our daughters graduated high school; the nest would be empty, and I would be free to try something new. Although my younger daughter was still in high school, we decided to take the leap at this time. I had a year of severance coming so we knew that there would be some money. I created a consulting company, working with area senior living communities to help them attract Jewish residents. Due to the Great Recession and my own inexperience as an entrepreneur, I shut it down after a year—just when the severance pay was ending. With fears of going broke, I lucked into a career as a pre-need funeral consultant. As a rabbi working with both pre-need and bereaved families, I was supposed to attract Jewish clients. While I was personally successful, Jewish clients did not seek me out; I signed up more Christian clients than Jewish ones. Frankly, Jews might ask me to conduct a funeral, but they did not want to talk about advance planning or how much money it might cost. Discussing money with a rabbi was, for them, distasteful. Yet, Christian clients were more than happy to work with me; they regarded my title as a sign of honesty in what is regarded, with just cause, as a dishonest business. I did a lot of praying in the meeting rooms but also met the family of a veteran who drove a tank for General Patton in the Battle of the Bulge, assisted a veteran who survived the Bataan Death March, and buried a man who was a liberator of Dachau. These experiences are priceless and have stayed with me for many years. They ameliorated much of the distaste I had for organized Judaism at the time.

After such a bitter separation, I had no desire to return to the pulpit. For a year or two, I didn't even attend a synagogue. After a time, a traditional colleague in town, a dear friend, convinced me to come to his synagogue, where I attended for several years. I have to say, he brought me back to Judaism. His congregation was, and still is, a throwback to the Conservadox congregation of my grandfather's day; the melodies were old fashioned and this Krakow-born rabbi, who grew up the son of a beloved rabbi in Jerusalem, portrayed himself as a latter-day Jackie Mason. He shared his infectious love of Judaism with me and gave me ample opportunity to chant Torah, to teach, and to reinvigorate my Judaism. But still, it was not enough for me to return to the rabbinate.

Then, a colleague was retiring from his small congregation nearby. He thought that I might conduct High Holy Day services in his stead as they were not hiring a full-time rabbi. I didn't want to do it, but we really needed the money. So, I accepted. Reluctantly. For two years, I was the High Holy Day rabbi at a URJ congregation that should have been in the USCJ; they had a Conservative cantor and used a Conservative *machzor*. Frankly, I hated doing it. But after being away, it was the first step in my return. I realized though it was the congregation that I disliked, not being on the pulpit. The spark was still there.

I gladly left that pulpit with the last shofar call of *N'ilah*, never to return. But even though those two years were trying, I felt ready emotionally and spiritually to return to the pulpit, if only in a part-time capacity. I was still working in the funeral business. I had also begun to teach in the Jewish Studies department at a local university. I loved working with the college kids and realized that the spark that had driven me at the start of my career was lighting up again.

That winter, I learned of a very part-time job in Jackson, Tennessee. Jackson is about one hour east of Memphis, where my wife grew up and where my in-laws still lived. My mother-in-law had grown up in the Jackson congregation. It was an unfamiliar city for me but well-known to my wife and family. I reached out and was hired almost immediately.

For three years, I led High Holy Day services and came for six to eight Shabbat weekends each year. The people in Jackson were the nicest, kindest people I had ever met. They were truly grateful for my presence, and I am still close to them today. It wasn't much of a pulpit, but I was working as a rabbi again.

After three years of flying and driving, I decided that I wanted more. I needed to spend more time in the pulpit. After so much time away, I wanted to work at what I know and love: being a rabbi. But soon I discovered, through multiple applications and interviews, that search committees felt that I was too old for a

full-time position. There is a real age bias among our congregations; none believed that a fifty-something rabbi could work with
kids or attract young families to their congregations. As a nation-
ally recognized Jewish educator (and a popular adjunct professor
teaching Gen-Z students), I found that offensive. But the reality
was that I was too old for youth work and too young to work in
retirement communities.

God works in mysterious ways. I went to Memphis for a regional
rabbinical conference, scheduled just before a Jackson weekend.
While I was there, I dropped in on a camp acquaintance who had
just started her first job as a Reform Jewish educator at Temple
Israel in Memphis, where my wife and I had met. After congratu-
lating her on her new position, she mentioned that her home pulpit in Odessa, Texas, was searching for a new rabbi. I knew several people in that congregation from Greene Family Camp and
could possibly leverage those connections. I asked her to make
the call. She called her mother (also a Greene acquaintance), who
then called the chair of the search committee. Within a week, I had
squared things with the placement commission and scheduled a
preliminary interview. The following month, I accepted the position: High Holy Days plus twelve Shabbat weekends per year. I
made my tearful good-byes in Jackson and moved on to the next
stage of my journey. I have happily been with Temple Beth El in
Odessa for the past nine years.

Fortunately, they did not ask me to move to Odessa. Odessa, and
its sister city, Midland, are midsize towns in the oil-rich Permian
Basin of west Texas. Jews have lived there for at least a hundred
years, ever since oil was discovered there. My congregants are the
typical mix: teachers, engineers, doctors, and the like. There are
not too many of them, but they are quite grateful for me when I
am there.

I fly from Dallas to Midland monthly. (Southwest Airlines considers me a valued customer, as does the Hilton Hotel chain.) I
leave for the airport on Friday morning and return on Sunday
afternoon; having spent a weekend leading *Kabbalat Shabbat* worship, Shabbat morning Torah study, a Saturday evening program,
and religious school on Sunday. Of course, I visit those who are
ill or elderly, counsel conversion students and, God willing, will
conduct two *b'nei mitzvah* in the coming years, the first at the synagogue since I came to town.

Commuting to my pulpit has its advantages. I joke that I get out of town before they get tired of me. But the reality is that the congregants understand they are a declining congregation, aging rapidly, and finding a successor will be difficult. So, they appreciate me. Coming monthly also greatly reduces my workload. Most weekends, I do not have to prepare much more than a sermon and Torah study. Sometimes we have an adult education program on Saturday night, and I try to do something fun with the kids on Sundays.

COVID has changed the congregation greatly. For two years, we held virtual weekly services and Torah study. Our kids joined with our sister congregation in Lubbock, creating an online school in the process. Several members contracted COVID but fortunately, nobody became too sick. We were fortunate.

But several congregants retired and moved away to be with their adult children. They scattered throughout the country and while they still love the congregation, they left us. They were all long-time and active members, with decades of institutional knowledge and activism. The newer members have not replaced them, either in numbers or in activity.

The online school was for us a failure. Most of the parents didn't push their kids to spend another morning looking at a computer screen. Some parents even put off joining the temple until this year, waiting for us to return to in-person schooling. This year, we are trying to revive our school. While we will still celebrate Chanukah and Purim with Lubbock, a "home and home" arrangement, we must teach our own kids once again. It's not a burden; it's our responsibility. But it is hard to start from scratch.

The COVID fallout has changed the congregation in many ways. Our religious school is now meeting on Friday afternoons. While this may not be practical in a larger congregation, it's common in small, isolated congregations; we held school on Friday afternoons in Jackson, for example. The parents will teach in their homes weekly and when I am in town, we'll meet at the temple for about ninety minutes, have a challah and pizza Shabbat dinner together and then, hopefully, the kids and their parents will stay for the service.

Another change is the financial fallout from so many members leaving the congregation. Aside from the two joint weekends with Lubbock, I'm leaving town on Saturday evening instead of on Sunday. On the one hand, if school is on Fridays, I don't need to be in town on Sunday. On the other hand, such financial difficulties do not bode well for the congregation or for how we will negotiate my next contract, should we agree that I will continue to serve them in the coming years.

While monthly commuting spares me a lot of the pain and agony of being a full-time rabbi, a job that cost me dearly in the past, there are still several disadvantages. Of course, I don't see my congregants enough—and COVID made it worse. If they don't come to services, it's hard to get to know them. It's also hard to do any kind of outreach to new families; they want to meet the rabbi but he's not there. I don't know any non-Jewish clergy or elected officials either in Midland or Odessa, which is a real detriment when trying to plan programs or to be involved in the larger community. Finally, my wife stays behind when I travel, except for the High Holy Days, when she sits in the pews, barely knowing anyone.

I don't know how much longer I will commute to Odessa. Perhaps this will be the last year; perhaps I'll stay another five years. If I am healthy and they keep liking what I'm doing, the *shiduch* will continue. But whether I stay or not, I truly hope that in the years to come, more of us will see this career path as one of great holiness and personal reward. Those of us serving smaller congregations in isolated areas have come to realize that we may be the last rabbis that these congregations will ever engage, be it due to their financial decline, aging congregants, or especially because student rabbis and newly ordained rabbis will not come to these small towns when more opportunity beckons in major metropolitan areas on the coasts. There are just not enough younger rabbis eager to serve these wonderful congregations.

But to end a career, serving a small, isolated congregation as an itinerant rabbi can't be beat. As the rabbinic shortage becomes more acute, I would encourage colleagues contemplating retirement to leave those big, stressful congregations (when ready) and spend a few years serving wonderful people in an underserved community. While you won't make the money that a full-time gig provides, you will have the freedom to travel, visit the grandkids, and write that book that you have been planning ever since your ordination. Perhaps you can draw from your pension to make ends meet, whether you move to the community or commute like I do. Most important, you will be valued and beloved, simply because you are present. It's a great retirement plan, without being fully retired.

An Unlikely Journey

Rabbi Neal Katz

I have been hesitant to tell the tale of my own career journey as a rabbi over the years because it is largely unremarkable. So, I'll start at the ending: I continue to serve the same pulpit where I started my rabbinate twenty years ago. I've seen colleagues change congregations, sometimes in search of a better professional fit and other times in an effort to enhance their careers. I have admired my peers who have climbed through the ranks to assume leadership positions in significant congregations or major organizations. Perhaps it is inertia, but I have never left my small East Texas congregation of seventy-five families. Though the events that brought me here may seem commonplace, they are worth recounting. And I appreciate the opportunity to share my unique journey with others through this journal.

I feel there were key moments that led me down this unlikely path. It was spring of the year 2000 at HUC-JIR in Cincinnati. My classmates and I were drawing numbers for the student pulpit lottery. As an entering third-year student, I knew that it was time to take on a biweekly pulpit. Fortunately, I got an early draw in the lottery, which meant I could get my top choice. I had spent weeks preceding that lottery researching the student pulpits for the coming year, and I knew a few things:

1. I wanted to fly to my student pulpit,
2. I wanted to have a soloist at the congregation, and
3. I did not want home hospitality.

After plotting out the matrix of possible congregations and ranking them according to my possible student lottery draw, my

RABBI NEAL KATZ (C03) has served as the rabbi of Congregation Beth El in Tyler, Texas, since his ordination from HUC-JIR in 2003. Neal is involved in many nonprofit agencies and is currently the Board chair of a local nonprofit journalism project called The Tyler Loop.

top choice was Tyler, Texas. It fit all my criteria. I had been to Dallas for a UAHC Biennial a few years prior, but other than that, I had no connection to Texas. Whatever this congregation was going to be, it was simply going to be a way-station on my journey to the ultimate goal: an assistantship in a large congregation in a big city. I was ambitious and wanted to serve in one of the large Movement congregations, full of resources and staff and with enough congregants so there could be a critical mass for doing innovative programs.

My second-year pulpit had been at a small community that met once a month in Great Falls, Montana. This biweekly was going to serve as the next step in my practical education.

A bit about Congregation Beth El in Tyler, Texas. It was founded in the spring of 1887 and spent its first thirteen years bringing in visiting rabbis and lay leaders. With a traditionalist break-off in the mid-1890s, the congregation began to raise funds to hire a full-time Reform rabbi. In 1900, they brought in Hungarian-born Maurice Faber. He had been serving a congregation in Keokuk, Iowa, at the time. Rabbi Faber stayed in Tyler until his death in 1934. And so began a run of wonderful rabbinic leadership at the congregation until Rabbi Steve Gold left in 1998. That was the year of transition.

Beth El found itself unexpectedly without a rabbi after ninety-eight years of mostly full-time rabbinic leadership (there were a few gaps). Unfortunately, Beth El in Tyler found itself in a doubly difficult situation: not only was it a small rural congregation (two hours east of Dallas), making it unattractive to rabbis seeking a large congregation in a big city, but 1998 also happened to be a year of a rabbi shortage in the Reform Movement. And Tyler was not a desirable market for many rabbis.

And so Beth El entered HUC-JIR's student pulpit program while they were searching for a full-time replacement for Rabbi Gold. The student-rabbi stretch lasted for five years. And for two of those five years, from 2000 to 2002, I served them as my biweekly pulpit.

My plan upon ordination in 2003 was to move to a large city and work in a large congregation. But a few things occurred during those years that led me on a much different career path than I had envisioned. I ended up coming back to Tyler full-time in 2003 and I have never left. I often joke that I am now in year twenty of a three-year contract. So what changed?

There were three distinct moments I recall that pushed me into a small solo pulpit two hours from the closest big city.

1. The Article

The first moment I began to think outside of the box began with an article by Rabbi Simeon Maslin *z"l* in the Summer 2001 *Reform Judaism* magazine. In the article, Rabbi Maslin, ordained in 1957, spoke about how his generation of rabbis were expected to serve in the military chaplaincy before serving in a congregational pulpit. This led him to two years in the military. Feeling called by service, he then moved his family to serve a small congregation in Curaçao. He wrote, "The salary was meager, but the satisfaction I derived from those years of service to a wonderfully appreciative community that might have disintegrated without rabbinic leadership more than made up for it."

As I read these words, something began to stir in me. In the year that article was published, 2001, the shortage of available rabbis was still a pressing issue. Rabbi Maslin lamented the misalignment of rabbinic resources. In that same article, he shared a text that could just as well have been written today. He wrote, "Even here in North America, where our congregations, camps, and day schools are flourishing, there are scores of historic congregations in the South and Midwest that lack rabbinic leadership and are fast fading away. And while some metropolitan congregations enjoy the services of two or three rabbis, there are communities on this continent and overseas that have been without a liberal rabbi for decades; some of them are simply giving up or turning to charlatans."

I know there are colleagues reading this article who are much better equipped than I to address the dynamics surrounding the rabbinic shortage of the late 1990s and early 2000s. But from my perspective as a rabbinic student, I was fascinated by the conversation. I saw Reform Movement congregations become agitated that the College-Institute was not producing enough rabbis to fill their pulpit needs. And to make matters more contentious, some of our colleagues, upon ordination from HUC-JIR, were opting to serve Conservative congregations, work at Hillels, or run community organizations.

And I appreciated the agitation. In the historical model of funding, as I understand it, the Union member congregations were patrons at some level of the College-Institute, the Sisterhoods offered a number of student scholarships, and there was plenty of fundraising from individual members of the Reform Movement. So the idea that the school that could not produce enough rabbis for the needs of the Movement that was funding it, and—*al achat kama v'kama*—was also ordaining rabbis for work outside the Movement—was upsetting.

I remember a powerful speech given by then HUC-JIR president Rabbi Shelly Zimmerman at a Movement event. The location escapes me. He was compelled to respond to the vocal concerns of those who blamed HUC-JIR for the shortage and for professional placements outside of the Movement. Rabbi Zimmerman responded forcefully that the College-Institute was not designed only to train Reform congregational pulpit rabbis. It was designed to produce a wide variety of leadership that served the Jewish community across a broad spectrum of roles. He went one step further and used this as an opportunity (correctly) to fundraise. He told the audience that at that moment, they needed to support the College-Institute even more than ever. It was a great way to flip the current crisis at that time into a fundraising opportunity.

And it was in this context that Rabbi Maslin's article appeared. He was offering the voice of an older generation of rabbis who felt duty-bound to work, at least initially, within the confines of the Reform Movement. And that spoke to me.

I grew up at Ohef Shalom, a wonderful Reform congregation in Norfolk, Virginia, led by Rabbi Larry Forman. The Reform Movement had a profound impact on my Jewish upbringing. I was heavily involved with both my local youth group and our NFTY region, where I served as vice president for two years. I spent my junior year abroad in NFTY's College and Kibbutz program (CAY), of blessed memory, and I worked for NFTY in Israel for three summers. I spent summers at Reform Jewish summer camps. And I met my wife through our synagogue youth group.

I was blessed with a rich tapestry of Jewish life that was provided through my local congregation and a national Movement. As an HUC-JIR student, I felt that part of my obligation in becoming a rabbi was to give back to that very same Movement. That is why Rabbi Maslin's article spoke to me in that moment. I was not planning on working outside the Movement, but I clearly heard the call of obligation.

2. The Money Idea

I remember there was a meeting on the Cincinnati campus between rabbinical students and Rabbi Steve Fox from the CCAR. And among the many topics covered was an emphasis by the CCAR leadership to encourage graduating rabbinic students to serve small, underserved communities. My ears perked up when I heard this, as I was already mulling over this idea after reading Rabbi Maslin's article. But what Rabbi Fox said next sweetened the deal. He shared an idea that was being floated around that for any new graduate that agreed to serve an underserved community for three years, there would be up to $50,000 of tuition reimbursement from the CCAR.

My mind immediately went to the fictional character of Dr. Joel Fleischman from the 1990s TV show *Northern Exposure*, who paid off some of his medical school debt by serving in a rural area of Alaska. I had amassed plenty of tuition debt before and during rabbinical school. And the idea that there could be some incentive that would help me pay down my debt was music to my ears. I pressed Rabbi Fox on some of the details and he admitted that it was just an idea being floated. He said that he shared that information with us to demonstrate how the CCAR was thinking creatively on how to address rabbinic shortfalls in certain demographic areas. He elaborated the proposal was to offer this to two students per year. And when I asked him what constituted an underserved community, he agreed that Tyler would be an example of such a community. It is two hours east of Dallas, an hour and forty-five minutes west of Shreveport, four hours north of Houston, and five hours southwest of Little Rock. If someone in East Texas needed a Reform rabbi, there was not one for hours. Even though there was no commitment by the CCAR at that point, I was intrigued by the prospect of a tuition reimbursement by serving a community that I already knew.

It turns out that the CCAR program never materialized due to a lack of funding. But at that formative time in my professional decision-making process, it made an impact on my thinking.

3. Herb Epstein

No one reading this article would know the name Herb Epstein; he was a congregant in Tyler. But Herb made the one statement that ultimately made my career decision for me.

Herb Epstein was a Bronx-born Jew who was raised in a traditional household. He left that community for military service and a life of business. Herb ended up working in the helicopter industry, eventually becoming the president of Aerospatiale Helicopter, an American Division of a European helicopter manufacturer. They were based in Dallas, Texas, and while he was president, this small company won a contract from the United States Coast Guard to build a fleet of their helicopters. Herb oversaw enormous growth for his company. Then he retired and moved to East Texas.

In his retirement, Herb, now in his seventies, returned to school and received his doctorate from Texas A&M. He did this because he wanted to teach at the local university, UT Tyler, which he did until he was about ninety years old. He taught in the business school and was a mentor to many students who were considering different career paths.

Herb's second marriage was to a lovely Methodist woman. They built a house on Lake Palestine in East Texas (it's pronounced with a long "e"—as in Palesteen). He named his lake house "Kinneret." Herb was an active participant in my adult study class during my student rabbi years and a regular Shabbat attendee. In 2005, he and his wife, in their early eighties, came on an Israel trip with me. Herb was not a high-maintenance congregant. He was always pleasant to be around, never got in my business, and was just happy to be connected to the Jewish community. Sometimes I pray for a hundred congregants like Herb Epstein.

In 2002, I was finishing up my student pulpit work in Tyler, and my mind was already swirling with the possibility of altering my plans for a large congregational pulpit. I was thinking about going to a small solo pulpit because of Rabbi Maslin's charge and the fanciful idea of tuition reimbursement by the CCAR. And the members of Beth El began hocking me about returning to Tyler the following year after ordination. I would just smile and nod and take it as a light ego boost, but I never took it too seriously. I still wasn't sure if Tyler would be the right landing spot for me.

And then one day in the spring of 2002, Herb Epstein took me to lunch at his favorite place, Applebee's. Even though I am a big guy, I don't eat a lot in one sitting. And yet eighty-year-old Herb would eat an entire steak, potatoes, a side of broccoli, and wash it down with a glass of red wine at lunch.

At that lunch, Herb did what I expected him to do: he began talking to me about coming back to Tyler full-time the following year. But he had an interesting approach that led to the one sentence that made the difference for me.

He asked rhetorically, "I guess people at the congregation are bugging you about coming back next year?" I replied, "Yes." He asked what I was thinking. I was upfront and told him that I had never considered it before but coming back to Tyler full-time was now in the mix because of an article that I had recently read plus the possibility of some tuition reimbursement. And then he asked me what my wife thought of the idea. She and I had discussed it and she was supportive of a possible move to Tyler—knowing that we would make up for the lack of a large religious community by connecting our kids to Jewish summer camps, youth group, Israel, and that we were only two hours from Dallas. But I still wasn't sure. And then came the statement.

He said, "Neal, you know I mentor a lot of different students who are planning out their careers." I nodded and acknowledged that I knew this.

And he said he would offer me one piece of advice: "When you map out all of the possible places you could go as a rabbi, and as long as all things are equal, and they have to be equal, in terms of commensurate pay, lifestyle, and so on, all things being equal . . . go to the place where you know you will be appreciated."

"Go to the place where you know you will be appreciated."

That's all my ears needed to hear. And I can say with confidence, that he was 100 percent right in that moment. And here twenty years later, Herb, of blessed memory, is still right.

I met with the administration at HUC-JIR to talk about the boundaries of my conversations with my student pulpit. They understood that the congregation was making a push to commit me to return there after ordination—but were also very clear about the rules. If it was a position advertised to CCAR rabbis (it was), I could not ethically interfere with the possible placement of a field rabbi in this congregation. And I did not want to. So, I was unable to commit to any offer of employment in Tyler. If they found a match before I was ordained, so be it.

And so, with the administration of HUC-JIR, we worked out the appropriate language for my reply whenever someone in Tyler would bring up the possibility of my coming back full-time. I would say, "If the congregation is still in placement next year, I will apply. And if I apply, it will be the only congregation to which I will apply." This allowed the congregation to continue their active search, but also be comfortable knowing that I was taking this seriously.

Congregation Beth El in Tyler did indeed have some rabbis apply for the position, but they were not good matches for the congregation. And when pulpit placement came in the spring of 2003, I did not join. I watched my classmates go through the angst of the placement process. I saw some of them go through the process successfully, while others had taken lower-ranked options as they made their way into the rabbinate. On the day that the list of matches was posted, I was not on the list since I had not gone through placement. I was a "free agent." And then I received a call five minutes later from a woman in Tyler who somehow could smell that that list had just been put on the door. She asked me if I wanted the job. I said, "Yes." And that was it. That was my interview. I often joke that I had no interview for this job. But in truth, I did have a two-year student pulpit interview. And so I came back to the place where I knew I would be appreciated.

I signed on to a three-year contract that began on July 1, 2003. Three years later, in the spring of 2006, Beth El held its annual meeting as my contract was nearing its end. The meeting was scheduled for 6:00 p.m. and I was in my office right before it started. At 5:55 p.m. three of the machers from the congregation came into my office and asked, "Do we have a contract for you when yours expires on June 30?" I said, "No, I've been asking you all about it for the past number of months." And they replied, "Well, we have completely dropped the ball on this."

Then they asked, "Are you leaving us?" I said, "No."

I asked, "Are you firing me?" They said, "No."

And we laughed.

They said, "We need to go down to the other end of the hall in five minutes and tell them that we have a renewed contract for you. Let's negotiate right now." I replied, "Okay."

"What do you want in your contract? Name your price. We are embarrassed. Just be fair. Do you want a bump in salary? Do you want to bump in COLA? Do you want a bump in benefits? Name your price."

I responded, "How about zero?" And they looked perplexed? "What do you mean?" they asked.

I said, "The contract that I signed in 2003 was fair and it had a built-in COLA. It covers all my benefits, and I would simply like an extension of that contract."

They pushed one more time. "Do you want a bump of 3 to 6 percent in salary from this year to next?" I said, "No, it's a fair contract for where I live and I would like an extension of that only."

They asked, "Can we say it's for five years?" I said, "Sure." And that was it. We shook hands and walked to the other end of the building for our 6:00 p.m. meeting.

I tell that story with pride, but I recognize that some rabbis don't like hearing the way that went down. And to make it crazier, that is the identical conversation I've had every five years. I refuse to take additional money. I just ask for extensions of the original 2003 contract. It was fair then, and it is still fair now.

I listen to my colleagues and some rabbis on the CCAR Facebook page talk about contract negotiations and they talk about bringing in mediators or lawyers. They talk about how it can get contentious and uncomfortable. And then once you are on the other side of those negotiations, how does that dynamic impact rabbinic work in the congregation? I admit that I am one of the lucky ones since I did not have to fight for any part of my initial contract. It was incredibly generous because they knew me for two years as a student.

When my first two children were born in Cincinnati, Beth El Tyler was generous with gifts and notes and genuine love. When my third child was born in Tyler in 2005, they were again menschen as they offered gifts and love. Over the years, my congregation has supported all my kids attending summer camp every year, they have given me wonderful Chanukah bonuses, and they have let me set my own schedule. If that is the case, why would I want to nickel-dime them in a contract negotiation? I feel like I landed in a wonderful community that understands *kavod haRav*. As Herb said, "Go to a place you know you will be appreciated." And it was never one-sided; I feel like I have paid my dues, like all rabbis, in terms of building those relationships that have sustained me in this small community.

I once sat down with a main macher of the congregation. He was president at the time. And I confided in him that I had a guilt complex. I told him that if I do all of my work at our seventy-five-family congregation, at best, I have a part-time job. I do work fifty to sixty hours a week, but most of those hours are outside of the congregation. I am heavily involved in local nonprofit work, I teach at the university, I perform music, and so on. And he said, "I know. That's why we love you. We need you to fill out those additional hours by being our voice in the community." I was shocked at his honesty, but it was exactly what I needed to hear. If I put the congregation and the members first, they were not going to micromanage my time. In fact, in one moment of crazy, they allowed me to run for a statewide office for an entire year. That's another article.

I was once at a conference when I ran into my former HUC-JIR professor, Rabbi Dr. Sam Joseph. He asked me how things were in Tyler. I told him that I felt like I was still in a honeymoon phase after many years in the same congregation. I also admitted that I was a little concerned. He smiled and said, "So, you landed in the right place. They like you and you like them. Don't take that for granted." I protested lightly, "Yeah, but I wonder what I could do with a larger congregation with more people and a bigger religious school and wider community reach."

He replied, "Rabbis suffer from the 'grass is greener-ism.' They think that it's always better somewhere else. And they chase after those opportunities—and sometimes they find it—sometimes they don't. But if you have already landed in a place where you are doing good work and they appreciate you, then count your blessings."

I heard an echo of Herb in Rabbi Joseph's remarks. And so, I have happily remained on the path that I never expected to take. It was those few key moments while at HUC-JIR that challenged my professional plans, and I opened myself up to a career in a small community that has, thus far, brought me personal and professional fulfillment.

General Articles

"Egypt Is Lost": Lessons for History and America

Rabbi Elaine Rose Glickman

The first fourteen chapters of the Book of Exodus comprise the Israelites' origin story. They also tell how a leader failed those over
whom he ruled, ignored calls for statecraft and prudence, and destroyed one of the greatest empires of all time.

In this article, I offer a commentary on selected passages from
Exodus 1:8 through 14:28, illuminating the motivations of Pharaoh
and how he views his people; highlighting examples of attempted
defiance; and delineating the gradual decline and then sudden
ruin of the kingdom of Egypt.

Exodus 1:8–11

The Pharaoh of the Joseph narrative held firm control over his nation. Even at a time of unprecedented crisis—lengthy and widespread famine, food insecurity, economic collapse, and an influx
of migrants seeking sustenance—his power remained unques-
tioned. The Egyptians did not challenge his rule or his decisions—
including what must have been the controversial appointment of
a foreigner as his second-in-command and master of the country's
wealth. The Book of Genesis refers to this ruler almost exclusively
by his title Pharaoh; on the few occasions in which the phrase
מֶלֶךְ מִצְרַיִם appears, the honorific Pharaoh immediately follows.

As related in Exodus 1:8ff, the emergence of a new ruler
brings an entirely different situation: [1] וַיָּקׇם מֶלֶךְ־חָדָשׁ עַל־מִצְרָיִם.
("A new king arose over Egypt.") The word that describes his

RABBI ELAINE ROSE GLICKMAN (C98) is the assistant executive director of the
Women's Rabbinic Network and a past editor-in-chief of the *CCAR Journal*.

ascension—וַיָּקָם—is not generally associated with kingship; it connotes simply "rising" rather than being appointed, acclaimed, or anointed for a position of power. Nor is this monarch immediately granted the title Pharaoh, or even a definite article; he is simply called מֶלֶךְ־חָדָשׁ ("a new king") .

How can מֶלֶךְ־חָדָשׁ establish power over the nation and achieve the corresponding title, Pharaoh? His method is unoriginal but effective; capitalizing on the increasing presence of Israelites in Egypt, this "new king" portrays them as the actual and more threatening "other." To unite himself with the Egyptian people as a "we," the aspiring Pharaoh warns of the danger that "they"—these foreigners—pose.

This danger, according to the new king, is twofold. He first raises the specter of war; his use of the passive voice (כִּי־תִקְרֶאנָה מִלְחָמָה²) and failure to name a specific enemy or menace, however, suggests that this threat is not imminent and perhaps not especially realistic. In fact, the peril of this war appears to come not from an external foe but from a change to the status quo—that is, a challenge to the current hegemony of the "we."

This new king cautions: If war is declared, the Israelites might join with those who hate us.³ And what will be the consequence? וְעָלָה מִן־הָאָרֶץ⁴. Although this passage is often translated to express fear that the Israelites will leave Egypt, a parallel use of the phrase in the Book of Hosea⁵—as well as Rashi's commentary—leads to a better understanding: that the Israelite community will "arise from the land"—that is, from their lowly station—among the Egyptians.

This tactic proves immediately effective. By the very next verse, the Israelites have been reduced from prolific landholders in the best part of Egypt to slaves—and this "new king" seems to have been accepted by the Egyptians and elevated to the status of Pharaoh.

Exodus 1:11–2:23

Although the new king has been named Pharaoh, his power is far from absolute. The astonishingly quick and complete enslavement of the Israelites is credited not to him but to the Egyptian people, as attested using the plural⁶—וַיָּשִׂימוּ—"they set taskmasters over [the Israelites]." When Pharaoh himself gives his first specific command to his subjects, he is disobeyed and foiled.

Pharaoh's first interaction with individual Egyptians proves illuminative. Addressing two midwives tending to the Hebrew women,[7] he instructs them to kill every boy they deliver. However, the audacity of this order is undermined by his approach: וַיֹּאמֶר, the root *amar*, not the stronger *tzevah* or even *dabar*—implies a conversation among equals rather than a monarch directing his subjects. The midwives not only refuse but boldly excuse their inaction with a lie that could be easily disproved, suggesting disrespect for the king's authority and what we might call a "deep state." And while his next step appears to be a compelling, universal command—now issued under the appellation Pharaoh—for all his subjects to engage in infanticide, no action seems to be taken;[8] his own daughter, in fact, will defy the order and bring a Hebrew boy into the royal palace, assimilating him so thoroughly that he will be mistaken for an Egyptian.[9]

Exodus 2:11–15 further illustrates the shortcomings of Pharaoh's knowledge and power. When Moses kills the Egyptian taskmaster tormenting a Hebrew slave, the Israelites know what he has done and speak about it openly the very next day. Although נוֹדַע הַדָּבָר ("the matter is known")[10]—Pharaoh remains unaware. Even his attempt to find and kill Moses is thwarted by "deep state"-style subterfuge as Moses finds shelter in Midian—a region ostensibly under Pharaoh's control[11]—with a priest who knowingly welcomes the fugitive into his family and gives him a daughter in marriage.

Chapter 2 draws to a close with the news that מֶלֶךְ מִצְרַיִם has died.[12] While the *p'shat* of this verse is clear and straightforward, Rashi cites *Sh'mot Rabbah* 1:34 to raise the possibility that the king only suffered a bout of leprosy but remained alive. Whether the Pharaoh who acts hereafter in our story is a new king (the fact that he is addressed almost exclusively as Pharaoh suggests this is the case) or not, we will find similar instability in his rule—and soon among not only his subjects but even among his courtiers and inner circle.

Exodus 4:19

Offering additional support for the idea that a new ruler sits upon the throne is this brief passage, which relates God's order that Moses return to Egypt: כִּי־מֵתוּ כָּל־הָאֲנָשִׁים הַמְבַקְשִׁים אֶת־נַפְשֶׁךָ ("for all the people who sought to kill you have died"). With these words, God not only reassures Moses that his pursuers are dead, but also hints that even with this new king Moses will still face a less-than-invincible foe. As Egyptian monarchs are generally presented as quasi-divine figures, an essential subtext of the Exodus narrative serves to remind the Israelites—and the reader—that Pharaoh is just an ordinary human being; God insinuates this for the first time by referring to Pharaoh as simply one of the people—הָאֲנָשִׁים—who wanted Moses dead.

Exodus 5:1–23

This first confrontation between Moses and Pharaoh begins abruptly; with no ceremony, Moses and Aaron are admitted to Pharaoh's presence and immediately make their petition. Although Pharaoh appears to react decisively—denying their request and knowledge of the One in Whose name it is made and ordering an immediate return to their labors—he is clearly rattled. Just as the earlier Pharaoh responded to the midwives' defiance by issuing a dramatic but impractical order, this Pharaoh ludicrously charges the taskmasters and foremen to cease giving the Israelites straw, but to require the same production of bricks.

This Pharaoh, however, proves far more capable of turning the situation to his advantage. Whereas the Pharaoh of Exodus 1 acceded to the midwives and appeared to leave unenforced his order that every Egyptian take responsibility for drowning baby Hebrew boys, this Pharaoh utilizes the impossibility of his command as an opportunity to consolidate his power.

First, Pharaoh renews the "othering" of the Israelites: When the Hebrew foremen rightfully blame the diminished production of bricks on the taskmasters' failure to provide straw, Pharaoh insists that the problem lies with the Israelites' laziness and delinquency, qualities that he expressly links with the worship of their particular God.[13] Next, he sows discord among the Israelites—blaming this punishment on Moses and Aaron's demand that the people be allowed to worship God, he weakens the solidarity of the oppressed by turning them against one another. Without a strong relationship with either God or with Moses and Aaron, the Israelites are vulnerable to these machinations; they leave Pharaoh's presence angry at Moses and Aaron—rather than Pharaoh—and blaming the brothers for their troubles. This exchange even causes division between Moses and God; still newly in relationship with *Adonai*, Moses lacks the confidence to defend God or even himself, instead turning on God and accusing: "From the time I came before Pharaoh to speak in Your name, he has brought even more evil upon this people—and You certainly have not saved Your people."[14]

Exodus 7:8–9:7

Moses and Aaron's next audience with Pharaoh brings the "divine signs and wonders" that God has promised—and first demonstrates Pharaoh's shortcomings as both a would-be god and a ruler.

Bearing his wondrous staff, Aaron follows God's command to throw down the rod, and it turns into a serpent before Pharaoh and his courtiers. Despite Pharaoh's supposedly supernatural powers, he does not even attempt to emulate the miracle; rather, he calls for חֲכָמִים וּמְכַשְּׁפִים ("his sages and magicians") to enact a similar transformation. Further emphasizing Pharaoh's weakness, God instructs Moses to intercept Pharaoh the next morning, as the monarch makes his way to the Nile to relieve himself in secret—delivering the message that while Pharaoh may be able to hide this physical need from the Egyptians who see him as divinity,[15] Moses is aware of his altogether human nature and limits.

A close reading of the account of the first plague introduces another weakness of Pharaoh and reveals the first cracks in the relationship between him and his subjects. This plague is comprehensive and devastating: The Nile, its canals and ponds, its waters collected in wooden and stone vessels—indeed כָּל־מִקְוֵה מֵימֵיהֶם ("every body of its waters")[16]—turn to blood; its fish die and stink; and blood flows throughout Egypt. Yet the moment that Pharaoh's magicians prove capable of imitating the miracle, Pharaoh loses interest. As the Egyptians suffer a river devoid of life, digging along its fetid banks in hopes of finding drinking water, Pharaoh retreats to his palace—apparently for a full week—and ignores the plight of כָּל־מִצְרַיִם (the entirety of his people).[17]

In response, God urges Moses to announce the second plague of frogs by emphasizing its effect not on the Egyptians but on Pharaoh himself: "The frogs will arise and come into *your* home and *your* bedroom, and upon *your* bed, and the houses of *your* courtiers and *your* people, and *your* ovens and *your* kneading-bowls. The frogs will come upon *you*, and upon *your* people, and upon all *your* courtiers."[18] And while תְּכַס אֶת־אֶרֶץ מִצְרָיִם (the frogs indeed cover the land of Egypt)[19]—they affect Pharaoh as the plague of blood did not, and he responds accordingly. This time, God does not need to command Moses and Aaron to confront Pharaoh; rather, Pharaoh summons them and begs first that the frogs be removed from him—and (only secondly) from his people. Once God grants Moses' request to ease the plague specifically אֲשֶׁר־שָׂם לְפַרְעֹה ("placed upon Pharaoh"),[20] however, Pharaoh again grows unconcerned. Even as the Egyptians drag dead frogs from their houses, their courtyards, and their fields—creating heaps so tremendous that the entire land reeks—Pharaoh is interested only in הָרְוָחָה ("the relief")[21] that he himself sees.

Although the third plague—lice—descends upon the entire land of Egypt, it appears like the first plague in that Pharaoh is not expressly affected—and Pharaoh does not expressly act. For the first time, however, those in his inner circle do; unable to replicate this affliction, Pharaoh's magicians warn: אֶצְבַּע אֱלֹהִים הִוא ("This is the finger of God.")[22] His response, however, is וַיֶּחֱזַק—confusing strength (חֵזֶק) with stubbornness, Pharaoh refuses to heed them.[23] This episode begins the process of dividing Pharaoh not only from his people but also from his inner circle; indeed, as Ramban observes, Pharaoh and his magicians do not speak to each other again.

God guides Moses to reclaim Pharaoh's attention with the fourth plague, commanding Moses again to intercept Pharaoh on his clandestine early-morning visit to relieve himself at the water, as well as emphasize how this plague will impact him and his inner circle. The swarms of insects will devastate *you*, *your* courtiers, *your* people, and *your* houses, Moses warns Pharaoh;[24] the homes of the Egyptians and their land are listed as apparent afterthoughts. God also turns Pharaoh's "othering" of the Israelites against him, sparing their historical region of Goshen from the plague. And once the insects are unleashed, Pharaoh's palace and the homes of his courtiers are expressly named as suffering the invasion.

Let us stop for a moment and envision the condition of Egypt: The Nile has just changed from blood back to water; presumably, there are not yet living fish in it, and holes remain along its banks from the Egyptians' recent and desperate attempts to secure drinking water. Rotting frogs lie in heaps, and—as the text does not describe an end to the third plague—the people may continue to struggle with lice; and הָאָרֶץ תִּשָּׁחֵת ("the entire land"),[25] except for Goshen, has been destroyed. And yet, in confronting this crisis —and the misery it has wrought on his community—Pharaoh centers his own concerns and suffering—addressing Moses and Aaron with the words: בַּעֲדִי. הַעְתִּירוּ ("Plead for me.")[26] Even the fifth plague—which will bring the death of מִצְרָיִם מִקְנֵה כֹּל ("all the livestock of Egypt")[27]—arouses Pharaoh's interest only enough that he asks if the Israelites' livestock has been killed; he does not inquire about, let alone comfort or aid, his own devastated people.

Exodus 9:8–10:20

Although Pharaoh has not been completely spared from the plagues, he has maintained his hold on the government and kept the apparatus of his regime functioning. However, with the arrival of the sixth plague—boils—the chaos engulfing Egypt finally reaches his palace and inner circle. Afflicted with inflammation, the court magicians are no longer able to appear before Moses; and when God announces that the next plague of hail will kill every person and animal left outside, some of Pharaoh's courtiers reveal themselves as יְהֹוָה אֶת־דְּבַר הַיָּרֵא ("one fearing the word of Adonai"),[28] and bring their slaves and livestock indoors.

The split that began with the falling-out between Pharaoh and his magicians during the third plague now deepens. Although the elite of Egypt do not yet dare to voice their concerns, the actions of some—declining to stand with Pharaoh against Moses as the sixth plague rages, and quietly attending to God's warning to save their possessions from the hail—show an estrangement between them and their leader, and a dawning awareness that despite Pharaoh's supposed divinity, the God of Israel is the One to be heeded. One might also suppose that the courtiers who remained loyal to Pharaoh —and whose slaves and livestock have consequently been destroyed by hail—are reconsidering their allegiances.

Perhaps aware of his inner circle's wavering support and the growing turmoil in his nation, Pharaoh again summons Moses and Aaron—and for the first time takes at least a bit of responsibility. הַפָּעַם חָטָאתִי, he confesses, I sinned this time—although these words are followed almost immediately with וְעַמִּי וַאֲנִי, as he shifts some of the blame by describing both himself and his people as "the wicked ones."[29] But for the moment, at least, Pharaoh's tactic is successful; Moses responds to Pharaoh's plea by calling for an end to the plague—and as soon as the hail stops, Pharaoh's beleaguered courtiers reunite with him and harden their own hearts.[30]

Pharaoh's renewed grip on power is short-lived, however. Moses and Aaron soon arrive before Pharaoh's court once more, bearing news of locusts that will cover the land, devour every remaining crop and foodstuff—and fill not only Pharaoh's house, but also the homes of his courtiers—a plague, they warn, that has not been seen "from the day [your ancestors] appeared on earth to this day."[31]

As soon as Moses and Aaron depart, Pharaoh's courtiers speak against him—for the first time, but in a way that suggests pent-up frustration and rage. "How long shall this one be a snare to us?" they demand—emphasizing their own unity and centering their own suffering. And they continue even more daringly, issuing an order to their ostensible divine leader: "Send הָאֲנָשִׁים ('the men') to worship יְהֹוָה אֱלֹהֵיהֶם ('*Adonai* their God')!" The Hebrew text underscores the significance of this outburst; referring to the Israelites as אֲנָשִׁים rather than slaves, the courtiers reveal their growing awareness of and respect for the humanity of the people whom Pharaoh has worked so hard to "other." Juxtaposed with the courtiers' first use of the name יְהֹוָה, by which God is known to the Israelites, the passage is an unmistakable rebuke. And the diatribe culminates in a stunning challenge that acknowledges the ruin already visited upon their country: "Do you not yet know that Egypt is lost?"[32] But Pharaoh again refuses to let the people go—and so, in a neat and surely intentional foil to Pharaoh's threat (in Exodus 1:10) that the Israelites might עָלָה מִן־הָאָרֶץ grow large, the locusts וַיַּעַל עַל כָּל־אֶרֶץ מִצְרַיִם arise upon the land of Egypt.[33]

Exodus 10:21–11:8

Before the ninth plague falls, the Book of Exodus has chronicled the tumult afflicting Egypt's natural world as well as the interpersonal tumult in Pharaoh's palace. With the commencement of the plague of darkness, the disruption of not only the natural and ruling order but also of familial and intimate relationships becomes complete.

Without warning, a darkness falls suddenly during daylight hours,[34] a darkness so alien that no light can shine against it and so thick that it can literally be touched. As Exodus 10:23b notes that the Israelites continued to have light in their dwelling-places, one infers that the darkness penetrated the homes of the Egyptians—rendering them unable to see each other, or even move about, for three days. This abrupt stoppage of human society and communication—people trapped in their workplaces or away from shelter, unable to prepare food, gather water, or relieve themselves in an appropriate location, and incapable of comforting one another—let alone their children—with a reassuring touch—is devastating to imagine.

Pharaoh's reaction, too, reflects the chaos that has overwhelmed his empire. While he has heretofore retained control over himself and his nation—demonstrating just enough remorse to halt a plague, just enough mastery of the situation to keep his inner circle from publicly challenging him, and just enough statecraft to continue providing at least a modicum of protection for his people—he reverts to issuing the type of blustering, impossible-to-take-seriously pronouncements we have not encountered since Exodus 1:22 and 5:7-8. Although Pharaoh has just summoned Moses,[35] he quickly turns on him and orders [36]לֵךְ מֵעָלַי, then—in an especially ridiculous outburst as the God Whom Moses represents has rendered Pharaoh and his people unable to see anything—threatens Moses with death if he sees Pharaoh's face again. It is Pharaoh's last attempt to maintain his façade as a divine power.

In a neat shift, the narrative now brings the reader out of Pharaoh's presence and into greater Egypt, where one can clearly see that Pharaoh's spell has been broken among his people. In Exodus 11:2, God commands Moses to tell the Israelites to request objects of silver and gold from the Egyptians—employing the Hebrew אִישׁ and אִשָּׁה to assert the full humanity of the former slaves (and perhaps to echo the word אֲנָשִׁים God had earlier used to describe Pharaoh) and רֵעֵהוּ and רְעוּתָהּ to emphasize the new parity between the Israelites and their former masters. But while God must act on behalf of the Israelites to ensure the Egyptians' favor, Moses himself needs no such intercession as he has become "a very great man in the land of Egypt." (Lest one wonder if only the downtrodden of Egypt have grown to admire Moses, the text concludes definitively: "in the eyes of the courtiers of Pharaoh as well as the eyes of the people."[37]) And just in case Pharaoh remains unaware of the shift in power that has taken place both inside and outside his inner circle, Moses offers these parting words to Pharaoh: "All of these courtiers of yours will come down to me, and bow low to me, saying: 'Go—you, and all the people who follow you.'"[38] It will be Moses and not Pharaoh to whom his supposed servants will pay obeisance; and the people whom Pharaoh supposedly rules will defy him and tell the Israelites to depart.

Exodus chapter 11 closes with the almost complete despoilation of Egypt; as the Israelites seize the precious metals and (presumably) other commodities that will be used in the building of the *Mishkan*, the nation is now devoid of private wealth as well as the crops, livestock, and fertile land that—under the Pharaoh of Genesis—made it perhaps the richest empire in the world. And at the head of this crumbling nation stands a ruler who has lost the regard of his courtiers and his people, and who is about to witness an additional—and almost unimaginable—devastation.

Exodus 12:29–36

The tenth and final plague strikes in the middle of the night, killing all of Egypt's firstborn—and completely destabilizing the hierarchy that once governed the nation. This מֶלֶךְ־חָדָשׁ who had worked so hard—and so effectively—to achieve the title Pharaoh is now listed alongside those who languish in prison, and even the cattle;[39] and the would-be divine monarch is forced to witness what he had intended to visit upon Israel—the death of its baby boys— unfolding upon his own people at the hand of Israel's God.

If only for the moment, Pharaoh reacts to this horror by showing engagement with his nation, summoning Moses and Aaron and ordering that the Israelites "depart from among my people"— although this care does not extend to his asking for a blessing for anyone but himself.[40] But the people he ruled have moved on; without looking to Pharaoh for guidance—let alone waiting for his order—the Egyptians are already urging the Israelites to leave, fearing כֻּלָּנוּ מֵתִים ("we will all die") and, thus, openly declaring their conviction that Pharaoh is powerless to protect them.[41]

Exodus 13:18–14:30

With Exodus 13:18, the climax of the action begins—with exactly the scenario Pharaoh had described when he first sought to ensure

his own power by "othering" the Israelites: עָלוּ בְנֵי־יִשְׂרָאֵל מֵאֶרֶץ.
("The Israelites arose from the land.") But now Pharaoh is the out-
sider—his nation stripped of its wealth, its land despoiled, its livestock devastated, its next generation slaughtered in the night, and its
respect transferred to his enemy Moses, who has become "a very great
man in the land of Egypt, in the eyes of the courtiers of Pharaoh as
well as the eyes of the people."[42]

But—although doing so is unquestionably best for Egypt—
מֶלֶךְ מִצְרַיִם refuses to accept his loss. Determined to re-establish
control over his people, Pharaoh exploits his command over the
military and demands they battle against the Israelites in his name.
Exodus 14:6–9 emphasizes that this is solely Pharaoh's fight: Literally every action is directed and undertaken by him alone. It
is Pharaoh who takes the chariots and places the officers within
them; it is Pharaoh—not the officers who would obviously be driving the chariots—named as the pursuer of the Israelites; and it is
Pharaoh named as the one to whom all the chariot-horses, the rid-
ers, and the soldiers belong.

And yet. Even as the text acknowledges the extent of Pharoah's
power over Egypt, Exodus 14 refuses to absolve the people of accountability. Exodus 14:5 relates that not only Pharaoh, but also his
courtiers, וַיֵּהָפֵךְ לְבַב ("reversed their hearts") and expressed regret
for releasing the Israelites; although the courtiers are not directly
charged with orchestrating the military campaign, the implica-
tion remains that they bear some responsibility. And while Exodus
14:6–9 rightfully underscores Pharaoh's dominion over the instru-
ments of war, the passage also acknowledges that rather than re-
volt against a command they know to be wrong and ruinous, the
Egyptians simply follow orders: וַיִּרְדְּפוּ מִצְרַיִם אַחֲרֵיהֶם ("The Egyptian people pursued the Israelites.")

It is an action they quickly come to regret. By the morning watch,
they are trapped in the sea, pinned by the gaze of God from the pil-
lar of fire and cloud. Again, the Egyptians beg Pharaoh to end his
doomed campaign against the Israelites, כִּי יְהֹוָה נִלְחָם לָהֶם בְּמִצְרָיִם
and to realize that *Adonai* is fighting Egypt for their sake[43]—but of
course it is too late. Delivered from Pharaoh and servitude, the tri-
umphant Israelites behold לְכֹל חֵיל פַּרְעֹה ("the entire army of Pharoah") perished—and lest one imagine that survivors might emerge
from the waters, Exodus 14:28 concludes: לֹא־נִשְׁאַר בָּהֶם עַד־אֶחָד
("not even one of them remained").

Postscript

A single leader can destroy a glorious nation. Advisors' statements of dissent and outrage—unaccompanied by action—make no difference. People will follow orders they know to be wrong and ruinous when someone in authority commands them to do so. Begging those in power to share their power is futile.

The persecuted and the marginalized can organize and change everything.

The relevance of Exodus 1–14 to what has happened (and might yet happen) in the United States of America is obvious.

May we choose leaders who will stand on the right side of the sea.

And if we do not: May we refuse to follow them into the depths.

Notes

1. Exodus 1:8.
2. Exodus 1:10.
3. Exodus 1:10. Again, these enemies do not necessarily come from outside Egypt; they could be, for example, the "mixed multitude" who will eventually join the Israelites in the Exodus.
4. Exodus 1:10.
5. Hosea 2:2.
6. Exodus 1:11.
7. Exodus 1:15. Despite Rashi and *Sotah* 11b's popular identification of Shifra and Puah with Yocheved and Miriam, I prefer Sforno's teaching that these midwives were Egyptian.
8. The abrupt ending of this narrative, the absence of references to widespread slaughter of Hebrew baby boys at the hands of ordinary Egyptians in the rest of the Torah, and the wistfulness with which our ancestors recall Egypt during our desert wanderings all underscore the unlikelihood that this command was ever carried out.
9. By the daughters of Reuel in Exodus 2:19.
10. Exodus 2:14.
11. Ibn Ezra on Exodus 2:15.
12. Exodus 2:23.
13. See Sforno on Exodus 5:17.
14. Exodus 5:23, with Rashi.
15. Rashi, quoting *Midrash Tanchuma Va-eira* 14 and *Sh'mot Rabbah* 9:8.

16. Exodus 7:19.
17. Exodus 7:24.
18. Exodus 7:28–29.
19. Exodus 8:2.
20. Exodus 8:8.
21. Exodus 8:11.
22. Exodus 8:15.
23. Exodus 8:15.
24. Exodus 8:17.
25. Exodus 8:20.
26. Exodus 8:24.
27. Exodus 9:6.
28. Exodus 9:20.
29. Exodus 9:27.
30. Exodus 9:34.
31. Exodus 10:6.
32. Exodus 10:7.
33. Exodus 10:14, excerpted.
34. Exodus 10:22, Rabbeinu Bachya.
35. Exodus 10:24.
36. Exodus 10:28.
37. Exodus 11:3.
38. Exodus 11:8.
39. Exodus 12:29.
40. Exodus 12:31–32.
41. Exodus 12:33.
42. Exodus 11:3.
43. Exodus 14:24–25.

Declarations of Dialogue: Christian, Jewish, and Muslim Overtures to the Religious Other

Rabbi Judith Schindler

In the mid-1990s, American political scientist and Harvard Professor Samuel Huntington coined the term "clash of civilizations" to advance his theory that wars in the post–Cold War period would be based on cultural and religious identities replacing the politics of ideology.[1] Despite the tragedy of September 11, Huntington's concept of irreconcilable differences as the basis for future conflict was rejected by Rabbi Jonathan Sacks, chief rabbi of the United Hebrew Congregations of the Commonwealth, who introduced a new paradigm to approach religious coexistence: the dignity of difference. Sacks argued that the shared reverence for one God mitigates against Huntington's view of inevitable clash. "A God of yours and mine must be a God of justice standing above both of us, teaching us to make space for one another, to hear one another's claims, and to resolve them equitably."[2]

This article sets forth the starting point for such a paradigmatic shift from interreligious conquest, conversion, or mere toleration to a deeper level of acceptance and inclusion: documents of dialogue. These religious ideological statements, grounded in philosophy and theology have been drafted by Jewish, Christian, and Muslim scholars and religious leaders from after the Holocaust to the present day. Often motivated by political realities, the authors

RABBI JUDITH SCHINDLER is the Sklut Professor of Jewish Studies and director of the Stan Greenspon Holocaust and Social Justice Education Center at Queens University of Charlotte and rabbi emerita of Temple Beth El in Charlotte, North Carolina. She co-authored *Recharging Judaism: How Civic Engagement is Good for Synagogues, Jews, and America* (CCAR Press, 2018) and was a consulting editor for *Deepening the Dialogue: Jewish-Americans and Israelis Envisioning the Jewish-Democratic State* (CCAR Press, 2019). She is currently pursuing a doctoral degree in Hebrew Letters from HUC-JIR/Cincinnati.

look inward to provide direction and motivation for restorative action, to build healing bridges between faith communities, and to ignite transformative change so different faiths can live together in peace. The political pressures that frequently propel these documents into creation, can come from internal denominational issues, interdenominational tension, and ever more frequently, arise from a sensitivity to the image of a denomination/religion in the eyes of the larger world.

From 1945 until 2022, religious communities have convened, at times as sole denominational or single religious bodies and, at other times, as ecumenical or interfaith associations, to foster the coexistence with different faith communities. Over nearly eight decades, Jewish, Christian, and, more recently, Muslim scholars and religious bodies/institutions have used their knowledge in the activist arena to promote peaceful interreligious relations.

Quoting the philosopher Friedrich Nietzsche's premise that "civilizations get sick and their physicians are their philosophers," Sheikh Abdullah bin Bayyah, the Muslim scholar and leader in interfaith dialogue, asserts that religious scholars "must descend from their ivory towers to help diagnose and treat societal diseases."[3] Such a descent happened initially after World War II.

Introducing a New Genre of Religious Literature

As each of the three monotheistic faiths of Judaism, Christianity, and Islam were birthed and matured, their communities of followers developed guides and boundaries regulating their relationship with the other tribes and communities with which they interacted. The emergence and canonization of the Hebrew Bible, the New Testament, and the Qur'an and their subsequent and respective realms of religious literature define the parameters for living those faiths. Each reflects the historical and political realities of their authors' and redactors' day.

Throughout the centuries spanning medieval and modern times, the relationship between the three faiths would, at times, know peaceful coexistence, and, at other times, would become marred by discord, intolerance, and ultimately violence. Conquests, forced conversions, the Crusades, the Spanish Inquisition, and pogroms of Eastern Europe aimed to terrorize minority religious communities —tainting both the pages of history and the image of religion. The

Holocaust reached a nadir, with Hitler's aim of erasing religious difference by making Europe *Judenrein* (free of Jews) for one thousand years.

Following World War II and in the aftermath of the Holocaust, international lawmaking and judicial preventive and restorative measures emerged to address the atrocities that had been perpetrated and the moral failures that enabled them. Among the post-Holocaust measures to create accountability, advance justice, and prevent future genocides were international, domestic, and military tribunals starting in 1945 and leading to the creation of the International Criminal Court that exists today; the creation of the United Nations (1945); the Nuremberg Code (1947), which created the first blueprint for principles of subjects' right in medical research (informed consent); the Nuremberg Principles (1947), which designated what constitutes a war crime; the United Nations Convention for the Prevention and Punishment of Genocide (1948); the United Nations Universal Declaration of Human Rights (1948); the establishment of the State of Israel (1948) providing a homeland and refuge for Jews globally and the UN Refugee Convention (1951) protecting those fleeing persecution.[4]

Correspondingly, some leaders of the religious communities in Europe and on the worldwide stage, convened to confront and redress the detrimental role religion had played by fertilizing the soil in which the seeds of Nazi ideology could so comfortably take root. Some faith communities began to acknowledge their guilt and complicity in the horrors of the Holocaust as their religious leaders crafted documents calling for atonement and accountability. They wrestled with teachings that had been misinterpreted to support religious and cultural supremacy and over the centuries had frequently led to violence.

The bold activism of a few individuals courageously compelling reluctant churches to engage in intense introspection and issue public proclamations of culpability calling for change would, over the course of decades, lead to a massive sea-change of religious leaders and institutions willing to engage in self-criticism and call publicly for accountability and activism. Eventually a new genre of literature emerged that can be categorized as documents of interfaith dialogue. These are statements of national and international religious organizations, orders, leaders, and scholars reflecting on guilt, atonement, theology, justice, education, dialogue, and cooperation in order to create a safer, more peaceful world of coexistence.

Surprisingly, hundreds of documents of dialogue would be created (a significant number stimulated by the Holocaust), each reflecting an evolving religious self-understanding in relation to other faiths. The most notable is the Roman Catholic Church Vatican II's 1965 *Nostra Aetate* Declaration, a brief document articulating a new understanding of the relationship of the Church to non-Christian religions. While it addresses Hinduism, Buddhism, and Islam, the heart of the message, and the motivating factor for its creation, was its statement denouncing antisemitism and withdrawing the accusation that Jews of Jesus's day or today are collectively responsible for Jesus's crucifixion. *Nostra Aetate* also set the standard for non-Catholic leaders in interreligious efforts. While volumes have been written on *Nostra Aetate*, many documents from other denominations and faiths are worthy of academic attention to guide interfaith engagement.

Holocaust refugee and publisher Helga Croner and Dr. Franklin Sherman, interfaith scholar and founding director of the Institute for Jewish–Christian Understanding at Muhlenberg College, collected these documents and organized them into volumes.[5] The categorization of documents in this article builds upon their work and that of international organizations devoted to the discipline of interfaith scholarship that have collections on their websites. Documents of Jewish–Christian–Muslim dialogue can be divided into several primary categories: Protestant, Roman Catholic, Orthodox Christian, Ecumenical, Jewish–Christian, Jewish, and Muslim. The themes range from atonement for the role their theology played in the Holocaust to renouncing the antisemitism of Martin Luther, and from denouncing terrorists to addressing the modern State of Israel.

This article explores the pioneering first documents penned by representatives of the Christian, Jewish, and Muslim faiths: the individuals who wrote them, the global conditions that inspired them, the issues they addressed, as well as their omissions—the subjects they failed to confront—all of which are instructive for us today.

> For congregations and communities engaged in interfaith activities and dialogue, they can skim the surface comparing sacred time and worship, or they can go far deeper in their shared

exploration. The latter approach requires reckoning with respective past divisive teachings as one journeys the path to reconciliation and restorative collaboration in the present. Naming and analyzing sources of difference are critical to the relationship building needed to prevent clashes that can have detrimental, destructive, if not devastating, consequences. Documents of dialogue can be used as source texts that reflect the breadth and depth of historical interfaith realities. From exploring the Gospel's view of Jesus's understanding of himself as a Jew (in relationship with the Jewish communities with which he daily interacted), to the early Jewish Rabbinic rejection of Christian cornerstones of belief, to Muhammad's seventh-century addressing of the Jews of Medina, interfaith relations are part of each faith's origin and evolving self-understanding. The "real miracle of monotheism," according to Rabbi Sacks, is "not that there is one God and therefore one truth, one faith, one way, but that unity above creates diversity here on earth."[6]

The Protestant Path to Reconciliation: Pastor Martin Niemöller and the "Stuttgart Declaration of Guilt" (October 1945)

In the immediate aftermath of the Holocaust, a monumental task was required of denazification of Germany, Austria, and of other Nazi occupied countries across Europe. This involved the purging of Nazi ideology from the culture, press, education, judiciary, government, and the Church. The process of religious redefinition began in Germany since Christian complicity, if not culpability, in that country was undeniable. When Hitler rose to power in 1933, apart from the less than one percent of the German population who were Jews, almost all Germans belonged to the Protestant Church (approximately 40 million) or the Roman Catholic Church (approximately 20 million).[7] Racialized antisemitic Nazi ideology was woven together with centuries-old European Christian antisemitism to produce a pseudo-scientific hierarchy of human value where Jews were deemed inferior and unfit for survival. This, coupled with anti-Jewish interpretation of Scripture within the Church, resulted in discrimination, dehumanization, and ultimately, the systematic state-sponsored murder of six million Jews just outside its walls.[8]

Shortly after the war, a semblance of ethical responsibility began to take hold among some Christians. In August 1945, a church meeting in the town of Treysa established a new beginning through the creation of a union called the "Protestant Church of Germany." This marked an intentional departure from the German Evangelical Church (within which a strong movement of German Christians supporting Nazi racism and nationalism had emerged).[9]

On the evening of October 17, 1945, a committee of twelve church leaders and laymen began to gather in Stuttgart. Upon arrival, German Lutheran pastor, and theologian Martin Niemöller, who had been recently released from seven years of imprisonment for his opposition to Nazi interference in the German Protestant churches (the majority of which were in Sachsenhausen and Dachau), was asked to preach at a service. His wife chose the text from Jeremiah upon which he would base his extemporaneous sermon: "Although our sins testify against us, O Lord, do something for the sake of your name!" (Jeremiah 14:7).[10]

In that sermon Niemöller said, "It is not enough to give the Nazis responsibility, it is also necessary for the Church to admit its responsibility." So passionate was Niemöller's indictment of the Protestant church that over the next two days of convening of the Council of the Protestant Church in Germany alongside representatives of the fledgling World Council of Churches (WCC), the first interfaith declaration of dialogue known as the "Stuttgart Declaration of Guilt" would be crafted.[11]

While the Declaration of Guilt, also known as the Stuttgart Confession, was not immediately disseminated to pulpits across the country, it gradually entered into the German church community consciousness. A memorial plaque in St. Mark's Church in Stuttgart provides the full wording of the "Stuttgart Declaration of Guilt" of October 19, 1945, noting that the impulse for this act of contrition came not from the German side but from the Oekumene (the WCC), and that this evening of transformative prayer reflected "the greatest hour in our St. Mark's Church."[12] This sentiment was not widespread, and the Declaration of Guilt was not universally applauded. Church leaders and many German citizens alike were not ready in 1945 to acknowledge that they carried some responsibility thus explaining the delayed publicizing of the Confession.

The Stuttgart Declaration acknowledged with great anguish the guilt of the Protestant Church: "Through us has endless suffering been brought to many peoples and countries. What we have often borne witness to before our congregations, we now declare in the name of the whole Church . . . we accuse ourselves for not witnessing more courageously." While they committed to cleansing themselves from influences alien to the church through a new beginning, this first interfaith document signed by Niemöller and nine others had a glaring omission—it failed to mention the Jewish people and the vast brutality and bloodshed to which they fell victim.[13]

Four months later, in February 1946, a second statement issued by the Provisional Committee of the World Council of Churches in Process of Formation in Geneva, Switzerland, entitled "Resolution on Antisemitism and the Jewish Situation" would right that wrong. It focused specifically, with horror, at the "unprecedented tragedy" that aimed to exterminate European Jewry, and the penitence required for the failures of the Churches to overcome the human evil that had threatened and continued to threaten "both Jewish and Christian communities."[14]

What transpired during those four months? First: the commencement of the Nuremberg trials, which focused a glaring spotlight on the atrocities and their perpetrators. And second, Niemöller's visit to Dachau—both of which happened in November 1945. In a July 1946 speech, Niemöller explains that he was driving by Dachau when his wife asked to see the cell where he had been imprisoned for four years. After seeing the cell, an American officer led them past an open gate enabling Niemöller to approach the crematory— a building he knew was there but had never seen. Before it was a sign reading: "Here in the years 1933 to 1945 238,756 people were cremated."[15]

Niemöller recalled that his wife fainted and sank trembling into his arms, which he believed was in response to the nearly quarter-million people murdered in that spot. He already knew that number. For him it was seeing the dates "1933 to 1945" that shook him to his core. His alibi claiming ignorance had been shattered.

In 1933, while Jews were being gassed, Niemöller had been an avid Hitler supporter. He challenged only those Nazi decrees connected to Church policy that excluded Christians with Jewish ancestry from being officers of the Church. It was only the imposition of Nazi policy on the Church that led Niemöller to form, in protest, the Pastors' Emergency League, which would become the Confessing Church in 1934.[16]

The stark evidence of the sign at Dachau produced the sudden contrition that led Niemöller to deliver many speeches of

confession from 1946 to 1979 acknowledging complicity, responsibility, and guilt. The often-quoted (and misquoted) Holocaust
poem attributed to him, "First they came for the Communists . . . ,"
came in many diverse forms. Niemöller shared the guilt of silence
and complicity in narrative form, always starting with Communists and ending with himself and/or the Church, using the collective "we." In varied extemporaneous speeches that Niemöller delivered throughout his life, he is reported to have included many
of the others who were targeted for whom he did not stand up.[17]

Over the courses of decades, the WCC declarations would evolve
on the issue of Christian supremacy and evangelism. It wasn't until the June 1977 WCC Committee meeting in Jerusalem that leaders, building upon their prior statements, acknowledged the world
of pluralism in which they live that upholds "religious liberty of
all." They made clear what this meant in terms of co-existence:
"We reject proselytism both in its gross and more refined forms.
This implies that all triumphalism, religious imperialism and every kind of manipulation are to be abrogated." The document also
explicitly affirms Israel's right to exist, respects the Jewish right to
self-determination while supporting the self-determination of Palestinian Arabs, and reiterates the WCC General Secretary's strong
concern about Zionism being equated with racism (a reference to
the 1975 UN Resolution 3379).[18]

The progression reflected in Niemöller himself, and that of his
WCC colleagues, typified that of some other Christian leaders in
this effort to rectify past wrongs and construct interfaith bridges.
In subsequent documents they confront the following issues: the
Churches' complicity with the Holocaust, historic antisemitism,
anti-Jewish theology, supersessionist doctrine, and the political
realities of the modern State of Israel with respect to Palestinians.
This introspection produced strategies for interfaith dialogue and
illuminated the need to revise materials to educate congregations.

Advances were not always enduring. In 1982, the WCC would
reverse its trend, on one hand acknowledging that "teachings of
contempt for Jews and Judaism" created a "spawning ground for
the evil of the Nazi Holocaust" while on the other, affirming their
obligation to witness and their support of the segment of their
constituents who understood the "salvific significance" of converting Jews so long as they embraced "non-coercive" practices.[19] In
2005, building on a July 2004 Presbyterian Church–USA General

Assembly watershed resolution supporting pro-Palestinian activism, the WCC urged its 347-member Protestant and Orthodox member churches representing half a billion Christians to divest from companies profiting from Israel's control of the West Bank and Gaza Strip.[20]

'A Word about Seelisberg (1947) and *Nostra Aetate* (1965): Jules Isaac as the Most Influential Actor on the Stage of Jewish–Christian Relations

While Niemöller was the first to utilize declarations of dialogue as a tool for transformation in the Christian–Jewish relationship, he was far from the most influential. That esteemed place in history is reserved for Jules Isaac, a distinguished professor and scholar of French history. Having lost his teaching post and forced into hiding by the Nazi regime, and with his knowledge of Greek and resources in hand provided by colleagues, Isaac immersed himself in the theological study of the New Testament. He sought to understand the soil that made Nazi ideology take root and spread like a deadly weed. In 1943, while Isaac was out for a walk, his wife, daughter, and son-in-law, were arrested by the Gestapo. They would eventually be murdered in Auschwitz. In a final note Isaac's wife managed to send, she urged him to finish his critical research: "My friend, take care of yourself, have confidence and finish your work, the world is waiting for it."[21]

The impact she knew his work could have was actualized. Isaac authored the first Jewish–Christian approach to atonement during the 1947 Seelisberg Conference in Switzerland that produced the "Ten Points of Seelisberg" outlining the most critical points confronting Christian teachings of contempt. Perhaps most remarkably, Isaac would gain audiences with two Popes—Pope Pius XII in 1949 and Pope John XXIII in 1960. The unprecedented dialogue during that latter meeting would lead to the watershed Catholic Vatican declaration *Nostra Aetate*, confronting its anti-Jewish teachings.

John L. Allen, Jr., the American journalist and Vatican correspondent, noted: "60 years ago, a Pope met a Jewish icon and the world changed." When Pope John XXIII announced his plans for Vatican II in January 1958, Isaac seized the opportunity to meet with the Pontiff, petitioning him to address Jewish–Christian relations with the world's bishops. He presented the eighteen points from his research, hopeful that they would "undergird Christian education about Judaism, such as 'Jesus was a Jew' and 'the trial of Jesus was a Roman trial, not a Jewish trial.'"[22]

Isaac's work and words would echo in the declarations of dialogue that would follow, and his influence on the academic study of the New Testament would be enduring. He coined the term "the teachings of contempt," and the term "supersessionism" appeared for the first time in the English translation of his six-hundred-page tome, *Jésus et Israel*.[23]

Jewish Words of Truth about Christianity Authored by Four Academics on Non-Jewish Campuses: *Dabru Emet* (September 2000)

After fifty-five years, with dozens of documents emerging from leaders of Christian denominations committed to reconstructing their theologies relating to Jews, but a notable dearth of interfaith declarations from the Jewish community, four Jewish scholars with an expertise in the field of theology supporting Jewish–Christian dialogue, formulated a Jewish response. The idea, conceived by Dr. Michael A. Signer of the University of Notre Dame, was developed into a declaration drafted by him alongside Dr. Tikva Fryer-Kensky of the University of Chicago Divinity School, Dr. Peter W. Ochs of the University of Virginia, and Dr. David Novak of the University of Toronto. Building on an original working paper crafted by Novak that provided a Jewish justification for dialogue within the context of Jewish law, the group would meet over the course of five years under the auspices of the Institute for Christian and Jewish Studies in Baltimore.[24]

The result of their collective thought leadership would be an historic first cross-denominational Jewish declaration of dialogue titled "*Dabru Emet*: A Jewish Statement on Christians and Christianity." On Sunday, September 10, 2000, it would be published as a full-page ad in the Sunday editions of both the *New York Times* and the *Baltimore Sun*.[25] In an article just prior to the document's release, Novak noted: "The reason we needed a statement is that major Christian groups and thinkers have in the past 30 or 40 years come up with a major rethinking about Jews and Judaism and have issued statements about how they can respect the legitimacy of Judaism. It seems to us to behoove Jewish thinkers to respond accordingly."[26]

Dabru Emet, a phrase emerging from Zechariah 8:16, means literally "speak the truth." The document's introductory paragraph acknowledged that its creation is in direct response to the growing number of Catholic and Protestant statements since the Holocaust expressing remorse and calling for reform; statements that acknowledge "God's enduring covenant with the Jewish people" and celebrate "the contribution of Judaism to world civilization and to Christian faith itself."[27]

Dabru Emet is comprised of eight claims recognizing the validity and value of Christianity. The following are the headings of each claim: "Jews and Christians worship the same God; Jews and Christians seek authority from the same book—the Bible (what Jews call 'Tanakh' and Christians call the 'Old Testament'); Christians can respect the claim of the Jewish people upon the land of Israel; Jews and Christians accept the moral principles of Torah; Nazism was not a Christian phenomenon; the humanly irreconcilable differences between Jews and Christians will not be settled until God redeems the entire world as promised in Scripture; a new relationship between Jews and Christians will not weaken Jewish practice; and Jews and Christians must work together for justice and peace."[28]

Its most controversial and highly debated statement asserted that "without the long history of Christian anti-Judaism and Christian violence against Jews, Nazi ideology could not have taken hold nor could it have been carried out . . . . But Nazism itself was not an inevitable outcome of Christianity. If the Nazi extermination of the Jews had been fully successful, it would have turned its murderous rage more directly to Christians."[29]

Signer shared that the document was written in the rhetorical form of a paraenesis, moral counsel of a religious nature, offering the readers "both 'yes' and 'no' about the Christian-Jewish relationship. A paranetic [sic] oration offers praise and blame and hope." The document is not made of platitudes but acknowledges the shared pain and offers "a path forward from the two millennia of violence and mutual recriminations."[30]

Signer further acknowledges that the document was seen by its authors as "an initial statement" and "never meant it to be a pesaq din (a legal decision), a Teshuvah (a rabbinical authoritative response to a query into Jewish practice), or a Fatwa." Other statements would be needed (including addressing the "situation in Israel"), and at the time of Signer's writing in 2002 were already underway.[31]

While *Dabru Emet* became a "first" because of its broader interdenominational backing, it was not the last. In August 2017, a declaration entitled "Between Jerusalem and Rome: Reflections on 50 Years of *Nostra Aetate*," would be issued by three major Orthodox Jewish organizations: The Conference of European Rabbis, the Chief Rabbinate of Israel, and the Rabbinical Council of America. It acknowledged the profound theological differences between Judaism and Christianity and applauded "the transformation of the attitude of the Church toward the Jewish community." It went on to echo Pope Francis's words upon visiting a synagogue (the third Pope to visit a Jewish house of worship) when he stated, "From enemies and strangers we have become friends and brothers. It is my hope that closeness, mutual understanding and respect between our two communities continue to grow."[32]

Why did it take five and a half decades for a Jewish document to be drafted by an interdenominational group of scholars and given authority by Jewish interdenominational leaders? Afterall, Jews were involved in the writing of Jewish–Christian documents from almost immediately after the war.[33]

First, misunderstanding, mistrust, and prejudicial attitudes have historically gone both ways in the Jewish–Christian relationship. The Midrash and Talmud have limited references (found only in uncensored versions) refuting Christian dogma, which only increase in medieval times.[34] The Rabbinical Council of America, the Rabbinical arm of the Modern Orthodox movement in the United States, issued an Orthodox statement against interreligious dialogue in 1964.[35] An influential 1964 article entitled "Confrontation" by Joseph Soloveitchik, a major American Orthodox rabbi, Talmudist, and modern philosopher, laid out the theological argument that unfortunately would deter rabbis from interfaith dialogue for decades afterwards.[36]

Second, there were issues of authority. Judaism does not have the authoritative, hierarchical structure of leadership that exists in many Christian denominations. Movement leaders could not speak for their congregations. In Franklin Sherman's two-volume collection of documents of dialogue spanning sixty-eight years, there is only one official statement issued by a Jewish denomination. The 1988 document *"Emet ve'Emunah* ['Truth and Faithfulness']: Statement of Principles of Conservative Judaism" issued jointly by five organizations within Conservative Judaism had a segment on "Relations with Other Faiths." It acknowledged the reciprocal relationship Jews have historically had, at times, with Christians, marked by fruitful exchange and mutual influence. In closing, the statement noted, "Theological humility requires us to recognize that although we have but one God, God has more than one nation."[37]

How then could *Dabru Emet* succeed in influencing the interfaith conversation? The four tenured faculty at non-Jewish institutions (each of whom addressed Christianity as part of their scholarship) had the academic knowledge, perspective, and freedom to speak. Their voices would become affirmed as authoritative by the 170 leading scholars and Reform, Conservative, Reconstructionist, and a small number of modern Orthodox rabbis who served as signatories.[38] Like the Muslim documents that would be written from 2004 to 2019, the authority of *Dabru Emet* would be affirmed most substantially by its signatories.

The lack of formal Jewish statements should not diminish the vital role that individual Jewish leaders and organizations have historically played. Starting in 1962, Rabbi Abraham Joshua Heschel, a prominent twentieth-century Jewish theologian, would be intimately involved in an exchange of ideas with Cardinal Augustin Bea (who was the primary author of *Nostra Aetate* and shepherd of the Catholic theological introspection leading to its proclamation).[39] Polish philosopher at the University of Warsaw, Stanislaw Krajewski, notes that "almost all the ideas" expressed in Abraham Joshua Heschel's groundbreaking 1965 lecture "No Man Is an Island" are included in the "unprecedented Jewish declaration on Christianity 'Dabru emet' [sic]."[40] The American Jewish Committee, likewise, played a pivotal role propelling *Nostra Aetate* to fruition.[41]

At the twentieth anniversary of *Dabru Emet*, scholar and interfaith activist Rabbi David Fox Sandmel reflected on its impact by asking and answering the question, "Is *Dabru Emet* the Jewish *Nostra Aetate*?" He concludes that in some ways it was far different than *Nostra Aetate*, as the academic authors went to great lengths to convey that they were speaking only for themselves as an interdenominational group of Jewish scholars. And in other ways, the similarities are strong: "*Nostra Aetate* has come to represent *all* of Christianity's post-Shoah reconsideration of its relationship to the Jews; since its publication, *Dabru Emet* has come to represent *the* Jewish reconsideration of post-Shoah Christianity."[42]

An Islamic Convening of Scholars in Response to Extremists: King Abdullah II and the Amman Message (2004–2005)

While it can be said that all documents of dialogue are political, those that originated in the Muslim community face the greatest scrutiny because of the strong engagement of Arab heads of state. Due to the fact that Islam has no centralized religious authority and more than one billion adherents, the vision, leadership, and support of political leaders alongside religious scholars was and continues to be required to make possible the major Muslim historic documents of dialogue.

The Amman Message was the first such Muslim effort envisioned by Jordan's King Abdullah II bin Al-Hussein and launched in the form of a press release during Ramadan on November 9, 2004. As was the case with the first and narrowly focused 1945 Protestant "Stuttgart Declaration of Guilt" that would lead directly into a broader and more intentional interfaith 1946 "Resolution on Antisemitism and the Jewish Situation," King Abdullah II's first effort on behalf of Muslims envisioning the Amman Message would lead directly to a more explicit call for interfaith dialogue with the October 2007 letter, "A Common Word Between Us and You."

The task of crafting interfaith declarations of dialogue requires very significant introspection. The theological grounding and religious record have to be set before overtures to the religious other can be made. The Amman Message earned accolades as "one of the most significant dialogue initiatives of our times" because of the blueprint it created for the many noteworthy interreligious statements and programs that would follow its path and build upon its work.[43]

The Amman Message sought to define normative Islam as it aimed to counter radical Muslim extremists, declaring what Islam is, what it is not, and what actions represent the faith. King Abdullah II had witnessed and been sickened by barbaric acts of Islamic extremist terrorism (with Muslims being the greatest number of victims).[44] There was a need to confront consequent accusations in the West (reinforced by the 9/11 images of the smoldering wreckage of the World Trade Center, the airplane crash at the Pentagon, and the crash of United Flight 93) that Islam is a faith of violence and extremism. King Abdullah II felt the imperative to fight those mispresenting the faith with every tool at his disposal—intellectual and military.

King Abdullah II explained in his 2011 autobiography that while Jordan had been a long-term partner and leader in the global fight against Al Qaeda and in efforts to save innocent lives, the struggle could not be won "by just winning tactical battles, using our military and intelligence service to take down cells and disrupt plots." Rather, Abdullah II recognized that to comprehensively defeat terrorists there was a need to "neutralize the appeal of their extremist ideology and combat the ignorance and hopelessness on which they thrive. This is not just a military battle; it is an intellectual one. And it is a battle we started a while ago."[45]

He was referring to late 2004, when he brought together leading Islamic scholars to explore how to combat terrorists and their dangerous ideas. King Abdullah II's cousin, advisor, and respected Islamic scholar, Prince Ghazi bin Muhammad, would lead the effort. They produced the Amman Message defining Islam and denouncing extremism, radicalism, fanaticism, and terrorism on religious and moral grounds.

The Amman Message affirmed Islam's pluralism, tolerance, and inclusion, noting that "Islam honors every human being, regardless of his color, race or religion." It noted that "Islam recognizes the noble station of [human] life, so there is to be no fighting against non-combatants, and no assault upon civilians and their properties, children at their mothers' bosom, students in their schools, nor upon elderly men and women." It noted the critical role that the scholars of Islam had to play in preventing youth "from the danger of sliding down the paths of ignorance, corruption, close-mindedness and subordination."[46]

King Abdullah II needed greater power beyond Jordan alone to counter Muslim extremist terrorists "who had spread their poison across the entire Muslim world."[47] Ghazi came up with three questions that would define normative Islam and undercut Islamic terrorists: Who is a Muslim? Is it permissible to declare someone an apostate (*takfir*)? Who has the right to issue *fatwas* (legal rulings)?

The questions were sent to twenty-four leading Muslim religious scholars from across the world representing all the branches of Islam, schools of jurisprudence, schools of thought, and religious orientations. King Abdullah II then hosted an international conference in Jordan of approximately two hundred leading Muslim scholars from fifty countries who unanimously agreed to the *fatwas* created by the great scholars. The statement issued at an International Islamic Conference held on July 4–6, 2005, would become known as "The Three Points of the Amman Message."

First, "The scholars recognized the validity of all eight *madhhab*s (legal schools) of Sunni, Shia, and Ibadhi Islam; of traditional Islamic theology (Ash'arism); of Islamic mysticism (Sufism), and of true Salafi thought; and came to a precise definition of who is a Muslim." Second, "Based upon this definition they forbade *takfir* (declarations of apostasy) between Muslims." Third, "They set forth the subjective and objective preconditions for the issuing of *fatwas*, thereby exposing ignorant and illegitimate edicts in the name of Islam."[48]

Over the course of 2005 and 2006, the Three Points were ratified by over five hundred global Muslim scholars. As explained on the official website of the Amman Message, the unanimity of endorsing the Amman Message and its Three Points amounted "to a historical, universal and unanimous religious and political consensus of the *Ummah* (nation) of Islam in our day . . . it is the first time in over a thousand years that the *Ummah* has formally and specifically come to such a pluralistic mutual inter-recognition."[49] According to the writers, this recognition was religiously legally binding based on the statement of Mohammad in the Hadith: "My Ummah will not agree upon an error."[50]

Tragically, on November 9, 2005 (notated as 9.11.05 in Jordan), on the year anniversary of the issuing of the Amman Message, Jordan experienced what Abdullah II and many others called "Jordan's 9/11." Abu Musab al-Zarqawi, then the head of Al Qaeda in Iraq (the precursor of the Islamic State), orchestrated three simultaneous suicide bombings at hotels, resulting in fifty-seven civilian deaths and approximately one hundred injured. The majority of those deaths occurred at a wedding party where thirty-eight friends and family of the bride and groom were killed.[51] This deadliest attack in Jordan's history only strengthened King Abdullah II's resolve to battle extremism militarily and fight fundamentalism intellectually by promoting pluralism and expanding the impact of the Amman Message.

Like the signature Christian documents before this watershed Muslim statement, what emerged was the imperative to revise the ways that religion is taught in order to turn "principles into practice."[52] The Amman Mandate included an extensive vision for its promulgation and implementation from legislation to media publications, from educational initiatives to preaching at local mosques. Abdullah II explained that after the Amman Message, "We started to do what we could to bring Muslims, Christians, and Jews together in peace as religions. We called the initiative the Amman Interfaith Message."[53]

A decade of global conferences, seminars, mass media campaigns, and efforts toward youth engagement and training religious leaders would bring the message to a global stage. In 2010, King Abdullah II proposed a World Interfaith Harmony Week to the UN General Assembly which was immediately adopted and is now annually observed during the first week of February. In 2013 and 2014, the annual initiative promoted the Amman Message.[54]

A Set Stage for Consequent Muslim Messages of Coexistence

The formula created through the Amman Message would enable the Muslim community to be responsive to future crises. In a September 13, 2006, speech at the University of Regensburg, Pope Benedict XVI intensified interfaith tensions when he appeared to argue that Islam is a violent religion, with a root cause being the character of the Muslim God. His speech created a reaction of outrage from Muslims around the world. In response, Prince Ghazi, with support from King Abdullah II, brought together thirty-eight Islamic authorities and scholars representing all denominations of schools and thought to agree to issue an "Open Letter to the Pope" exactly one month later. The statement would articulate the common ground between Muslims and Christians.[55]

Exactly one year later, the message would be expanded with the October 13, 2007, letter, "A Common Word Between Us and You," signed by 138 Muslim leaders. In what would become known as the Yale response, an ecumenical group of Christian scholars issued a letter, "Loving God and Neighbor Together: A Christian Response to 'A Common Word Between Us and You.'"[56] Soon after, interfaith conferences and academic courses would be offered, and numerous articles and books would be written exploring the contents of this landmark document in Christian-Muslim relations that centered upon the two fundamental shared religious teachings: love of God and love of the neighbor.[57]

From 2004 to today, utilizing the structure crafted through the Amman Message, eight Muslim documents of dialogue have been created.[58] Each document responded to the crises of its day calling Muslim scholars to develop an action plan grounded in theology and actualized through international educational and interfaith initiatives.

In reflecting on the first of the Muslim declarations, the Amman Message, Michaelle Browers, professor of Politics and International Affairs at Wake Forest University, deems it more political than religious. She writes, it was "constructed as a debate within Islam, among Muslims, yet it is clear that it contains an awareness of a non-Muslim audience. The text of the Message, as well as the discourses surrounding its subsequent propagation, reveal additional impetuses that are more political than religious."[59] The same can be said for many, if not most, of religious statements emerging from all three faiths, including Vatican II. Political realities influence religious proclamations and one could challenge whether objectively determining where a document falls on a political versus religious spectrum is feasible.

The efforts to redeem Islam from the hands of violent extremists and free its true adherents from being victimized were critical in 2004, as they are today. Preventing violence not only by Muslim terrorists who have tried to hijack Islam, but by non-Muslims who prey on Muslims post 9/11 and have become prejudiced by corrupt and dangerous misinterpretations of Islam, remains essential to global religious freedom and safety. Despite the best efforts from Muslim scholars and political leaders, the tragic reality remains of Muslim extremists engaging in acts of violence under the banner of Islam and of misinformed and biased journalists who report that Islam is a violent religion. A critical need remains to support and expand strong counternarratives to Islamic Fundamentalism.[60]

Conclusion

When society is sick, religious scholars need to "descend from their ivory towers."[61] The urgent need for this work remains as true today as it was in the years and decades following World War

II as the German Protestant Church and Catholic Church sought to atone for their sins in allowing Nazi ideology, policy, and practice to permeate its walls.

Christian scholars addressing their own responsibility and complicity in the Holocaust was the original motivation for drafting documents of dialogue. The end of World War II and its judicial as well as ethical reckoning was cataclysmic in birthing an internal Church reckoning to lay out the roadmap for repairing/bridging interfaith relations.

Jewish silence in confronting its own historic prejudicial attitudes toward Christianity compelled a group of four scholars to lead the way in addressing this disconcerting omission in the Jewish theological world. The Muslim confrontation with Islamic terrorism that not only attacked its own (and those of other faiths) but also distorted and devalued Islam as a religion in the eyes of the world led King Abdullah II and Prince Ghazi to create a theological and educational platform for change.

Religious declarations of dialogue offer one significant entry point for interfaith reparative work.[62] The authors vary; religious leaders, academics, and political heads of state have all engaged with this work. The creators of each document were constrained by the political realities of their day; hence each statement inevitably fell short. In Christianity's first statement, the post-Holocaust 1945 "Stuttgart Declaration of Guilt," Jews are not mentioned. In the 2000 Jewish statement, "*Dabru Emet*," only four individuals claim authorship, rather than influential Jewish institutions or organizations. In the 2004 Muslim "Amman Message" and its corresponding Three Points, the lens primarily centers on intra-Muslim relations and only afterwards does it broaden to include the interfaith community as a primary part of its focus.

Some documents are narrow in scope, while others are expansive, providing solid roadmaps to transformative dialogical encounters. Some are more introspective, reflecting internal struggles within their own denomination surrounding the interfaith encounter with other faiths, while others are more global. Yet when seen as a whole, the documents of dialogue build upon one another and have influenced each other—even across lines of faith.

Despite best efforts, religion-based hate and violence remain a reality today. Teachings of contempt that degrade Judaism need to be eradicated from pulpits and classrooms. Transformative interfaith education remains a priority for adherents of all faiths—from the training of religious leadership to the laity to youth education and university courses. As was called for through the Amman Declaration and afterwards, the use of publishing and all forms of multimedia are also needed to advance messages of pluralism.

Theologian and scholar Dr. Susannah Heschel explains that "Theology is never written in a vacuum."[63] Each document of dialogue tells a story. While each new declaration is written to ground a response in the theology of a particular faith and denomination, each is attempting to create a bridge that will heal a wound with a faith or community different from its own.

The work is evolving, and while political realities will necessarily limit the word choices one may make in crafting documents, the possibilities for repairing the harm created in the name of religion through the articulation of a vision for interfaith relations are great. This work is critical to ensuring the safety, security, and success not only of one's own faith adherents but of all. It is essential for reinforcing the moral authority of religion in general, redeeming it from the harm believers have caused over centuries.

As global conditions change, there will be a need to craft new documents. The premise that words have transformative power grounds the sacred scriptures of Judaism, Christianity, and Islam. Modern declarations of dialogue by theologians and religious leaders similarly seek to use words to dismantle antisemitism, Islamophobia, and religiously based extremist radicalization and violence and promote the power of interfaith relations to be utilized for good. The clash of civilizations predicted by Huntington can indeed be countered by an interreligious collaboration and conspiracy for good.

Acknowledgments

Special thanks to Dr. Reuven Firestone for his guidance and to Amy Lefkof and Anita Strauss LaRowe for their editorial wisdom.

Notes

1. Samuel Huntington (1927–2008) was an American political scientist and academic who spent more than fifty years at Harvard University as a professor and director of Harvard's Center for International Affairs. Samuel P. Huntington, "The Clash of

Civilizations?" *Foreign Affairs* 72, no. 3 (1993): 22–49, https://doi.org/10.2307/20045621.

2. Jonathan Sacks (1948–2020) was an English Orthodox rabbi, philosopher, theologian, and author. Sacks served as the chief rabbi of the United Hebrew Congregations of the Commonwealth from 1991 to 2013. Jonathan Sacks, "The Dignity of Difference: How to Avoid the Clash of Civilizations," Foreign Policy Research Institute, Templeton Lecture on Religion and World Affairs, June 27, 2013, https://www.fpri.org/article/2013/06/the-dignity-of-difference-avoiding-the-clash-of-civilizations/.

3. Sheikh Abdullah bin Bayyah, is a global thought leader, respected as a Muslim scholar by "all the Muslim sects and schools." He is currently the president of the Forum for Promoting Peace in Muslim Societies, and he has worked as an activist since 2013. In 2016, he convened one hundred religious leaders (fifty Muslim and fifty non-Muslim) in Marrakesh for a summit leading to the Marrakesh Declaration on the rights of religious minorities in Muslim majority countries. "His Eminence Sheikh Abdullah bin Bayyah," The Muslim 500: The World's Most Influential Muslims, accessed May 1, 2022. https://themuslim500.com/profiles/abdullah-bin-bayyah/. Susan Hayward, "Understanding and Extending the Marrakesh Declaration in Policy and Practice," United States Institute of Peace, Special Report 392, September 2016, https://docplayer.net/24925399-Special-report-2301-constitution-ave-nw-washington-dc-fax.html.

4. "A Changed World: The Continuing Impact of the Holocaust," United States Holocaust Memorial Museum, accessed April 28, 2022, https://www.ushmm.org/m/pdfs/20120405-aftermath-brochure.pdf.

5. Franklin Sherman, *Bridges: Documents of the Christian-Jewish Dialogue: Volume One, the Road to Reconciliation* (Mahwah: Paulist Press, 2011); Franklin Sherman, *Bridges: Documents of the Christian-Jewish Dialogue: Volume Two, Building a New Relationship* (Mahwah: Paulist Press, 2011); Helga Kroner, *Stepping Stones to Further Jewish-Christian Relations* (London and New York: Stimulus Books, 1977); Helga Kroner, *More Stepping Stones to Jewish-Christian Relations* (New York and Mahwah, NJ: Paulist Press, 1985); See also the Stimulus Foundation created by Helga Kroner to further publications on Jewish–Christian relations, The Stimulus Foundation, accessed May 14, 2022, *https://www.stimulusfoundation.org/.* The International Council of Christians and Jews website holds a collection of more than two hundred statements along with other global resources and articles on the topic of Jewish–Christian Relations. "Statements," International Council of Christians and Jews, accessed May 14, 2022, https://www.jcrelations.net/statements.html.

6. Sacks, "The Dignity of Difference: How to Avoid the Clash of Civilizations," Foreign Policy Research Institute, June 27, 2013, https://www.fpri.org/article/2013/06/the-dignity-of-difference-avoiding-the-clash-of-civilizations/.

7. "The German Churches and the Nazi State," The United States Holocaust Memorial Museum, accessed May 11, 2022, https://encyclopedia.ushmm.org/content/en/article/the-german-churches-and-the-nazi-state.

8. Centuries old European antisemitism included the unfounded accusations of the blood libel (claiming Jews slaughtered Christians to use their blood for ritual purposes), that Jews poisoned the wells during the Plague, and host desecration. Robert Chazan, *From Anti-Judaism to Anti-Semitism: Ancient and Medieval Christian Constructions of Jewish History* (New York: Cambridge University Press, 2016), x.

9. Matthew D. Hockenos, *A Church Divided: German Protestants Confront the Nazi Past* (Bloomington: Indiana University Press, 2004), 42–46.

10. Historical background from St. Mark's Church, Stuttgart. Translation by Harold Marcuse, Professor of History at UC Santa Barbara. "The Stuttgart Declaration of Guilt by the Council of the Protestant Church of Germany, October 19, 1945," UC Santa Barbara, March 2005, https://marcuse.faculty.history.ucsb.edu/projects/niem/StuttgartDeclaration.htm.

11. The formal title of the Stuttgart Declaration of Guilt is the "Declaration to the Representatives of the World Council of Churches." The World Council of Churches (WCC) was voted into existence by one hundred leaders in 1937–1938; yet the 1939 outbreak of World War II postponed its inauguration to 1948 (with 147 member churches). Today it has a membership of 352 churches from more than 120 countries representing over 580 million Christians. Niemöller was elected as one of six presidents of the WCC serving from 1961 to 1968. The 1948 Stuttgart Declaration of Guilt is categorized as Protestant; however, after the Russian Orthodox Church joined the WCC in 1961, their statements would thereafter be categorized as ecumenical. "History," World Council of Churches, accessed May 14, 2022, https://www.oikoumene.org/about-the-wcc/history.

12. Text from memorial plaque at St. Mark's Church, Stuttgart. Translated by Harold Marcuse, accessed May 11, 2022, https://marcuse.faculty.history.ucsb.edu/projects/niem/StuttgartDeclaration.htm.

13. "Stuttgart Declaration of Guilt," in Sherman, *Volume One*, 41–42.

14. Sherman, *Volume One*, 43–44.

15. Martin Niemoller, *Der Weg ins Freie* (Stuttgart: F. Mittelbach, 1946), 17–20. Translated by Harold Marcuse, "The Origin and Reception

of Martin Niemöller's, 'First they came for the communists . . . ,'"
in *Remembering for the Future: Armenia, Auschwitz, and Beyond*, ed.
Michael Berenbaum, Richard Libowitz, and Marcia Sachs Littell
(St. Paul, Minnesota: Paragon House, 2016), 177–78.

16. Marcuse, "The Origin," 189–90.

17. Marcuse, "The Origin," 191.

18. Sherman, *Volume One*, 305–6.

19. Sherman, *Volume One*, 322–23.

20. "The Presbyterian Church's General Assembly voted 431 to 62 in
    July [2004] to 'initiate a process of phased selective divestment
    in multinational corporations operating in Israel' and also de-
    cided to continue funding messianic congregations that target
    Jews for proselytizing." Alan Cooperman, "Israel Divestiture
    Spurs Clash," *The Washington Post*, September 29, 2004. "World
    Council of Churches Endorses Divestment From Israel," Religion
    News Service, February 23, 2005, accessed July 18, 2022, https://
    religionnews.com/2005/02/23/news-story-world-council-of-
    churches-endorses-divestment-from-israel/. While many prior
    Presbyterian Church (USA) General Assemblies offered up single
    resolutions related to the Israeli–Palestinian conflict, the 2004
    General Assembly created five resolutions criticizing Israel. This
    essay cannot treat Boycott, Divestment and Sanctions (BDS). For
    resources on the history of BDS and Christian denominational in-
    volvement in it see Cary Nelson and Michael C. Gizzi, *Peace and
    Faith: Christian Churches and The Israeli-Palestinian Conflict* (Phila-
    delphia and Boston: Presbyterians for Middle East Peace, October
    2021).

21. "A Short Introduction to Jules Isaac," Jules Isaac Founda-
    tion, accessed May 21, 2022, https://julesisaacstichting.org/
    a-short-introduction-to-jules-isaac/.

22. John L. Allen, Jr., "60 Years Ago, a Pope Met a Jewish Icon and the
    World Changed," *Crux*, accessed May 15, 2022, https://cruxnow.
    com/news-analysis/2020/06/60-years-ago-a-pope-met-a-
    jewish-icon-and-the-world-changed.

23. Isaac identified three teachings of contempt rooted in the teach-
    ings of the early church: Jewish dispersion was providential
    punishment for the crucifixion, the deterioration of Judaism
    was due to the legalism of the Pharisees, and the Jews were re-
    sponsible for deicide. The term "supersessionism, often used
    interchangeably with "replacement theology," is the claim that
    God's covenant with the Jews has been replaced by a new cov-
    enant through Jesus and with the Church. R. Kendall Soulen,
    professor of Systematic Theology at Wesley Theological Semi-
    nary writes: "Although never formally defined as a doctrine
    by the early Church, supersessionism has stood at the centre

of Christianity's understanding of its relationship to the Jewish people from antiquity until recent times." Jules Isaac, *The Teaching of Contempt: Christian Roots of Anti-Semitism*, (New York: Holt, Rinehart and Winston, 1964). R. Kendall Soulen, "Supersessionism," in *A Dictionary of Jewish-Christian Relations*, ed. Edward Kessler and Neil Wenborn (Cambridge: Cambridge University Press, 2005), 413–14.

24. The Institute for Christian and Jewish Studies is now the Institute for Islamic, Christian, and Jewish Studies. David Novak, *Jewish-Christian Dialogue: A Jewish Justification* (Oxford: Oxford University Press, 1989). David F. Sandmel, Rosann M. Catalano, and Christopher Magee Leighton, *Irreconcilable Differences?: A Learning Resource for Jews and Christians* (Boulder, CO: Westview Press, 2001).

25. "Dabru Emet: A Jewish Statement on Christians and Christianity," *Institute for Islamic, Christian, and Jewish Studies*, accessed June 29, 2022, https://icjs.org/dabru-emet-text/.

26. Laurie Goodstein, "Leading Jewish Scholars Extend a Hand to Christians," *New York Times*, September 8, 2000.

27. "*Dabru Emet* ['Speak the Truth']: A Jewish Statement on Christians and Christianity," Sherman, *Volume Two*, 511.

28. Sherman, *Volume Two*, 511.

29. Sherman, *Volume Two*, 513.

30. Michael Signer, "Dabru Emet: Sic et Non," Council of Centers on Jewish-Christian Relations, October 28, 2002, https://www.ccjr. us/dialogika-resources/documents-and-statements/analyses/dabru-emet-signer.

31. Signer, "Dabru Emet: Sic et Non."

32. "Between Jerusalem and Rome: Reflections on 50 Years of *Nostra Aetate*," Center for Jewish-Christian Understanding and Cooperation, accessed May 30, 2022, https://www.cjcuc.org/2017/08/31/between-jerusalem-and-rome/.

33. In August 1947 at the Seelisberg Conference, a significant group of Christian and Jewish leaders assembled including the presidents of national Jewish–Christian organizations, the chief rabbis of Budapest and Bucharest, and representatives of the World Council of Churches. Christian Rutishauser, "The 1947 Seelisberg Conference: The Foundation of the Jewish-Christian Dialogue," *Studies in Christian-Jewish Relations* 2, no. 2 (2007): 34–53.

34. The third-century Talmudic Sage Rabbi Abbahu comments: "'I am the first,' for I have no father, 'and I am the last,' for I have no son, 'and beside Me there is no God,' for I have no brother." (Midrash, *Sh'mot Rabbah* 29:5). See Louis Jacobs. "Christianity," *The Jewish Religion: A Companion*. (Oxford: Oxford University Press, 1995), 79–80.

35. "Statement adopted by the Rabbinical Council of America [the Rabbinic arm of the modern Orthodox movement in the United States] at its Midwinter Conference, February 3–5 1964," in *Sherman, Volume One*, 418.

36. Joseph B. Soloveitchik, "Confrontation," *Tradition: A Journal of Orthodox Jewish Thought* 6, no. 2 (1964).

37. "*Emet ve'Emunah* ['Truth and Faithfulness']: Statement of Principles of Conservative Judaism (excerpt)," in Sherman, *Volume 2*, 494–96.

38. The number of signatories would grow to 220 a month later. "Dabru Emet: A Jewish Statement on Christians and Christianity."

39. Abraham Joshua Heschel, "On Improving Catholic-Jewish Relations: A Memorandum to His Eminence Agostino Cardinal Bea President The Secretariat for Christian Unity," May 22, 1962, *American Jewish Archives*, MS-603: Rabbi Marc H. Tanenbaum Collection, 1945–1992, series C: Interreligious Activities, 1952–1992, box 12, folder 8, Bea, Augustin [Cardinal], 1962–1963.

40. Stanislaw Krajewski, "Abraham Joshua Heschel and the Declaration 'Dabru Emet,'" *Shofar* 26, no. 1 (2007): 154–68, http://www.jstor.org/stable/42944652.

41. Magdalena Dziaczkowska notes that when the center of Jewish diaspora life moved to North America in the postwar era, many American Jewish organizations became engaged in interreligious conversations surrounding Vatican II. "Although initially unclear which Jewish organization would fill this role, the American Jewish Committee (hereafter AJC) became the most significant Jewish voice during Nostra Aetate's drafting and promulgation." Magdalena Dziaczkowska, "American Judaism and the Second Vatican Council: The Response of the American Jewish Committee to Nostra Aetate," *U.S. Catholic historian* 38, no. 3 (2020): 26. "AJC and Vatican II: A Chronology of the Agency's Involvement," 1984, Rabbi Marc H. Tanenbaum Collection, series C, box 11, folder 4.

42. Rabbi David Fox Sandmel also managed the publication of *Christianity in Jewish Terms* (2000), and *Irreconcilable Differences: A Learning Resource for Christians and Jews* (2001). David Fox Sandmel, "Is *Dabru Emet* the Jewish *Nostra Aetate*? Sic et non," American Religion, accessed May 15, 2022, https://www.american-religion.org/dabruemet/sandmel.

43. Mike Hardy, Fiyaz Mughal, and Sarah Markiewicz, eds., *Muslim Identity in a Turbulent Age: Islamic Extremism and Western Islamophobia* (Philadelphia: Jessica Kingsley Publishers, 2017), 3.

44. In September 2004, Abdullah II had been in Russia visiting President Vladimir Putin, when Islamist separatists captured a school in Beslan, a North-Ossetian town, taking 1,100 hostages, two-thirds

of whom were children. The terrorists demanded Russian's withdrawal from Chechnya. After three days, the Russians ended the siege and three hundred were killed—half of whom were children. Hardy, Mighal, and Markiewicz, eds., *Muslim Identity*, 19.

45. King Abdullah II, *Our Last Chance: In Pursuit of Peace in a Time of Peril* (New York: Viking, 2011), 256.

46. "The Amman Message," *The Official Website of the Amman Message*, accessed May 30, 2022, https://ammanmessage.com/the-amman-message-full/.

47. King Abdullah II, *Our Last Chance*, 257.

48. King Abdullah II, *Our Last Chance*, 258.

49. "On the Amman Message," *The Official Website of the Amman Message*, accessed June 29, 2022, https://ammanmessage.com/on-the-amman-message/.

50. "Anas bin Malik said: 'I heard the Messenger of Allah say: My nation will not unite on misguidance, so if you see them differing, follow the great majority.'" Ibn Majah, *Sunnan,* book 36, hadith 25, as cited by Imam Muhammad Bin Yazeed Ibn Majah Al-Qazwini, *English Translation of Sunan Ibn Majah, Volume 5* (Riyadh: Darussalam, 2007), no. 3950, 174–75. The translation in this article is from *The Official Website of the Amman Message.*

51. Brent Sadler, Barbara Starr, Nic Robertson, Henry Schuster, and Kristen Gillespie, "Jordan 'failed bomber' confesses on TV," CNN.com, November 14, 2005, http://www.cnn.com/2005/WORLD/meast/11/13/jordan.blasts/.

52. "Introduction by HRH Prince Ghazi bin Muhammad," *The Official Website of the Amman Message*, 7.

53. King Abdullah II, *Our Last Chance*, 259.

54. The conclusion of promoting the Amman Message was marked by a two-day seminar in September 2014. *Muslim Identity in a Turbulent Age*, 36–37.

55. "Introduction to A Common Word Between Us and You," *A Common Word*, accessed June 30, 2022, https://www.acommonword.com/introduction-to-a-common-word-between-us-and-you/.

56. Miroslav Volf and Melissa Yarrington, *A Common Word: Muslims and Christians on Loving God and Neighbor*, (Grand Rapids, MI: Eerdmans Publishing House Co., 2010), xiii.

57. Prince Ghazi notes that "'A Common Word' was *not* intended to exclude Judaism as such or diminish its importance. We started with Christianity bilaterally simply because Islam and Christianity are the two largest religions in the world and in history . . . Jewish observers have been invited attendees of the conferences in [sic] Yale and Cambridge." Volf and Yarrington, *A Common Word: Muslims and Christians*, 11.

58. The Amman Message (November 2004), The "Common Word" Open Letter (2007), The Washington Declaration (2013), The Marrakesh Declaration for the Rights of Religious Minorities in Muslim-Majority Lands (January 2016), Human Fraternity Declaration (February 2019), the Washington Declaration of the Alliance of Virtue for the Common Good (February 2018), The Makkah Declaration (2019), and the Charter of the New Alliance of Virtue (December 2019). The Marrakesh coincided with the 1,400th anniversary of the Charter of Medina, a constitutional contract between Muhammad and the people of Medina.

59. Michaelle Browers, "Official Islam and the Limits of Communicative Action: The Paradox of the Amman Message." *Third World Quarterly* 32, no. 5 (2011): 944.

60. Moh'd Khair Eiedat, "The Amman Message: A Counter-Narrative to Islamic Fundamentalism," Hardy, Mighal, and Markiewicz, eds., *Muslim Identity, Muslim Identity in a Turbulent Age*, 151.

61. See note 3.

62. Grass-roots interfaith volunteering such as working in soup kitchens and homeless shelters, interfaith education, and collaborative advocacy on issues of social justice can be other meaningful starting points for reparative work.

63. Susannah Heschel, "Interfaith Begins with Faith," American Religion, accessed May 31, 2022, https://www.american-religion.org/dabruemet/heschel.

M'gillah and Machiavelli: Esther's Political Science

Rabbi Leigh Lerner

Introduction

In Tractate *M'gillah* of the Babylonian Talmud, the Rabbis analyze the practical politics of Esther's strategic dealings with Ahasuerus and Haman. "Unlike most modern commentators to Esther, whose concerns are mainly for the psychological . . . motivations or . . . the literary considerations . . . of the narrative, the Talmudic opinions all relate to the strategic wisdom of Esther's actions."[1] The tractate offers useful political thinking, provides guidance to future Jewish struggles for survival, and makes Talmud *M'gillah* (hereafter BTM) 15b[2] deserving of careful analysis as an early text in political science. Like Machiavelli's *The Prince*,[3] its message speaks to secular public life.

Talmud far predates Niccolò Machiavelli's seminal Renaissance work, *The Prince* of 1532, which arose in a time of autocratic kings and a few proto-republics, yet it has stunning similarities that validate Esther's strategy. Comparing Machiavelli's advice with the political implications of Esther's artifice of inviting Haman to the wine banquet with Ahasuerus demonstrates not only commonalities of thought in the two works, but also significant differences.

In Esther, a tale of intrigue and deception unfolds before the reader. Consider Esther's statement asking the king and Haman to come to the feast "prepared for him" (Esther 5:4; all biblical quotations JPS, 1985). For whom? For the king? For Haman? The referent *lo* is not clear. Insofar as the Jews are concerned, just as Amos the prophet conspired against Jeroboam and his minion Amaziah (Amos 7:10), so Esther conspires against Ahasuerus and Haman.

RABBI LEIGH LERNER (C72) is rabbi emeritus of Temple Emanu-El-Beth Sholom, Montreal, Canada. From 2012 to 2019, he served as volunteer rabbi to Shir Hadash Firenze and other Italian Reform congregations and still teaches in Italy online. He is the author of *The Mossad Messiah: A Novel of Israel* and numerous articles.

Meanwhile, Haman conspires with Ahasuerus to destroy the Jews, and now, because Haman is invited to the wine feast, the king may begin to believe that Haman conspires against him with his Number One Wife. The Book of Esther grabs the reader's attention with its palace politics and intrigue.

When Esther appears before Ahasuerus, her wine feast is ready. "Let Your Majesty and Haman come today to the feast that I have prepared for him" (Esther 5:4). At the wine feast, the king asks Esther her wish, up to half the kingdom. She simply invites the two to return for another day of the wine feast and promises to "do Your Majesty's bidding" (Esther 5:8). Rashi thinks that means she will reveal her nationality and lineage to Ahasuerus, which certainly plays into the grand finale at the end of the second day's feasting. Ibn Ezra takes a more nuanced view. He suggests that during the first day Esther looked for an opening to accuse Haman and bring the subject of the fatal decree before the king, but she did not find the proper moment and wanted to try again. In the text she speaks of a banquet that "I will prepare" (Esther 5:8), indicating that Esther needed to redo the task perhaps originally planned for only one day.

How does Ibn Ezra's comment jibe with the Talmud? Like Ibn Ezra, in BTM 15b the Rabbis also emphasize Esther's powers of observation and ask an unexpectedly basic political question that touches on both days of the queen's festivities: "What did Esther see to invite Haman to the banquet?" After all, she could have invited the king alone and appealed to him for mercy once he was sufficiently warmed by the wine and perhaps by her caresses. Then, in one brief, powerful paragraph, the Rabbis of BTM 15b explain the many political facets of which Esther had to be aware in order to put an end to Haman's hold on the king and his plot against the Jews.

Babylonian Talmud *M'gillah* 15b

Rabbi Elazar says: She hid snares for him, as it is stated: "May their table be a trap for them" (Ps. 69:23). Rabbi Yehoshua says: She learned to do this from the Jewish teachings of her father's house, as it is stated: "If your enemy be hungry, give him bread to eat, [and if he is thirsty, give him water to drink]" (Prov. 25:21). Rabbi Meir says: She invited him in order that he be near her at all times, so that he would not take counsel and rebel [against Ahasuerus]. Rabbi Yehuda says: She invited Haman so that it not be found out that she was a Jew. Rabbi Nechemya says: She did this so that the Jewish people would not say, "We have a sister in the king's house," and consequently remove their mind from [the need to pray for] divine mercy. Rabbi Yosei says, [she acted in this manner] so that Haman would always be on hand for her. Rabbi Shimon ben Menasya says, [Esther said to herself]: "Perhaps the Omnipresent will feel compassion, and God will perform a miracle for us." Rabbi Yehoshua ben Korcha says: She said to herself: "I will act kindly toward him in order that both he [Haman] and she [Esther] would be killed." Rabban Gamliel says, Ahasuerus was a fickle king. Rabban Gamliel said: We still need the words of Rabbi Eliezer HaModa'i. As it is taught in a *baraita*, Rabbi Eliezer HaModa'i says, "She made the king jealous of him, and she made the other ministers [or, the princes[4]] jealous of him." Rava says: Esther invited Haman to her banquet in order to fulfill that which is stated: "Pride goes before destruction [and a haughty spirit before a fall"] (Prov. 16:18). Both Abaye and Rava say that she invited Haman in order to fulfill the verse: "When they are heated, I will make feasts for them" (Jer. 51:39–40).

Each Rabbinic statement expresses profound political insight and strategic awareness, and each is worthy of consideration.

1. **Snares and Traps:** Rabbi Elazar ben Shamua (2nd c. CE) says she hid snares for him, as it is stated, "'May their table be a trap for them'" (Psalm 69:23).

Rabbi Elazar's assertion that Esther hid snares and traps requires review of the verses that follow in the psalm: "May their table be a trap for them, a snare for their allies. May their eyes grow dim so that they cannot see; may their loins collapse continually. Pour out Your wrath on them; may Your blazing anger overtake them." How could this happen? Adin Steinsaltz comments that Esther assumed she could trip up Haman during the feast,[5] ensnaring the prime minister at the table by his own misbehavior, eliciting the king's wrath.

Psalm 69 charges Esther to become the messenger of destruction to Haman and his war against the Jews. Yet there is more to it. The references in the psalm are in the plural, to "them." Esther's table must become a trap not only for Haman, but for Ahasuerus, too, so that she must be aware of the critical time when she has both enemies in hand in order to bring the king to her side and send the evil prime minister to his downfall.

To be clear, Talmud sees Ahasuerus as an enemy with whom Esther must deal. The famous "Mound and Ditch" parable of BTM 14a indicates how strongly the Rabbis felt that Ahasuerus was no friend of the Jews:

> Rabbi Abba offered a parable comparing Ahasuerus and Haman to explain how we might understand them: Once two people owned adjacent fields. One had a mound of earth in the middle of the field, and the other's field had a ditch in the midst of it. The owner of the ditch saw the neighbor's mound and thought, "I'll gladly pay whoever will give me that mound to fill in this ditch." The owner of the mound saw the other's ditch and thought, "I'll gladly pay whoever will let me use that ditch so that I can fill it with this useless mound and thus remove it from my property." One day the two encountered each other. The owner of the ditch said to the owner of the mound, "Sell me your mound so I can fill in my ditch." The owner of the mound, who wanted rid of it, said to him, "Take it for free. *Halevai*, if only you had asked me sooner."

We can identify the players by their actions. The ditch owner is Haman. How do we know? The owner of the mound, who does not offer to lift a finger, tells the ditch owner, "take it for free," just as Ahasuerus refused money from Haman (Esther 3:11). The ditch owner must do the work, just as Haman must manage the destruction of the Jews. Thus, the owner of the mound is Ahasuerus, who apparently views the Jews as an unnecessary heap of dirt in his kingdom. Because they are dirt, he wants them removed, revealing his wickedness, but he does not wish to get his hands soiled in the process, neither by labor nor by money. Like so many other malefactors, he wants a "front man" to bear the blame, Haman. Therefore, Ahasuerus did not really need Haman's convincing. Instead, he delighted that Haman had become the tool by which he could remove the Jewish problem from his midst, exactly as he desired. Esther had to consider snares and traps for this enemy as well as for Haman.

Just as Rabbi Elazar speaks of snares, *The Prince* (*TP*) speaks to the general idea of snares awaiting the ruler. If people were all good, the law would be sufficient help to avoid the snares, but people are not always law abiding. Frequently one must resort to the behavior of the beast to deal with traps set by the lawless (*TP*, 18).

Though Ahasuerus rules the empire and Haman rules the king, Esther rules the banquet of wine as queen. Her overarching stratagem relates to Machiavelli's reference to the behavior of the beast. In Esther of the Old Greek Septuagint, she turns to God to ask for support in prayer: "O King of the gods and Master of all dominion! Put eloquent speech in my mouth before the lion, and turn his heart to hate the one who fights against us so that there may be an end of him and those who agree with him."[6] Esther refers to Ahasuerus as "the lion." As director of events at the banquet of wine, however, it is Esther who must be the lion and more.

Machiavelli believes that rulers must sometimes play the role of two beasts at once: the fox and the lion. A fox can find the snares, but cannot defend against the wolves. The lion cannot defend against the snares, but can scare off the wolves. Together, the wily fox and the powerful lion make the perfect bestial combination (*TP*, 18). Yes, Esther must set snares for her guests, but she must also outfox any traps they may set for her, even as she summons the courage and strength of a lion to overcome the wolves, her foes.

Perhaps the Talmud put Rabbi Elazar's opinion first because he chose a psalm which can serve as the keynote expression of Esther's and the Jewish people's situation in the Persian Empire and beyond. Consider Psalm 69 in its entirety and marvel at its application across Jewish history, not just the moment of the wine feast. Here are a few examples of its thrust:

69:2–3a "Deliver me, O God, for the waters have reached my neck. I am sinking into the slimy deep and find no foothold." Midrash on Psalms 69:2 considers the exile in Persia to be precisely such a situation: "The words 'and find no foothold' allude to the exile in Media and in Persia." Esther's attempt is a last-ditch effort not only for her, but for the entire Jewish people drowning in despair. She knows that life itself depends on her success.

69:4 "My eyes fail while I wait for God." God seems absent from Persian Jewry in its plight. Indeed, God's name does not appear in the Book of Esther.

69:5 "More numerous than the hairs of my head are those who hate me without reason; many are those who would destroy me."

This verse describes the feelings of Esther's Jewry and countless Jews across generations of antisemitism, ghettos, and pogroms. Esther must stare down this feeling to win the day, as have others after her.

69:9 "I am a stranger to my brothers, an alien to my kin." Having married the king of Persia, Esther lives in an entirely non-Jewish world. To some of her community she may seem a self-hating Jew who has given up her heritage in favor of the delights of palace life as a royal consort. They may despise her, not honor her for having accepted and assimilated into her royal estate.

69:19 "Do not hide (אל תסתר פניך) Your face from Your servant, for I am in distress; answer me quickly." Yes, Esther feels that God has abandoned her, but this verse suggests an answer to her prayer. God's work is hidden *in her*, for re-pointing of her very name testifies to that fact: not Esther—אֶסְתֵּר, but *Esater*—אֶסָתֵר, "I will be hidden."[7] In Esther's deeds, God's hidden redemption will be found, and in the end, she should look in the mirror and accept her role as the answer to her prayer.

69:36 "For God will deliver Zion and rebuild the cities of Judah; they shall live there and inherit it." When Ahasuerus promises Esther up to half his kingdom (Esther 5:3), he establishes a critical limit, half and nothing further. Rashi comments that חצי (half) has its root in חצץ, *ch-ts-ts*, which means "to drive a wedge in" or "to divide off." Jews consider Jerusalem the middle of the world. Imagining Ahasuerus agrees, were he to allow the rebuilding of the Temple, that would overweight Jerusalem's centrality in his empire beyond the middle point, becoming a thing that חוצץ, obstructs his kingdom, which he could not allow.[8] In Jewish eyes, Ahasuerus's refusal to permit the rebuilding of the Temple defines his enemy status. The psalm, however, ends on a note of hope and restoration, and Esther must acknowledge that possibility through the fullness of her deeds on God's behalf and for the Jewish people so that Jerusalem restored can remain the people's aspiration.

Rabbi Elazar sets the tone for all the Rabbinic opinions that follow. His choice of Psalm 69 captures Esther's feelings and spirit, helps the reader imagine Esther or ourselves emerging successfully from an abyss, and instills in us the same power, confidence, and bravery of Esther.

2. **Dissemble to Your Advantage**: Rabbi Yehoshua ben Hananiah (ca.100 CE) says: She learned to do this from the Jewish teachings of her father's house, as it is stated: "If your enemy be hungry, give him bread to eat, [and if he is thirsty, give him water to drink]" (Proverbs 25:21).

Esther was an orphan adopted by her foster father Mordecai (Esther 2:7), a leader in the Jewish community (*Esther Rabbah* 6:2). She lived in his Jewish home, observed his teaching of Jewish tradition, and witnessed how he handled the politics of leadership and the interactions necessary to guide a stiff-necked people toward the Torah's goals. One useful method across the ages has always been to influence others by dining with them. Congeniality, good food, some wine, and relaxed conversation almost never fail to lead to warmer, more personal, trusting relationships.

For Rashi, the enemy of Proverbs is one's evil inclination. Water means Torah, and that will control the *yetzer hara*. Commentators like Ibn Ezra and Malbim believe that the verse urges treating enemies with generosity and kindness to overcome their aggressive impulses. Rabbi Yehoshua comprehends the straits in which Esther finds herself, and his use of Proverbs 25:21 can be understood as a hint to take seriously the verse that follows: "You will be heaping live coals on his head, and the Eternal will reward you" (Proverbs 25:22).

If Esther knows Proverbs 25, she can also find this advice: "It is the glory of God to conceal a matter, and the glory of a king to plumb a matter" (Proverbs 25:2). Esther, working on God's behalf, must conceal her intent, whose practical outcome will cause Ahasuerus to plumb the malevolence of Haman. Esther's task? "Remove the wicked from the king's presence, and his throne will be established in justice" (Proverbs 25:5). "Defend your right against your fellow, but do not give away the secrets of another" (Proverbs 25:9). If in defense of one's own rights the secrets of another must be guarded, how much the more so must Esther guard her true identity, a personal secret, until the propitious time to reveal it. Once again, the Talmudic Rabbi selects a quotation from a text replete with pragmatic advice for Esther.

If Esther must then play the fox, Machiavelli explains that "it is necessary to know well how to disguise this characteristic, and to be a great pretender and dissembler; and men are so simple, and so subject to present necessities, that he who seeks to deceive will always find someone who will allow himself to be deceived" (*TP*, 18). Having succeeded in entertaining her two men on the first day, she must follow with another day of dissembling and playing the fox in order ultimately to become the lion.

In addition, Rabbi Yehoshua extends the meaning of Rabbi Elazar's observation that the dining table must provide snares and traps for the two guests. He suggests that Esther, having observed Mordecai's leadership, saw the opportunity to be a generous hostess. Offering plenty to eat and drink along with good conversation elevates Esther's status in the men's minds even as she relaxes the guard of her two guests as she awaits the required opening to attack Haman.

3. **Keep your enemies close:** Rabbi Meir (ca.145 CE) says: She invited him in order that he be near her at all times, so that he would not take counsel and rebel [against Ahasuerus].

Why should Esther worry about Haman's taking counsel or initiating rebellion? Haman listened to his wife, Zeresh; his friends; and his official advisors (Esther 5:14; 6:13). They instigated the making of the gallows for Mordecai. Thus, Haman has a following with whom he could rebel, and he gives them ear, as well.

The *m'gillah* speaks to Haman's personality at the same time it presents us with his counselors. When invited to Esther's feast, he brags to them that only he and the king will be there with the queen. He vaunts his wealth,[9] boasts of his children, and presents himself as a man of great power, but the sight of the Jew Mordecai in the King's Gate weighs on his heart. Mordecai's seeming disrespect makes all Haman's achievements worthless in his eyes. We are given a man of inordinate egotism and pride, a man whose ego cannot stand the idea of anyone, particularly a Jew, disrespecting him.

Is Mordecai just a lowly Jew? What does it mean to sit in the King's Gate? Robert Gordis explains that "throughout the ancient Near East 'the gate' was the area where trials were conducted and justice was dispensed." Gordis posits the idea that "after Esther becomes queen, she has Mordecai appointed a magistrate or judge, a lesser position in the elaborate hierarchy of Persian officials. Not only is this a recognition of what Mordecai has done for her, but it gives him easier access to the royal quarters."[10] Whether Esther urged the king or his representatives to elevate Mordecai remains conjecture, but if the gate in Shushan served as a place for cases to be adjudicated, it is not just any Jew who disrespected and infuriated Haman, but a government official setting an example of insolence for all the Jews. Surely that would intensify Haman's bitter antisemitism, a fact which his wife, friends, and advisors understood and to which they allied themselves by urging Haman to erect the gallows for Mordecai (Esther 5:11–14).

The Rabbis discern Haman's authority as the most influential of government ministers, in full possession of the king's signet ring to do as he pleases. Facing a threat to his power, given Haman's many political connections and his wealth, it remained possible for him to rebel against the king and attempt a palace coup. We have evidence that he was considering that possibility in Esther 6:8, when Ahasuerus asked what should be done to the man he wants to honor. Haman decides that the king meant to honor him. He advises the king to "let royal garb which the king has worn be brought, and a horse on which the king has ridden and on whose head a royal diadem has been set"[11] (Esther 6:9). Haman wants to make a public appearance like royalty, allowing the public to imagine him as such. The king may understand Haman's egotistical yearnings, since his command concerns the clothing and the horse but omits Haman's suggestion of the crown (Esther 6:10).

According to Rabbi Meir, in the face of Haman's active advisory group and his own pretentions to rulership, Esther was wise to follow the dictum of Sun Tzu[12] made popular by a remark of the Godfather in the film of the same name: "Keep your friends close and your enemies closer." For that judicious reason she invited Haman to the wine feast with her husband the king. If Esther confronted the prime minister in the very presence of the king, Haman could not arise and rush off to piece together a coup nor gather his advisors without greatly disturbing his relationship with Ahasuerus. Esther understood Haman's ego and ambition and how to use them to her own ends.

There is a further political issue, as Machiavelli points out in chapter 2 of *The Prince*. Ahasuerus is a hereditary prince, which puts him in a preferred position because "the hereditary prince has less cause and less necessity to offend, hence it happens that he will be more loved." But Machiavelli offers one proviso: "unless extraordinary vices cause him to be hated." A hereditary prince's acceptance can be diminished by his own exaggerated behavior, and a king who gives banquets of six months' duration, a king who entertains the conquered nobles at virtually endless luxurious festivities while the people of his own city watch the foreigners come and go—such a king may be said to have extraordinary vices and be ripe for overthrow. Bigthan and Teresh plotted against the king, but Mordecai's effort stopped them (Esther 2:21). Haman, the power-hungry observer of all this, may see an opportunity to snatch the empire away from Ahasuerus. Esther's invitation holds him in check if only for the time necessary to bring about his downfall.

4. **Maintain Your Disguise**: Rabbi Yehuda bar Ilai (2nd c. CE) says, She invited Haman so that it not be found out that she was a Jew.

Adin Steinsaltz comments that if Esther distanced herself from Haman, he might be suspicious that she was a Jew,[13] particularly since she may have intervened to put Mordecai in the King's Gate as an official. Joshua Kulp states that had Haman suspected her Jewishness, with the possibility that she would appeal to Ahasuerus to stop the fatal decree, Haman might have hastened to complete his murderous plans.[14] Both explanations are politically astute.

Machiavelli adds, "Everyone sees what you appear to be, few really know what you are" (*TP*, 18). If this is the rule for kings, it is also the rule for queens who seek to control a situation that threatens them and which includes the necessity to withhold some vital information from government leaders, whether the king or his prime minister. If Esther's Jewishness were discovered before she herself admitted of it, not only would her scheme fail, but any favorable view of her and support for her cause by the king would vanish. She would no longer appear to be a disinterested party, and without Haman's presence, the wine banquet's goal would fail, if it took place at all.

5. **Don't Discount the Spiritual Factor**: Rabbi Nechemya (ca. 150 CE) says: She did this so that the Jewish people would not say, "We have a sister in the king's house," and consequently remove their mind from [the need to pray for] divine mercy.

Nechemya advocates not for violence, but for prayerful fasting. Since the time of Jeremiah, when Jews were bidden to "seek the welfare of the city to which I have exiled you and pray to the

Eternal in its behalf" (Jeremiah 29:7), Jews have prayed for the welfare of the government for their own sake, but Jews also have acted to secure it. From the sixteenth to the eighteenth centuries in Eastern Europe, the *shtadlan*, "a well-connected, culturally adept, linguistically capable person" had the "official function . . . to intervene on behalf of . . . Jewish communities and . . . officials on all matters that the . . . community board and the intercommunal . . . council deemed appropriate."[15] Communities looked after their welfare by putting representatives in high places. In ancient days, Jews living as a minority community had comparable practices.

Esther Rabbah 10:14 relates that Rabbi Hiyya the elder and Rabbi Simeon bar Halafta once were together when they saw the dawn come up. Rabbi Hiyya said to Rabbi Simeon, "The greatness of Israel is like this: it commences almost imperceptibly, but becomes continually more and more powerful. What is the proof? 'Though I have fallen, I rise again; Though I sit in darkness, the Eternal is my light' (Micah 7:8). Just so, at first, Mordecai sat in the King's Gate (Esther 2:21); then, Mordecai returned to the King's Gate (Esther 6:12); then, Mordecai went forth from the presence of the king (Esther 8:15); and finally, the Jews had light and gladness, and joy and honor" (Esther 8:16).

Why did the Jews have joy and honor? "For Mordecai was now powerful in the royal palace, and his fame was spreading through all the provinces; the man Mordecai was growing ever more powerful" (Esther 9:12). And how did Mordecai become so powerful? In part by his own actions in saving the king's life, and in large part because Esther was the Jews' "sister in the king's house." Esther is secretly *in loco shtadlan*, the influencer Jew closest to the king. Mordecai is *shtadlan*-in-waiting, importantly the male counterpart of Esther, both of whom win the trust of the king in different ways. In the end, it is Mordecai who possesses the king's signet ring.

Given the practices of the Achaemenid kings of Persia[16] and in the face of Haman's decree, the Jewish community of Shushan and Persia could, indeed, have said to itself, "Esther is Ahasuerus's Number One Wife. We are fortunate to have an influencer at the top of the chain of household command, a woman who has the king's ear. What have we to fear? She will act on our behalf to put a stop to Haman's plan."

If we extend Nechemya's comment into the moment when Esther invited Haman, what did she see? Esther saw that Haman's egotism would spread the word to his many friends about his upcoming appearance with the king at the queen's feast. They, in turn, would gossip, and soon all Shushan would know of it. Therefore, by inviting Haman to the wine feast, Esther makes it seem as if she wants the dreaded prime minister at her side, falsely giving the impression of a self-hating Jew who has forgotten her origins and taken up with the Persian majority. She appears not to be their sister in the palace at all, but on the side of the enemy. Jews might even misconstrue the three-day fast[17] that she commanded (Esther 4:16) as exaggerated religiosity meant to make herself seem Jewishly motivated. The Jews might conclude that their only hope for survival lay in prayers asking God's mercy, prayers that Esther has imposed on them by openly inviting Haman.

The comment of Rabbi Nechemya shows that he wants to put God and prayer directly into this Talmudic discussion. Gersonides and Ohr Chadash say that Esther's three-day fast includes prayer to God. Ibn Ezra and other commentators make it clear that fasting is a prayerful act on behalf of Esther, so that Nechemya is not alone in this consideration. Esther, however, did not ask the people to pray, but only to fast.

Fasting on behalf of Esther also supports Esther in her ruse to keep her Jewishness undisclosed before the king and Haman, since the Jews must know that the king would not have a Jew for a queen. The fast encourages them to support Esther by remaining silent about her Jewishness. Nechemya's response, then, may also be interpreted as an augmentation of Rabbi Yehuda's argument, that Esther did not want her Jewishness discovered.

Nechemya's words come also as a potent warning. He reminds us that, while secular strategy is necessary in many a crisis of governance, in every severe political confrontation there exists the spiritual factor, the yearning for the divine path, the soulful and prayerful hope for the upright of heart to prevail by encouraging and enhancing human life.

Machiavelli makes an assumption similar to Nechemya's idea that the Jews of Shushan might say, "We have a sister in the king's house." Promoting Italian unity, *The Prince* endorses Giuliano de Medici's possible leadership as Pope Clement VII, whom Machiavelli considers a brother in the Vatican. He writes, "Nor is there . . . at present one in whom she [Italy] can place more hope than in your illustrious house, with its valor and fortune, favored by God and by the Church of which [you are] now the chief, and which could be made the head of this redemption" (*TP*, 26). Machiavelli wants the Pope, leader of the Church's prayers, to let his religiosity inspire him to action in order to become the prince of a united Italy, a hope unfulfilled during the Renaissance. That achievement would have answered the prayers of Machiavelli and of many other Italians for the granting of divine mercy. Machiavelli, however, urges neither prayer nor fasting, but war. Only when Mordecai ascends to power does Machiavelli's advice prevail, when Mordecai wages war against Persia's antisemites.

6. **Time and Timing**: Rabbi Yosei ben Chalafta (2nd c. CE) says, [she acted in this manner] so that Haman would always be on hand for her.

Differing from Rabbi Meir, Rabbi Yosei views Esther's need to keep Haman close at hand not in order to stifle any possibility of his running to co-conspirators for a rebellion, not to make sure that he can't access advisors, but entirely for the queen's own purposes.

Time and timing must play a major part in Rabbi Yosei's reasoning. Regarding these, Mordecai is Esther's sole advisor and conspirator. He has impressed upon her how important her role has become in the salvation of the Jewish people, a task she can only escape at her own peril. Regarding time: "If you keep silent in this crisis, relief and deliverance will come to the Jews from another quarter, while you and your father's house will perish" (Esther 4:14). Regarding timing: "And who knows, perhaps you have attained to royal position for just such a crisis" (Esther 4:14).

The time is now, Mordecai declares, and your timing has to be perfect to end the crisis. Esther accepts the challenge set by her foster father and immediately issues an order to him, for she is, after all, the Queen of Persia. She commands Mordecai to gather the Jews and declare a three-day fast, which she will also endure, following which she'll go to the king. As the decision-maker, Esther's actions conform to Machiavelli's observation in chapter 23, "good counsels, from wherever they come, are born of the wisdom of the prince, and not the wisdom of the prince from good counsels."

Esther's actions after the encounter with Mordecai reflect respect for his advice, but ultimately, she is in control. Good fortune seems to have placed Esther in her royal estate. "If, to one who governs himself with caution and patience, times and affairs converge in such a way that his administration is successful, his fortune is made; but if times and affairs change, he is ruined if he does not change his course of action" (TP, 25). That is precisely what Esther has determined to do, to change her course of action from being the receiver of good fortune to the creator of it.

But what about time and timing? Why must they be perfect? By keeping Haman present throughout the gathering with the king, Rashi suggests that at some point she may be able to trip up the enemy of the Jews, showing him to Ahasuerus for exactly what he is. That takes timing. So also, an appeal to Ahasuerus requires perfect timing, for he must seem to be in either a merciful mood or angry at Haman. Ben Yehoyada thinks the intention is to let Haman feel secure enough that he would not prepare for himself a safe house to which he could escape.[18] That requires time. If Esther failed to set up Haman for a fall or find the appropriate moment to reveal the prime minister's weaknesses to the king, perhaps she could finally appeal to Haman for mercy—not a pleasant option, but one whose timing awaits the end of an unsuccessful wine feast.

7. **God's Intervention Is Only a "Perhaps"**: Rabbi Shimon ben Menasya (2nd–3rd c. CE) says, [Esther said to herself]: "Perhaps the Omnipresent will feel compassion, and God will perform a miracle for us."

Interpreting the statement of Rabbi Shimon presents difficulties. On the surface, it seems to go hand in hand with Rabbi Nechemya, who explains that Esther invited Haman as a means of encouraging the Jews to pray for God's help. Now from Rabbi Shimon we surmise that Haman's very presence at Esther's feast would arouse God's sympathy for her and for the Jewish people so that sending a divine miracle might be the sole solution. It is not, however, clear for whom the sympathy would be aroused.

The text of BTM 15b states *veyaaseh lanu nes*, [Perhaps . . . God] "will make a miracle for us." To whom does the word "us" refer? Is it all the Jews, or is Queen Esther using the majestic plural? Rashi and Ohr Chadash think it's the latter. Rashi to BTM 15b: "God will notice that I have to flatter the wicked one, disregarding my honor." And Ohr Chadash: "Esther was honoring Haman too much, and such greatness was unsuitable for this wicked one. Therefore, let

God make a miracle to bring down and destroy the evil one."[19] Steinsaltz views praying for a miracle to include the whole Jewish people, but with Esther as the pivot point. "Perhaps the Omnipresent will take notice that all are supporting Haman and nobody is supporting the Jewish people [in which Esther clearly includes herself], and will perform a miracle for [all of] us."[20]

Miracles, however, remain in the hands of God. To this point among the Rabbis of BTM 15b, the preponderance of reasoning is entirely political. Even Steinsaltz's view can be seen as Jewish politics between Esther and God, forging a deal with the Eternal for aid. Septuagint Esther 8:8–10 puts those divine politics into a prayer that Esther sends to God: "It does not satisfy them that we are in bitter captivity, but they have struck a deal with their idols. They will abolish the purpose that you with your mouth have ordained, and destroy your inheritance, and silence the mouth of those who praise you, and quench the glory of your house and of your altar, and open the mouths of the heathen to bring forth the praises of the idols, to magnify a fleshly king forever."[21]

Although the Septuagint's words are a prayer, the prayer argues with God. It recalls to God the *b'rit* (the "covenant") and its promise to safeguard the Jewish people, demanding the ancient contract's fulfillment not simply for a miracle to save Persian Jewry, but in order to save God's own reputation. It turns a miraculous intervention into divine self-interest and the "compassion" mentioned by Shimon ben Menasya into divine self-compassion.

Shimon ben Menasya's statement brings a religious element into Esther's strategy. What does Machiavelli think is the role of religion in matters of state? The prince should "appear to him who sees and hears him altogether merciful, faithful, humane, upright, and religious. There is nothing more necessary than to appear to have than this last quality, inasmuch as men judge generally more by the eye than by the hand" (*TP*, 18). Esther fasted for three days and asked the community to join her. She could be seen as religious and upright, despite possible doubts about her faithfulness because she invited Haman to the feast.

What does Machiavelli finally conclude about all the appearance of religiosity? Referring to Ferdinand the Catholic of Spain, he writes, "One prince of the present time[22] . . . never preaches anything else but peace and good faith, and to both he is most hostile, and either, if he had kept it, would have deprived him of reputation and kingdom many a time" (*TP*, 18). Esther will not save the Jewish people with peace and good faith, and Mordecai will not deal with bloodthirsty antisemites as a humane, merciful minister to the king. Still, a distinction must be drawn, for Machiavelli describes King Ferdinand as duplicitous for the sake of power, while any dissembling by Esther and Mordecai aims to promote their people's safety.

In *The Prince* we read, "You must know there are two ways of contesting, the one by the law, the other by force; the first method is proper to men, the second to beasts; but because the first is frequently not sufficient, it is necessary to have recourse to the second. Therefore, it is necessary for a prince to understand how to avail himself of the beast and the man" (*TP*, 18). Thus, BTM 15b is Machiavellian in its practical politics, leading to strong state or communal action for Jewish self- preservation, and "perhaps" that must be taken as a miracle, what Max Kadushin called the "normal mysticism"[23] of the Rabbis. BTM 15b leads us to a crescendo of awareness that Esther rejects the pettiness of self-preservation and personal power in order to validate the Torah's command to save the lives of her community.

8. **Use Any Vice**: Rabbi Yehoshua ben Korcha (2nd c. CE) says: She said to herself: I will act kindly toward him in order that both he [Haman] and she [Esther] would be killed.

Esther already put her life on the line in going to the king without an invitation: "And if I perish, I perish" (Esther 4:16). We know that she is prepared to risk all to save the Jews. Rabbi Yehoshua ben Korcha plays on this fact with his comment. He indicates that if Esther becomes too cozy with Haman in the presence of Ahasuerus, the king may suspect that they are having an affair and kill them both. With Haman out of the picture, there would be no follow-through on the decree of death to the Jews, since Ahasuerus had no desire to take personal charge of the genocide,[24] and in ancient times, often when the person who originated a decree died, the decree died with him.[25]

Daniel 6:6–9, however, indicates that once a Persian king made a decree, he could not reverse it. Nevertheless, it was possible to counteract a decree by the issue of new ones. If Esther could cause Ahasuerus to eliminate Haman, the antisemites would not only lack their leader, but might be considered followers of a rebel and suppressed. This occurred when the king appointed Mordecai in Haman's stead (Esther 8:2), along with permission for a preemptive strike against the antisemites (Esther 8:11). The new decrees counteracted the royal decree promoted by Haman.

Why does Yehoshua ben Korcha have Esther speak about herself in the third person when she creates a situation that risks her life? To take such a bold step as feigning an amorous interest in Haman requires that Esther distance herself from her own soul. She would have to overcome anxiety and distasteful thoughts to see herself not as a Jewish woman, not as a human being, but as a material object, an instrument necessary to save the lives of her community. A study by Moser et al. suggests that "third-person self-talk may constitute a relatively effortless form of self-control."[26]

Suppose Esther decided to make eyes at Haman. She would be correct in assuming it would be the end of Haman and of herself. Just as Vashti's misbehavior became well known in Shushan, so also would Esther's. Her respect in the Jewish community would fall to zero. As Benedict Arnold became a byword for traitor in America, Esther would become a byword for the self-hating Jewish traitor who consorted with the enemy. There would be no Book of Esther, even though her actions would have saved the Jewish people. Esther was willing to go to any length to save the Jews of the Persian Empire, as Yehoshua ben Korcha explains.

Would Mordecai have been able to explain away Esther's actions in such a case? People would say, "Why listen to him? He's her foster father, *nogéa badavar,* not a disinterested party." The Jewish community might say that God had intervened, or that Esther deserved her fate, and we are simply fortunate. Machiavelli would say that "Men more quickly forget the death of their father than the loss of their patrimony" (*TP,* 17). On this basis, perhaps Esther would be forgotten, but the inheritance of the Jewish people, their covenant and hope for redemption in the Land of Israel and for re-establishment of the Davidic monarchy would not have been lost, and Jewish life would continue.

Machiavelli relates that a prince "need not make himself uneasy at incurring a reproach for those vices without which the state can only be saved with difficulty, for if everything is considered carefully, it will be found that something which looks like virtue, if followed, would be his ruin; whilst something else, which looks like vice, yet followed brings him security and prosperity" (*TP*, 15). With Esther, it is not a state that she wants to save, but the lives of her community. If the "vice" of a feigned affair is required to manipulate the king's attitude toward Haman, so be it, no matter the cost.

9. **Play on the King's Changeability**: Rabban Gamliel (1st c. CE) says, Ahasuerus was a fickle king.

How does Rabban Gamliel know that Ahasuerus is a fickle, unstable king? Because he killed his wife Vashti to please his admirer Haman, and then killed his admirer Haman to please his wife, Esther.[27] And what does that instability have to do with Esther's invitation of Haman to the banquet of wine? Steinsaltz comments that Esther hoped for Ahasuerus to see Haman many times in order that familiarity might breed contempt, and he would change his mind about him.[28] Rashi to BTM 15b is similar, thinking that perhaps in his fickleness, the king would go back on his word [to kill the Jews]: "Esther said, maybe I can lure him, i.e. Ahasuerus, to see Haman's true nature, and he'll execute him. Were Haman not invited, the optimum time would pass and the king would go back on his word to do so."

The opinion of commentators old and new leads to the conclusion that Esther herself could not become the new Jael, who killed General Barak in Judges 4. Esther must arrange for Ahasuerus to remove his prime minister or change his decree. That meant she had to deal with the king's changeability and seek an instantly accomplishable decision.

Machiavelli sheds light on Esther's reasoning when he distinguishes between the Turkish and the French monarchies of his day: "The Turk is governed by one lord, the others are his servants . . . [he] shifts and changes them as he chooses. But the King of France is placed in the midst of an ancient body of lords, acknowledged by their own subjects, and beloved by them; they have their own prerogatives, nor can the king take these away except at his peril" (*TP*, 4). Esther knows that Haman's governmental position comes directly from the absolute monarch of Persia, whom she has no intention to dethrone or slay.

However, Machiavelli believes "it makes [a prince] contemptible to be considered fickle, frivolous . . . irresolute." "Instead . . .

in his private dealings with his subjects let him show that his judgments are irrevocable, and maintain himself in such reputation
that no one can hope either to deceive him or to get round him"
(*TP*, 19). Esther wants the king to revoke his judgment of death to
the Jews, and Gamliel sees Ahasuerus's fickleness as an opportunity to prompt that change. Esther knows that Haman has thrown
the king deep into the pit of deception, exacerbating his prejudice.
She must be ready on the spur of the moment to use her husband's
fickle nature in order to turn him to her side and against his prime
minister.

Were Ahasuerus to remove the decree of death, he would be
returning to *status quo ante* Haman. The Shushanites, originally
"dumbfounded" (Esther 3:15) by that decree against the Jews, might
think the king had rejected his fickleness and returned to ways that
endeared him to the populace. Machiavelli would approve: "He
who is highly esteemed is not easily conspired against; for, provided
it is well known that he is an excellent man and revered by his people, he can only be attacked with difficulty" (*TP*, 19).

10. **Instigate Suspicion or Jealousy**: Rabban Gamliel said: We still
    need the words of Rabbi Eliezer HaModa'i (ca. 80–110 CE). As
    it is taught in a *baraita*, Rabbi Eliezer HaModa'i says, She made
    the king jealous of him, and she made the other ministers [or,
    the princes] jealous of him.

Yehoshua ben Korcha suggested that if Esther treated Haman
kindly, the king's jealousy would bring about their execution. But
need she go that far? Rabban Gamliel believes that merely inviting
Haman would inflame the king's jealousy.

After the first day's banquet, fear and jealousy particularly agi-
tate King Ahasuerus. That night, the king could not sleep. BTM
15b suggests that his sleep was disturbed because Haman was
invited to the wine feast, eliciting jealousy or suspicion of a plot
afoot against him.

Esther Rabbah 10:1 indicates that his sleep was disturbed "because in a dream he saw Haman seizing a sword to kill him. Awak-
ing in terror, he commanded his scribes to bring the book of the
chronicles to see what events had occurred. They opened the book
and found how Mordecai had informed against the threat of Bigthan and Teresh [to Ahasuerus]. Thus, when they said to the king,

'It is Haman standing in the court' (Esther 6:5), the king said: 'What I saw in my dream is true; this fellow has only come at this time of day to kill me.'" Fear of Haman's growing avarice for power may be poisoning the king's attitude toward his prime minister.

Talmud joins itself to this midrashic theme of kingly fear in BTM 15b: "[Ahasuerus]said to himself, 'What's unique about the fact that Esther invited Haman? Perhaps they are conspiring against that man to kill him.'" If "that man" refers to Haman, what follows makes no sense. The king has put himself in third-person, just as when, according to Yehoshua ben Korcha, Esther did so in thinking about being killed for an ostensible affair with Haman. "[Ahasuerus] said again, if this is so, is there no one who loves me and would inform me [of this conspiracy]?" He continued, "Maybe there is some man who did me a favor, whom I have not rewarded, and because there is no financial benefit for them, people refrain from revealing [plots] to me."[29] At that point the king called for his chronicles to be read.

The mere fact that Esther only invited one additional guest beside Ahasuerus to dine with her does, indeed, point to a plan to instill jealousy in her royal husband. Unlike kings and generals, the power of the king's royal consort over her husband stems from beauty, femininity, sexuality, fecundity, and her organizational skills regarding the household. These powers draw the king towards her so strongly that, at her request, he is willing to give her up to half his kingdom, far more than a mere token of his love for Esther. But Esther's beguiling attributes can easily charm others, as well. Yehoshua ben Korcha has already posed the possibility of a feigned affair with Haman as a way to cause both her own and Haman's death. Now Rabbi Eliezer HaModa'i modifies Yehoshua's comment.

If the king trusts Esther sufficiently to believe that there is no current affair with Haman, he may still be at the stage of jealous worries that disturb his sleep on the eve of the second wine feast. But why be jealous of a man who serves at the king's whim? He could simply eliminate him, which plays well into Esther's hands. In addition, Eliezer's comment brings in the other ministers, or even the princes, those young men preparing to battle for the throne of their father. They all realize that alone among them, only Haman has been invited to the wine feast with the royal couple; only Haman appears to have the ear of the king. They, too, might want to eliminate the prime minister out of jealousy. It's a simple but compelling, impressive, and risky formula for success that Esther applies by inviting Haman with the king.

Does *The Prince* understand Esther's risk? Machiavelli speaks almost nothing of a queen and her power, but fortune receives feminine referent: "I hold it to be true that Fortune is the arbiter of one-half of our actions, but that she still leaves us to direct the other half, or perhaps a little less" (*TP*, 25). Similarly, in the *m'gillah*, Esther represents the Jewish nation dispersed in Persian lands, and Eliezer HaModa'i understands that Esther's toying with Ahasuerus's emotions by inviting Haman to the banquet stands not only as a brilliant ploy, but like all the other reasons for inviting the prime minister, also relies in part on fortune, since the results of the invitation are to some extent out of her control.

Esther, however, understands the role of fortune in life. Had Vashti not refused to appear before Ahasuerus at his gala party, no opening for Number One Wife would ever have occurred. Fortune alone determined that possibility. Had Esther's persona not been attractive to the cosmeticians in the king's harem, perhaps her beauty would not have shined brightly enough to attract the king. Had the king not extended his scepter to permit her uninvited entry into the throne room, Esther would be the next Vashti, simply gone, and so on. Esther understands the idea of fortune and realizes that she must carefully manage the part of the situation that is under her control.

11. **Take Advantage of Overweening Pride**: Rava (Abba ben Joseph bar Chama), (ca. 280–352 CE) says: Esther invited Haman to her banquet in order to fulfill that which is stated: "Pride goes before destruction [and a haughty spirit before a fall"] (Proverbs 16:18).

Moshe Alshich suggests that those of haughty and prideful spirit try to hide their personality trait from others, but the world sees right through their efforts and knows who they are at heart.[30] The *m'gillah* clearly portrays Haman's vainglory, but in pointing to pride as a route to self-destruction, Rava underscores how Haman's attendance at the banquet with the king and no other minister amplifies his pride. Haman's egotism is well-illustrated in Esther 5:11–12, so that he will not be able to hide his truest self from the king, particularly in comparison to Esther's modest, understated self-awareness. Haman's pride thus does precede and lead to his fall.

In a later work, "The Life of Castruccio Castracani," Machiavelli relates what he thought a truly fortunate and virtuous politician would do.[31] When the papacy was in exile in Avignon, Castracani (1284–1328), who favored a strong relationship to the Holy Roman Empire, was made a Roman senator in a fashion fully comparable to Haman. He assumed his office "with the greatest pomp, Castruccio being clothed in a brocaded toga, which had the following words embroidered on its front: 'I am what God wills.' While on the back was 'What God desires shall be.'" Moreover, Castracani was "a man willing to overcome by fraud those whom he desired to subdue, because he was wont to say that it was the victory that brought the glory, not the methods of achieving it" (TP, *Castracani*). While Machiavelli fawningly imagines the man's virtues, still, this very man prevented the Pope's return to Rome and died before his children suffered for their father's deeds at the hands of the Guelphs, the pro-papacy party that did not forget their father's prideful malevolence. Similarly, BTM 15b states that Haman had thirty sons. Ten died, ten were hanged, and after their father's death, ten had to beg from door to door. Ben Yehoyada asks if that was sufficient punishment. Talmud N'*darim* 7b might respond, "Poverty leads to death." Pride and its politics thus brought about both the fall of the House of Haman and of Castracani.

12. **Inebriate the Enemy**: Both Abaye (Nachmani ben Kaylil, ca. 278–337 CE) and Rava say that she invited Haman in order to fulfill the verse: "When they are heated, I will make feasts for them, [and I will make them drunk, that they may rejoice, and sleep a perpetual sleep and not awake, said the Eternal. I will bring them down like lambs to the slaughter, like rams with male goats]" (Jeremiah 51:39–40).

Again, our Rabbis cite verses that refer to "they." Abaye and Rava aver that Esther's wine feast was meant to intoxicate both the king and Haman in order to accomplish her goal of saving the Jewish people. Use of third-person plural indicates that Esther saw Ahasuerus as an enemy even at the last minute.

In *Yalkut Shimoni*, Rabbi Eleazar said that when the king asked Esther who threatened her and her people, she would have pointed at Ahasuerus, but an angel came and slapped her hand in the direction of Haman.[32] In this midrash of divine intervention, heaven considered Haman the root of the threat to the Jews, or the easiest target to end the potential genocide, a pragmatic strategy.

According to Abaye and Rava, Esther wanted Haman present in order to intoxicate him. Indeed, imbibing wine at banquets was an Achaemenid Persian custom, as evidenced by Esther 1:10 and explained by historians.[33] Machiavelli writes that when someone boasted of his ability to drink much without becoming intoxicated, Castruccio Castracani commented that an ox could do the same, thus condemning drunkenness (*TP, Castracani*). Perhaps what enhanced Castracani's control of every situation was his sobriety.

In the scene of the wine feast, for the sake of self-control, Esther, too, needed to stay sober while both Ahasuerus and Haman drank. Alcohol loosens the tongue and clouds judgment, giving Haman the opportunity to make a fool of himself before the king. Alcohol also increases aggressive behavior,[34] and Esther may have seen that occur in the Persian court.

Wine augmented the aggressiveness of both Haman and the king. When Haman threw himself upon the queen to beg for mercy, he committed an aggression against her person that the king, returning from the garden, observed with horror. Haman's act piqued the royal fury, and it is possible that the king's inebriated state pushed him to react more violently to Haman's threat to Esther than he would have if sober. Abaye and Rava know the effects of alcohol on personality and remind us that it can be used to advantage in politicking.

Elijah's Wisdom

The paragraph of opinions offered by thirteen Rabbis in Talmud *M'gillah* 15b comes to a surprising conclusion with the addition of Elijah's wisdom for the Rabbis:

> Rabba bar Avuha (active ca. 250–290 CE) once happened upon Elijah the Prophet. He said to him: In accordance with whose understanding did Esther see fit to act in this manner [i.e. to invite Haman to the banquet of wine]? Elijah, said to him: Esther acted

according to all the reasons previously stated by the Tana'im and all the reasons stated by the Amora'im.

Instead of refusing to answer and leaving the question a *teiku*, a Rabbinic disagreement awaiting solution for the time when Elijah returns to earth to solve all the Rabbis' unresolved disputes, Elijah responds. His answer seems like the old joke about a rabbi's solution to a tiff between husband and wife: "You're right . . . and you're right." Later the rabbi's wife says, "They can't both be right," to which the sage responds, "You're right, too." Elijah, however, has not merely avoided mixing into the Talmud's logical melee. Elijah has made two radical assertions.

First, thirteen Rabbis offered their opinions as to what Esther saw that made her invite Haman. All thirteen were men, and all they could offer was one opinion each, or a shared opinion. Elijah, however, indicates that Esther, a Jewish woman, foresaw all their opinions, and taken as a whole, she decided to invite Haman to the wine feast. Elijah's answer tells us that one Jewish woman, Esther, had vision that far exceeded all the thirteen Sages of the Talmud. In short, the ancient prophet Elijah and the ancient Rabbis who wrote BTM 15b have given sufficient reason to justify the end of male hegemony over Jewish life, for might there not be other courageous and visionary Esthers in every generation?

Elijah's assertion also stands as a radical endorsement of Gersonides's answer to the problem of God's foreknowledge. In *Wars of the Lord*, treatise 3, chapter 4,[35] Gersonides contends that God has a general knowledge of what actions it is possible for an individual to choose, but no foreknowledge of which choice that human being will make. Once that choice is made, God has foreknowledge of all possible choices that follow from it, but again, does not know beforehand the next human decision. Contingency is the issue, and if God knew the person's decisions ahead of time, there would be no contingency, no possible outcomes for which persons could be held responsible because of their choices. If God had foreknowledge of choice, it would be required to consider that knowledge as a *force majeure* relieving the individual of personal responsibility on Yom Kippur or any other day. In this way, Gersonides explains how "all is foreseen, yet free will is given" (*Mishnah Avot* 3:15). Thus, what matters is not that Elijah thinks that all the Rabbis are correct in their opinion of why Esther invited Haman to the wine feast with the king. What matters is Elijah's implied assertion that these Rabbis elucidated Esther's every imaginable contingency in planning her goals for the banquet of wine and inviting Haman to it.

God does not know which policy or effort will yield the desired outcome of saving the Jews of Persia, nor does Esther, at least not until the moment that she puts a choice into play. Furthermore, she was not only dealing with trying to trap Haman, use Haman, and expose Haman. She was dealing with Ahasuerus, whose reactions also had to be elicited and directed to her ends. Esther was managing a complex situation. Any or all of the Rabbis' reasons for inviting Haman could have led to certain choices by Esther that would either succeed or fail.

The Rabbis ask, "What did Esther see?" Taken together, Elijah answers that, like a champion chess player, she saw all the possible moves and their possible outcomes in order to outplay her opponents, while keeping her endgame in mind. It was *imitatio Dei* of the highest order, for, like God, she had to know all the choices she could make and their probable consequences while continually having to choose life for the Jewish people. Esther, therefore, provides an example of detailed planning, complex thought, and mental gymnastics while calculating strategy on the fly during the banquet. Esther triumphs over Ahasuerus and Haman with a victory won on a battlefield of wits, even as she outwitted thirteen Rabbis.

Esther vs. Machiavelli

In many ways, Esther's moves were Machiavellian, but Esther and Machiavelli differ in one fundamental way. Machiavelli wrote *The Prince* to suggest how a ruler might retain, extend, and sometimes seize power. Though he wanted princes to be loved by their people and to act as ethically as possible, morality did not constrain him. For example, speaking of princes who obtained power by wickedness, he wrote, "injuries ought to be done all at one time, so that, being tasted less, they offend less; benefits ought to be given little by little, so that the flavor of them may last longer" (*TP*, 8).

Esther, on the other hand, rules Ahasuerus and Haman only momentarily, at her wine feast. Her power stems from her relationship to the king and the power of hosting the two guests who determine the future of her community. She wields that power not to keep it nor to obtain more of it, but to save the lives of thousands of Jews. Because Persian Jewry had been doomed to a Final Solution, Jewish tradition gives Esther full permission to trap, dissemble, entice, mislead, impede, control, pray, convince, prey on weakness, instigate emotions, incite rebellion against Haman by minister and prince, intoxicate her guests, and even martyr herself and her reputation. Her wine feast is Machiavellian precisely because, in the critical life-or-death moment for her community, she must follow the Jewish ethic that puts the highest value on saving lives.

Esther's Political Science for Today

Is there a message for today? Israel, home to half the world's Jews, bears the same responsibility as Esther: to save Jewish lives, the lives of its citizens, and as Israel has often done, save also its potential citizens—Jews in mortal danger. In a crisis, Israel must swiftly examine all the possibilities of action and all their possible results before choosing its course, and then be strategically wise enough to change course midstream. If some of those choices appear Machiavellian in scope, sometimes it must be that way to save lives.

Similarly, when Diaspora Jewry faces serious new challenges, just as thirteen Rabbis across generations recount in Talmud every possible reason Esther saw to invite Haman to her banquet, so Jewish leadership must weigh its courses of action, examining their every possibility and nuance, even dealing directly with malefactors and those whose power permits them to exist. The Rabbis of BTM 15b are like a think tank opening doors of thought, planning, action, and reaction. Every Jewish community, local and national, needs such a council that, like Esther, *sees*, has the necessary vision to assess and constructively foresee future possibilities, and if necessary, to be a quick reaction force for the saving of Jews and Jewish communal life.

When thirteen Rabbis ask, "What did Esther see?" they ask a mystical question, for Talmud says *Ta sh'ma* ("Come and hear"), while Zohar emphasizes, "*Ta chazi* ("Come and see"). Machiavelli tells us that in a place where a citizen becomes ruler, that person requires "a happy shrewdness" (*TP*, 9). "Happy the one who finds wisdom (*chochmah*), happy the one who attains understanding (*t'vunah*)" (Proverbs 3:13). Was that not Esther? In the mystical *s'firot*, Wisdom, *chochmah*, represents the germ of an idea, often taken as masculine. Birthing it into usable, applicable form is *binah* ("understanding"), often taken as feminine. Together they become *daat* ("knowledge"), a fulsome, conscious idea including self-awareness.[36]

Come, then, and see what the Rabbis saw in Esther: a woman of wisdom, understanding, and knowledge, and the vision to apply them in ways pragmatic and spiritual, widely communal, yet with flexible single-mindedness of purpose. She did it with knowledge of self and knowledge of her antagonists.

Can we find such women and men with the powers of Esther? Can we find leaders of "happy shrewdness," people of vision and sound political judgment capable of evaluating and acting, as did Esther? This is the challenge of today and of every Jewish era.

Notes

1. Eliezer L. Segal, "The Tide Turns," *The Babylonian Esther Midrash: A Critical Commentary: Esther*, Vol. 3, *Chapter 5 to End*, Brown Judaic Studies (2020), 20–21, https://www.jstor.org/stable/j.ctvzpv4t6.5.

2. BT *M'gillah* 15b, *The William Davidson Talmud* (Koren–Steinsaltz) (hereafter BTM and page #), https://www.sefaria.org/Megillah.15b.12?ven=William_Davidson_Edition_-_English&vhe=William_Davidson_Edition_-_Vocalized_Aramaic&lang=bi&with=all&lang2=en.

3. References to *The Prince* by Niccolò Machiavelli, first published in 1532, are to Gutenberg.org edition, https://www.gutenberg.org/files/1232/1232-h/1232-h.htm#pref04 abbreviated as *TP* with the chapter number. References to "The Life of Castruccio Castracani," which follows *The Prince* are referred to as *TP, Castracani*.

4. Was Haman a prince? BTM 12b: A Sage taught in a baraita: Memucan is Haman. And why is Haman referred to as Memucan? Because he was prepared [*muchan*] to bring calamity upon the Jewish people. Others, like Rav Kahana, see him as a common man, an advisor to Ahasuerus (BTM 12b).

5. BT *M'gillah* 15b, Commentary, https://www.sefaria.org/Megillah.15b.12?ven=William_Davidson_Edition_-_English&vhe=William_Davidson_Edition_-_Vocalized_Aramaic&lang=bi&with=Steinsaltz&lang2=en.

6. International Organization for Septuagint and Cognate Studies, *Esther, A New English Translation of the Septuagint* (New York: Oxford University Press, 2007), 432, Greek, left column, 22:24, http://ccat.sas.upenn.edu/nets/edition/17-esther-nets.pdf.

7. This is a well-known interpretation. See, for example, Shimon Matisyahu, "Revealing Torah Secrets," Gematriot, no. 22, March

12, 2009, http://gematriot.blogspot.com/2009/03/22-last-letter.html.

8. See also *Esther Rabbah* 1:1 where Ahasuerus is credited with stopping the rebuilding of the Temple.

9. How wealthy was Haman? He offers Ahasuerus ten thousand talents of silver that he might destroy the Jewish community of Persia, the equivalent in today's exchange rates of $280,000,000. See "Weights and Measures (in the Bible)," *New Catholic Encyclopedia, Encyclopedia.com, https://www.encyclopedia.com/religion/encyclopedias-almanacs-transcripts-and-maps/weights-and-measures-bible*.

10. Robert Gordis, "Studies in the Esther Narrative," *Journal of Biblical Literature* 95, no. 1 (1976): 48.

11. Sandra Berg, in *The Book of Esther: Motifs, Themes and Structures* (Missoula, MT: 1979), 61, writes that "at Nineva and Chorsabad stone bas-reliefs on the palace wall show a horse wearing a crown."

12. 5th c. BCE Chinese military leader and author of *The Art of War*.

13. BTM 15b, commentary, https://www.sefaria.org/Megillah.15b.14?ven=William_Davidson_Edition_-_English&vhe=William_Davidson_Edition_-_Vocalized_Aramaic&lang=bi&with=Steinsaltz&lang2=en.

14. BTM 15b, commentary, https://www.sefaria.org/Megillah.15b.14?ven=William_Davidson_Edition_-_English&vhe=William_Davidson_Edition_-_Vocalized_Aramaic&lang=bi&p2=Daf_Shevui_to_Megillah.15b.15&lang2=bi.

15. Scott Ury, "Shtadlan," *YIVO Encyclopedia of Jews in Eastern Europe*, 2010, https://yivoencyclopedia.org/article.aspx/Shtadlan.

16. Harem1: In Ancient Iran. "Herodotus (1.135), who wrote in the time of Artaxerxes, testifies that each (notable) Persian man had several wives, and a still larger number of concubines—(Strabo, Geography 15.3.17, adds: 'for the sake of having many children'). This was the case with the Persian king as well (see Brosius, pp. 13–20, 204–5). Wives came to the husband on a well-regulated turn-basis (Herodotus 3.69). They exercised total control over the family's children until these were five years old (Herodotus 1.136), and they customarily accompanied their husband at dinner banquets (ibid., 5.18) but left when 'women entertainers' of the harem came in and the men began merrymaking (Plutarch, Moralia, 140B). The chief consort, the wife, who as a rule was the daughter of a Persian prince and the mother of the heir to the throne (Rawlinson, pp. 216–18), controlled the household." https://www.iranicaonline.org/articles/harem-i.

17. The three-day fast as described in the Book of Esther is highly unusual and taxing. The executive committee of the editorial Board, Julius H. Greenstone, Emil G. Hirsch, and Hartwig Hirschfeld

explain in Fasting and Fast-Days (צוֹם = "fasting"; עִנּוּת נֶפֶשׁ= "affliction of soul"; later Hebrew [Ezra ix. 5] and Talmudic) how a three-day fast is traditionally performed. "In the Book of Esther an additional fast is recorded (ix. 31; comp. iv. 3, 16), which is commonly observed, in commemoration of the fast of Esther, on the thirteenth of Adar, although some used to fast three days—the first and second Mondays and the Thursday following Purim (Soferim xvii. 4, xxi. 2)." *Jewish Encyclopedia*, the unedited first text of the 1906 *Jewish Encyclopedia*, .https://jewishencyclopedia.com/articles/6033-fasting-and-fast-days.

18. BTM 15b, commentary, https://www.sefaria.org/Megillah.15b.14?ven=William_Davidson_Edition_-_English&vhe=William_Davidson_Edition_-_Vocalized_Aramaic&lang=bi&with=Ben%20Yehoyada&lang2=en.

19. BTM 15b, commentary, https://www.sefaria.org/Megillah.15b.14?ven=William_Davidson_Edition_-_English&vhe=William_Davidson_Edition_-_Vocalized_Aramaic&lang=bi&with=Daf%20Shevui%20to%20Megillah | Quoting&lang2=en.

20. BTM 15b, commentary, https://www.sefaria.org/Megillah.15b.14?ven=William_Davidson_Edition_-_English&vhe=William_Davidson_Edition_-_Vocalized_Aramaic&lang=bi&with=Steinsaltz&lang2=en.

21. http://www.magister.msk.ru/library/bible/english/web/GkEsther.htm.

22. His Most Catholic Monarch, King Ferdinand of Spain. *The Prince*, Page by Page Books, Chapter 18, n. 5: Ferdinand of Aragon, "When Machiavelli was writing 'The Prince' it would have been clearly impossible to mention Ferdinand's name here without giving offence," Burd's *Il Principe*, 308, https://www.pagebypagebooks.com/Nicolo_Machiavelli/The_Prince/CHAPTER_XVIII_footnotes.html.

23. Max Kadushin, *The Rabbinic Mind*, Chapter VI, "Normal Mysticism" (Waltham, MA: Blaisdell Publishing, 1965).

24. Esther 5:11: And the king said [to Haman], "The money and the people are yours to do with as you see fit."

25. For a biblical example, see I Kings 2:2–9, wherein David makes certain requests of Solomon to be accomplished by his son after his death. David could have issued a decree to slay the various victims, but dying, he knew that the decree might die with him. Therefore, he asks Solomon to finish the work of vengeance for him.

26. Jason S. Moser et al., "Third-person Self-talk Facilitates Emotion Regulation without Engaging Cognitive Control: Converging Evidence from ERP and fMRI," *Scientific Reports* 7, no. 4519 (July 2017): 1–9, https://www.nature.com/articles/s41598-017-04047-3.

27. Barry Dov Walfish, "Ahasuerus. Judaism," *Encyclopedia of the Bible and its Reception*, vol. 1 (Berlin: De Gruyter, 2009): 627–28.

28. BTM 15b, commentary, https://www.sefaria.org/Megillah.15b.15?ven=William_Davidson_Edition_-_English&vhe=William_Davidson_Edition_-_Vocalized_Aramaic&lang=bi&with=Steinsaltz&lang2=en.

29. Ibid., https://www.sefaria.org/Megillah.15b.21?ven=William_Davidson_Edition_-_English&vhe=William_Davidson_Edition_-_Vocalized_Aramaic&lang=bi&with=Steinsaltz&lang2=en.

30. Moshe Alshich, comment to Proverbs 16:18, https://www.sefaria.org/Proverbs.16.18?ven=Tanakh:_The_Holy_Scriptures,_published_by_JPS&vhe=Miqra_according_to_the_Masorah&lang=bi&with=Alshich&lang2=en.

31. Catherine Zuckert, "The Life of Castruccio Castracani: Machiavelli as Literary Artist, Historian, Teacher and Philosopher," History of Political Thought 31, no. 4 (2010): 577–603, abstract by Michael Zuckert.

32. See Eliezer L. Segal, *The Babylonian Esther Midrash: A Critical Commentary*, vol. 3, 104.

33. Joshua J. Mark, Ancient Persian Culture (November 27, 2019), https://www.worldhistory.org/Ancient_Persian_Culture/.

34. Anne Beck, and Andreas Heinz, "Alcohol-Related Aggression: Social and Neurobiological Factors," *Deutsches Arzteblatt international* 110, no. 42 (2013): 711–15, https://www.ncbi.nlm.nih.gov/pmc/articles/PMC3820993/.

35. Levi ben Gershon (Gersonides), *Sefer Milhamot haShem* (1329) (Riva di Trento, 1560; Leipzig, 1866, Berlin, 1923), translated into English as *The Wars of the Lord* by Seymour Feldman, 3 vols. (Philadelphia: Jewish Publication Society, 1984–1999), https://www.sefaria.org/The_Wars_of_the_Lord%2C_Third_Treatise.4.4?vhe=Milhamot_Hashem,_Leipzig,_1866&lang=bi.

36. David A. Cooper, *God Is a Verb*, (New York: Riverhead Books, 1997), 91, and Laibl Wolf, *Practical Kabbalah: a Guide to Jewish Wisdom for Everyday Life* (Harmony/Rodale, 2010), 86.

Challenges and Opportunities for Change: Biblical Models

Rabbi Steven Bob

The times are always changing. The key challenge for me as a rabbi has been knowing when and how to adjust to the changes. We need to determine when to go with the current of the culture and when to follow a countercultural course. As the Bard wrote: "May you have a strong foundation/When the winds of changes shift."

I am mid-century modern. I was born at the high tide of the baby boom in 1950. I began my studies at HUC-JIR in Jerusalem in 1972, fifty years ago. We are aware of how the world has changed over these past fifty years. For added perspective, we can ask how did the world change during the fifty years before 1972?

In 1972 Jewish life was not like it had been in 1922. In 1972, we understood that the destruction of European Jewry and the establishment of the State of Israel were "epoch making events" that reshaped the Jewish world. It was clear to us as young rabbinic students that we needed to be different kinds of rabbis than of those of the previous age.

One should not expect that Jewish life in 2022 should be like it was in 1972. The changes in Jewish life over the fifty years since 1972 have been of a different nature than those of the 1922-1972 era. The leaders of the American Jewish community of 1922 did not foresee the events to come over the next fifty years. In 1972, we did not know how the world would change during the next fifty years. It is certainly not my place as a retired congregational rabbi to suggest specific ideas as to how the rabbis of this generation should respond to current and future challenges. But I can point to the ways in which the *Tanach* can guide us. The Bible provides

RABBI STEVEN BOB (C77), rabbi emeritus of Congregation Etz Chaim, Lombard, Illinois, is completing a new book on Ezra and Nehemiah. He is the author of *Jonah and the Meaning of Our Lives* (JPS, 2016) and *Go to Nineveh* (Pickwick, 2013).

significant examples of visionary leaders taking bold steps to re-shape the religious life of the people.

To help us understand how to respond to major shifts in our world, let us look at a pivotal chapter in the Hebrew Bible. If I ask you to list the key sections of the Hebrew Bible, you might mention the Exodus from Egypt or revelation at Mount Sinai. If you want to go for ideas rather than events, you might point to the Holiness Code in Leviticus 19. The eighth chapter of Nehemiah probably did not come to mind, although it stands as one of the key pivotal chapters of the entire Hebrew Bible. It describes the rededication of the people following the return from exile. It begins:

> When the seventh month arrived—the Israelites being [settled] in their towns—the entire people gathered as one person into the square that was before the Water Gate; and they asked Ezra the scribe to bring the scroll of the Torah of Moses with which the Eternal had charged Israel. On the first day of the seventh month, Ezra the priest brought the Torah before the congregation, men and women, and all who could listen with understanding. (Nehemiah 8:1–2)

One might expect that the ceremony of national rededication would take place at the recently rebuilt Temple. But instead, it takes place outside the Temple at the Water Gate. These two verses mention that Ezra is a priest, but the ceremony does not feature Ezra putting on the official garments of the priesthood and the offering a sacrifice. Instead, the ceremony of national rededication features the first public reading of the Torah by Ezra the scribe. Nowhere in the Hebrew Bible is there a record of any of the kings, prophets, or priests of the First Temple period convening the public to hear them read the Torah.

It is no exaggeration to view this moment of Ezra reading the Torah, as the beginning of Judaism as we know it. For Ezra and Nehemiah, the Torah, not animal sacrifice, stood at the center. The text specifically identifies Ezra as a "Cohein" and as a "Sofeir." And then describes Ezra the Sofeir reading from the *sefer Torah*. The English word "scribe" does not fully capture Ezra's relation-ship to the Torah. I see him as the "scroll former."

In history, change generally occurs slowly but significant turn-ing point moments do emerge. For example, from the beginning of time until the mid-eighteenth century, the only way to convey a message to another person was by speaking it or by writing it down and having it hand delivered. Then in 1844 Samuel Morse sent a telegraph message from the Capitol in Washington to the Mt. Claire Depot in Baltimore proclaiming, "What hath God wrought." In 1876 Alexander Graham Bell used the telephone to summon his assistant from the next room, saying, "Watson come here, I want to see you." The telegraph and the telephone began a process of innovation that led to our current ability to be in contact with anyone anywhere in the world via the smart phone in our pockets. The days on which Morse and Bell sent their first messages are remembered as turning points in human history. The Rosh HaShanah day on which Ezra read from the Torah at the Water Gate was such a turning point day in Jewish history.

Throughout the Second Temple period our people read Torah and offered sacrifices. We know from Josephus that in the final decades of the Second Temple era some of our people, Sadducees, focused their lives on the sacrifices, and some of our people, the Pharisees, focused their attention on the Torah. The Judaism that guides our lives today grew out of the foundation created by the Pharisees. In reading these verses in Nehemiah, we witness the laying of the cornerstone of that foundation. Our work as rabbis rest on the foundation created when Ezra read from the Torah scroll on that Rosh HaShanah.

Civic events and religious rituals often include a recitation of "sacred history" laying out the past and the purpose of the community. Abraham Lincoln began his Gettysburg Address with a review of the sacred history of the United States to clearly define the purpose of the Civil War:

> Four score and seven years ago our fathers brought forth on this continent, a new nation, conceived in Liberty, and dedicated to the proposition that all men are created equal. Now we are engaged in a great civil war, testing whether that nation, or any nation so conceived and so dedicated, can long endure. We are met on a great battle-field of that war. We have come to dedicate a portion of that field, as a final resting place for those who here gave their lives that that nation might live. It is altogether fitting and proper that we should do this.

Each spring during our Passover seder we read a familiar paragraph from the Book of Deuteronomy describing the sacred history of the Jewish People:

> My father was a fugitive Aramean, and he went down to Egypt with meager numbers, and sojourned there; but there he became a great and very populous nation. The Egyptians dealt harshly with us and oppressed us; they imposed heavy labor upon us. We cried to the Eternal, the God of our ancestors, and the Eternal heard our plea, and saw our plight, our misery, and our oppression. The Eternal freed us from Egypt with a mighty hand, by an outstretched arm and awesome power and by signs, and portents. He brought us into this place, and gave us this land, a land flowing with milk and honey. Wherefore, I now bring the first fruits of the soil, which You, O Eternal, has given me. And you shall leave it before the Eternal your God and bow low before the Eternal your God. (Deuteronomy 26:5–10)

The connection of this passage to Passover grows out of its vivid description of the Exodus from Egypt. We also encounter this text as part of the annual cycle of Torah readings as the summer turns to fall. It is in the first chapter of the Torah portion *Ki Tavo* read a few weeks before Rosh HaShanah. In its original context in Deuteronomy the paragraph is part of the "First Fruits" ceremony. These are the words that we are instructed to recite as we place the first fruits of the land in the hands of the priests at the Temple in Jerusalem.

We may be so familiar with this version of our sacred history that we do not notice that it omits an important stop on our way from being slaves in Egypt to bringing first fruits to the Temple in Jerusalem. What is missing? Not a minor detail but rather a major foundational event in Jewish history, the revelation of the Torah at Mount Sinai! For the author of the Deuteronomy text, the entire saga of our people leads to bringing sacrifices to the Temple in Jerusalem. From this point of view the bringing of sacrifices to the Temple in Jerusalem is the fulfillment of our destiny.

Chapter 9 of the Book of Nehemiah includes another version of our sacred history. It is not part of our annual religious life, so it remains far less well known. The entire section is thirty verses long. It begins:

> You are the Eternal the God, who chose Abram, who brought him out of Ur of the Chaldeans, and changed his name to Abraham. Finding his heart true to You, You made a covenant with him to

give him the land of the Canaanite, the Hittite, the Amorite, the Perizzite, the Jebusite and the Girgashite—to give to his descendants. And you kept your word. (Nehemiah 9:7–8)

The text retells the Exodus from Egypt and then continues:

You came down on Mount Sinai and spoke with them from heaven; You gave them right rules and true teachings, good laws and commandments. You made known to them Your holy sabbath, and You ordained for them laws, commandments, and Torah through Moses Your servant. (Nehemiah 9:13–14)

This version of our sacred history includes the revelation of the Torah to Moses at Mount Sinai in contrast to the version in Deuteronomy. The earlier versions of the Sacred History ignored the Revelation at Mount Sinai because Torah was not yet a core concern. Torah had not yet become a central means of connecting with God. In the pre-exile era, the Temple sacrifices were the single means of expressing connection with God. In contrast, Torah stands as a central focus in Ezra/Nehemiah. The experience of exile brought on a major shift in the religious life of our people. This major change can serve as a model to us in making major changes in responding to the challenges of our time and in responding to the challenges that will arise in the times to come.

As Reform rabbis we appreciate the ongoing dynamic nature of Jewish ritual life. We understand that the meaning of rituals evolve and that new rituals arise. One of our challenges as rabbis is to navigate this process to create new ritual moments that resonate as authentic and deeply rooted in tradition. Ezra/Nehemiah provides a model for creating new rituals in response to shifts in the life of our people.

After the public reading of the Torah scroll, the people began to study the contents of the text. They discovered a commandment to build sukkot (booths):

The whole community that returned from captivity made booths and dwelt in the booths—the Israelites had not done so from the days of Joshua the son of Nun to that day. And there was very great gladness. (Nehemiah 8:17)

This verse seems to say that building a sukkah was a new ritual created in the time of Ezra and Nehemiah by the generation that had returned from exile. It seems to say that the Judges and the Kings, Deborah, Gideon, David, and Solomon had not built sukkot. It seems to say that all the prophets of the First Temple period from Elijah and Elisha to Isaiah and Jeremiah had never entered a sukkah. Could this be true? Is it possible that this verse means exactly what it says?

Over the centuries many voices have been raised to argue that this verse should not be taken literally. They insist that it could not be possible for the construction of the sukkah to be something new in the time of Ezra and Nehemiah. Accepting the plain meaning of this verse would upset their method of understanding the Bible. We find this type of response in Rabbinic sources and among academic Bible scholars. We will look first at Rabbinic authorities.

The Sages address this question in the Babylonian Talmud *Masechet Arachin* 32b. The Talmud explains that we should not take Nehemiah 8:17 to be talking specifically about who built a sukkah. It contends that the reference to Joshua in the Nehemiah verse reflects the dedication of the Land of Israel to God as holy by Joshua. This dedication ceased to be in effect when the Babylonians destroyed the First Temple. Now through the efforts of Ezra and Nehemiah, the land was once again dedicated to God.

As often is the case in the Talmud, a second voice objects to this first opinion. This second voice says that the holiness of the land endured even after the destruction of the Temple. The change expressed in the Nehemiah verse is that during the First Temple period the people regularly gave in to the temptation to engage in idolatry. But by the Second Temple period this problem had disappeared. The Talmud argues that the description of Ezra and his followers dwelling in sukkot should be understood as metaphoric language expressing that they remained loyal to the One God of Israel. They did not serve other gods, as had the previous generations.

The Talmud points out that in the Nehemiah verse Joshua's name is spelled without a *hei*. It is rendered Yeishua rather than the typical spelling Yehoshua. The removal of the *hei* in this context is to express Joshua's lack of full devotion to God in that he allowed idolatry to continue to exist in the land. Since the letter *hei* is one of the four letters in the Divine Name, its inclusion in a person's name often expresses that person's deep devotion to God.

While the later Rabbinic authorities Ralbag, Metzudat David, and Malbim each followed their own creative path in explaining away this apparent addition of new ritual created at the time of the return from exile, they all began with the assumption that the verse could not be literally true.

Some modern academic Bible scholars have also wrestled with this verse in a similar way. I will share two examples from prominent authorities. H. G. H. Williamson wrote:

> Even if booths were erected at the festival before Ezra's time, they were merely part of the harvest aspect of the festival . . . Now, however, the significance of the booths in terms of Israel's history were introduced. For the first time in centuries, they were erected in Jerusalem as a reminder of the wilderness wanderings.[1]

Joseph Blenkinsopp wrote:

> If, therefore, we are to look for any historical innovation, it is not in the celebration of the festival itself, which already was well established or even in the dwelling in booths implied in the very name of the festival but in the use of the species to construct and cover the *sukkah*.[2]

Both Williamson and Blenkinsopp create arguments to avoid taking Nehemiah 8:17 at face value. The scholarly discourse and the Rabbinic tradition both work hard to reject the point the Nehemiah text proclaims.

I see this key verse in Nehemiah in a completely different way. I have no problem accepting Nehemiah 8:17 as it is written. I read the verse as accurate reporting of the creation of this new ritual of building sukkot.

We have known the meaning of a sukkah since we were children. To understand what is truly going on here please set side those childhood lessons and follow the creation of the ritual step by step.

Step One: Before Nehemiah Nobody in the Bible Built a Sukkah

Deuteronomy 16 mentions the festival and calls it the festival of Sukkot, but it does not mention anybody dwelling in a sukkah:

> After the ingathering from your threshing floor and your vat, you shall hold the Feast of Booths for seven days. You shall

rejoice in your festival your son and your daughter, your male and your female slaves, the Levite, the stranger, the fatherless, and the widow in your communities. You shall hold the festival for the Eternal your God in the place that the Eternal will choose for the Eternal your God will bless all your crops and all your undertakings and you shall have nothing but joy. (Deuteronomy 16:13–15)

Judges 21:19 attests to the celebration of *chag* ("festival") but does not mention the construction of actual booths. I Samuel 1:3 describes Elkanah making an annual pilgrimage to Shiloh to offer sacrifices. Most readers assume that this refers to Sukkot but the text does not specifically mention a *chag*. Nowhere does this story describe the construction of actual booths.

The only place the Hebrew Bible mentions the actual construction of a sukkah on Sukkot is Nehemiah 8:17 and Leviticus 23:42–43, which is a late addition to Leviticus based on the Nehemiah verse.

Leviticus 23 contains the commandments concerning the various holidays. The section on the holidays begins and ends with a bookend phrase. The section begins in verse 4: "These are the appointed feasts . . . ." We then see a paragraph for each of the festivals. Sukkot is described in verses 33–36 but the building of booths and gathering the four species are not mentioned in that paragraph. It describes the length of the festival and the sacrifices to be offered. The section on the festivals concludes with a repetition of the bookend phrase in verse 37: "These are the appointed feasts . . . ."

Then beginning with verse 39 we can find an extra paragraph tacked on that mentions the new Sukkot rituals described in Nehemiah 8:14–17.

On the first day you shall take the product of the goodly trees, branches of the palm trees, boughs of the leafy trees and the willows of the brook and you shall rejoice before the Eternal your God seven days . . . You shall live in sukkot seven days; all citizens in Israel shall live in sukkot in order that future generations may know that I made the Israelite people live in sukkot when I brought them out of the land of Egypt, I the Eternal your God. (Leviticus 23:40, 42–43)

This additional paragraph of Leviticus could not have been written before the time of Ezra and Nehemiah because it contains commandments that were unknown before that time. The fact that these verses are added in after the second bookend verse (v. 37), "These are the appointed feasts . . . ," reveals the seam joining the new Sukkot material created during the time of Ezra/Nehemiah to the older preexisting section on the holidays.

The entire Hebrew Bible describes only one person dwelling in a sukkah. In the fourth chapter of the Book of Jonah, the prophet builds a sukkah to protect himself from the sun. That event has nothing to do with the festival.

So why doesn't the Bible mention anyone building a sukkah to celebrate Sukkot before the exile? The ritual did not yet exist.

Step Two: The Bible Stresses the Connections between the Temple and Sukkot

King Solomon dedicated the First Temple on the Festival of Sukkot:

> Then Solomon convoked the elders of Israel—all the heads of the tribes and the ancestral chieftains of the Israelites—before King Solomon in Jerusalem, to bring up the Ark of the Covenant of the Eternal from the city of David, that is Zion. All the men of Israel gathered before King Solomon at the Feast [of Booths] in the month Ethanim—that is the seventh month. (I Kings 8:1–2)

When the Maccabees cleansed the Temple, they wanted to follow King Solomon's example and rededicate it on Sukkot, but it was not ready in time. So, they created a "second Sukkot" later in the fall patterned on Sukkot:

> They rededicated the Temple on the twenty-fifth day of the month of Kislev, the same day of the same month on which the Temple had been desecrated by the gentiles. The happy celebration lasted eight days, like the Festival of Booths, and the people remembered how only a short time before, they had spent the Festival of Booths wandering like wild animals in the mountains and living in caves. But now, carrying green palm branches and sticks decorated with ivy, they paraded around, singing grateful praises to Him who had brought about the purification of His own Temple. Everyone agreed that the entire Jewish nation should celebrate this festival each year. (II Maccabees 10:5–8)

Many Jews today do not know that Chanukah grows out of Sukkot. But it is clear from these two stories of the dedication of the Temple and the rededication of the Temple that we should see the close connection of the Temple and the Festival of Sukkot.

Step Three: The Meaning of Living in Booths in the Wilderness

The section of Leviticus 23 that I have identified as having been composed in the time of Nehemiah includes a reference to the forty years in the wilderness:

> You shall live in booths seven days; all the citizens in Israel shall live in booths; in order that future generations may know that I made the Israelite people live in booths when I brought them out of the land of Egypt, I am The Eternal your God. (Leviticus 23:42–43)

I do not understand this verse to be referring only to the years the Israelites lived in the wilderness following the exodus from Egypt. I think that it is referring to years in exile in the wilderness of Babylonia.

Why did the custom of build sukkot arise during the exile? I believe that during the years in Babylonian exile, the people built booths on the festival of Sukkot to recall the destroyed Temple, which had originally been dedicated on that festival by King Solomon. The booths were a *zeicher l'mikdash* (a "memorial for the Temple"). Building a sukkah each fall for the festival of Sukkot helped the exiles maintain their religious identity in Babylonia.

When the people returned from exile, they continued this ritual that they had begun in Babylonia. They read into it the additional meaning of the earlier forty years in the wilderness. This connection between the two periods in the wilderness served to create a useful way of understanding their recent suffering in Babylonia.

During the years in Babylonia the sukkah reminded the people of the Temple they hoped to rebuild when they would return to Jerusalem. Once they returned to the land and rebuilt the Temple, they continued to annually construct a sukkah and began to dwell in it to remind them of their years in exile and the forty years in the wilderness.

In our time we have been creating new rituals and imbuing old rituals with new meaning.

Ezra/Nehemiah mark the beginning of a major shift in Jewish life from sacrifices to Torah.

Responding to the destruction of European Jewry and the creation of the Jewish state was the work of the rabbis one generation before us. I and many of the rabbis of my generation devoted ourselves to responding the to the needs of the Jewish People by saving Soviet Jewry, rescuing the Jews of Ethiopia, helping American Jews develop strong connections with the people, land, and State of Israel. We spent countless hours in youth activities and at summer camps. We navigated changes in culture and structures of society. I saw my central task as bringing Torah to the people and the people to Torah. Throughout my thirty-nine years as a congregational rabbi, I sought new ways to strengthen the Jewish people and increase their Torah knowledge and devotion to learning. The rabbis of each generation can, in their own ways, follow the example of Ezra and Nehemiah by creating new paths of responding to realities of their generation.

Notes

1. H. G. H. Williamson, *World Biblical Commentary, Volume 16: Ezra, Nehemiah* (Waco, TX: Word Books, 1985), 296.
2. Joseph Blenkinsopp, *Ezra-Nehemiah: A Commentary*, Old Testament Library (Philadelphia: Westminster Press, 1988).

Interpersonal *T'shuvah*

Rabbi Neil Hirsch[1]

That *t'shuvah* is necessary is clear; how to do it is not so simple. For all we talk about *t'shuvah*, how well do we really understand how it works? Our personal experiences and our best Jewish textual sources on the topic are imprecise do-it-yourself manuals.

T'shuvah is fiercely personal. Hearing of wrongdoing, we are reminded of what was done to us, or how we erred. As expressed in Jewish literature, *t'shuvah* is an experience carried out *bein adam l'chaveiro*, between individuals. The sibling who never returned the loan, the spouse who violated the marriage, the friend who lied, the student who posted something regrettable online: Who among us can say that we have not sinned, erred, or gone astray? Who among us can say that we have not suffered or been harmed?[2] *T'shuvah* is a topic that our congregants come to discuss with us. And, as of late, the Reform movement has begun a process of institutional *t'shuvah*, as we publicly reckon with decades-long patterns of wrongdoing. How does one repair after experiencing a rupture in one's life? Can an organization make *t'shuvah*? If forgiveness is possible, how do we achieve it? These questions are more than just Jewish ethical dilemmas. Forgiveness affects one's psyche, and it plays out in community.

Mining our classic texts on *t'shuvah* reveals the process to be inherently interpersonal. The way the tradition speaks about *t'shuvah* implies that a wrong has been committed between two or more parties. The Jewish bookshelf on how to offer an apology and how to forgive is vast. Though additionally, by approaching the topic through psychological and sociological lenses, we can deepen our understanding of how one can perform, as Maimonides put it, a *t'shuvah g'murah*, a complete repentance.

RABBI NEIL HIRSCH (NY10) serves Hevreh of Southern Berkshire, in Great Barrington, Massachusetts. He is a current DHL candidate at HUC-JIR, researching a variety of voices on accountability, justice, *t'shuvah*, and forgiveness.

Cornerstone Texts on *T'shuvah*

For transgressions between God and a person, Yom Kippur atones. But for transgressions between one person and their friend, Yom Kippur does not atone until one has sought forgiveness from the other. (Mishnah Yoma 8:9)

Mishnah Yoma 8:9 stands as the cornerstone text on interpersonal *t'shuvah*, reminding us to tend to our relationships with God and with our neighbors simultaneously. One of the gifts of this mishnah is that it frames *t'shuvah* relationally: Yom Kippur atones for sins between God and Israel because of the sacred relationship established in covenant. Yom Kippur does not atone for interpersonal wrongdoing, though, until we wrongdoers have sought to repair the harm we did to others. Yom Kippur does not do its task until we have done our own.

One performs *t'shuvah* in relationship with others. Although Yoma 8:9 directs us to engage with one another in *t'shuvah*, it does not tell us how. It does not provide directions on how to say, "I am sorry," nor does it give us any sense of how to receive those words. The mishnah's silence on how to perform *t'shuvah* invites more conversation.

Several assertions in the Jerusalem Talmud expand on and respond to Yoma 8:9 by describing the actions one can take to affect *t'shuvah*.[3] There, Sh'muel argues that one who sins against their fellow must go and confess. If the other accepts the confession, then the offender has performed *t'shuvah*. However, suppose the victim rejects the offender's approach; what then? In that case, the offender then brings others along, again confessing in their presence, evidencing both the remorse that motivates the apology and the communal impact that the offense against the individual had.

In recognizing a valid apology, the Sages are not of one mind. Again, the same halacha from the Jerusalem Talmud gives us guidance. R' Yehudah ben B'teirah declares that one should detail their wrongdoing in confessing, while R' Akiva makes a counter-argument.[4] Siding with R' Yehudah ben B'teirah, Maimonides, in *Hilchot T'shuvah*, writes that the offender confesses verbally to the victim about the wrongdoing. For one to have performed *t'shuvah g'murah*, they must accompany their oral confession with an objective change of heart, demonstrated by behavioral changes.[5]

Perhaps these principles are enough of a handbook for *t'shuvah*. When a person wrongs another, that person apologizes verbally and changes their behavior. *T'shuvah*, then, is seemingly self-evident. We know what an apology is supposed to sound like, how it is supposed to happen, and what it looks like when a repentant person has changed their ways.

Yet, we are the ones who complicate *t'shuvah*. A victim or witness may find themselves judging the sincerity of the apology. Others avoid the pain of confrontation, rationalizing their unwillingness to engage in a forgiveness process. The act of apologizing is seemingly direct, but the complication of interpersonal relationships is what proves so challenging. We may be able to generalize the rules for an apology, but every offense has a specific narrative, particular players, and defined social context. *T'shuvah* may be straightforward, but our relationships and our feelings regarding the transgression problematize the situation.

What is curious about the literature on *t'shuvah* is that much of the conversation focuses on the spiritual or philosophical nature of repentance, with little said on how to engage in a *t'shuvah* process—the *halacha l'ma'aseh*. Jonah, the biblical book most closely associated with *t'shuvah*, serves as a debate between the prophet and God about the use of Divine judgment and mercy. Maimonides' *Hilchot T'shuvah*, Rabbeinu Yonah's *Shaarei T'shuvah*, and the Meiri's *Chibur HaT'shuvah* all offer extensive thought on the concepts of apology and forgiveness but are not easily accessible. Moreover, modern philosophical and theological treatments on the topic like Rav Kook's *Orot HaT'shuvah* and Soloveitchik's teachings recorded by Pinchas Peli keep the topic in the rafters, making it difficult to navigate what we are to do when we have wronged another, or when we ourselves are survivors of profound transgressions. The problem with all these texts is their relative de-codability, making it difficult for a person to know when they or someone else has performed *t'shuvah*.

For that reason, turning to the psychological and sociological literature on forgiveness and apology informs a contemporary *halacha* of *t'shuvah*. Terminology, processes, and scenarios from these fields fill out the picture.

How Forgiveness Operates

Dave, an active member of my congregation, is someone who knows how forgiveness operates.[6] Several years ago, his mother was struck and killed by a truck while crossing the street, having headed out to take her dog for a walk. The accident was just that, a complete accident. Dave's mother had been looking at her phone when she stepped off the curb. The man driving the oncoming truck could not see her. He was blind in one eye, and she literally stepped into the spot where he could not see her. In Vermont, where she lived, a person can legally drive even with sight deficits as severe as this man's.

Dave and his family were devastated. Once the family gathered on the afternoon of the accident, Dave's father called a family meeting. The police asked if he wanted to press charges. Dave's father asked each of his children their opinion, remarkably, they were all of one mind. They saw the situation for what it was, a tragic accident. The driver was doing nothing criminal when he came upon their mother. Yes, it could be seen as involuntary manslaughter, but Dave and his family could not imagine punishing someone who by misfortune had taken another person's life. That is punishment enough, they figured. They chose to forgo criminal charges, believing that would not address their hurt, and that it would only add to the injustice of the circumstance.

At the memorial service, a friend of the family approached Dave's father. This friend let them know that the driver and his wife had come to pay their respects. The driver wanted to know if he was welcome there. Dave's father turned to his children to see how they felt about it. Again, they said yes. The man approached the family, coming up to Dave's father with tears in his eyes. "I am so sorry," was all the man said, and all he needed to say. Dave's father shook the driver's hand and accepted the apology. The driver repeated this ritual with each of the children. And each child responded with acceptance.

Dave was never angry at the driver, but he was angry that his mother had died a tragic death. Upon hearing the apology, Dave's anger over the circumstances lessened. The driver's apology helped him accept the reality of the situation.

Nobody ever expects a tragedy. Yet, we know that, too often, these situations happen. What plays out after the tragedy shows how *t'shuvah* can operate psychologically. In causing the accident, the driver created a massively tragic conflict between himself and Dave's family. In the time between the accident and the memorial service, Dave and his family lived with unforgiveness and grief, where a host of negative emotions associated with suffering are found. The driver offered the apology in earnest. By saying nothing more than, "I am sorry," he recognized that there was nothing he could do to repair the breach. But when he shared his heartfelt apology, conveying his regret over the circumstances, the family connected with him empathically, seeing his suffering along with their own. In connecting during this moment of apology, Dave and his family, along with the driver, were able to shift their emotional energies from the resentment and hurt that come with tragic grief and move toward acceptance and compassion.

When we do wrong, the apology—and the acceptance of the apology—happens when we pivot from the negative experience of the transgression toward a new chapter, a restored state, even though we know we can never fully repair that which has been broken. The Stress-Coping Theory of Forgiveness, framed by psychologist Everett Worthington, captures Dave's experience well and is helpful when taken in partnership with Jewish perspectives on *t'shuvah*. Worthington describes a transgression as a psychological stress. Forgiveness thus serves as a coping mechanism, bringing the individual back to a sense of internal balance.[7] When a transgression occurs, it transforms or even ruptures the relationship between or among the parties involved. The transgression creates a vacuum in the relationship that demands to be filled.

And, at first, *unforgiveness* is what fills the void. Those are the feelings of resentment, bitterness, hostility, hatred, anger—a range of negative emotions. It is in unforgiveness that we explore our desires for vengeance and voice our frustration that we cannot go back to before everything went wrong.[8] Unforgiveness is where we deeply feel the injustice of the circumstances.[9]

Worthington defines *forgiveness* as the opposite of unforgiveness. He understands forgiveness as the release of the host of negative emotions associated with unforgiveness. If wrongdoing generates feelings of unforgiveness for the victim, then forgiveness is the process that proposes transformation and healing for those involved. Dave made a deliberate, emotional choice to forgive. This is a power that lives exclusively with the victims of wrongdoing.[10] Significantly, the victim holds the power. Forgiveness allows the victim to find restoration while transitioning toward a new stage after the transgression occurred. Dave found compassion for the driver, transforming his grief.

Importantly, unlike in Dave's situation, some cases of wrong-doing are not accidental. There are those who act out of malice. Worthington's framework is admittedly optimistic, promising a new chapter if only the victim and offender are to engage with one another. Though we are not to be naïve. The decision for victims and survivors to sit down with an offender is not to be taken lightly, especially in cases involving trauma, crime, or other heightened transgressions.[11] We hear today about placing the needs of the survivors first, bringing trauma-informed perspectives to any conversation about wrongdoing. Regardless of the circumstances being addressed, Worthington's framework contributes to a survivor-first way of thinking.

For any victim, according to Worthington, the question of forgiveness operates along two planes: decisional and emotional. Forgiveness is never the exclusive property of only one of those planes. Someone may choose to forgive another but continue to harbor resentment. Alternatively, it is also possible for victims to unburden themselves from the feelings of unforgiveness without ever really deciding to do so. Forgiveness, then, is the braiding together of a victim's thoughts and feelings toward the offender and toward the harm that offender committed.

Decisional forgiveness is an internal experience, held by the one who suffered harm. It is understood as "a behavioral intention statement to treat the transgressor as a person of value, to forswear revenge, and to act in ways that forbear expression of anger about the transgression."[12] The ways that we decide to forgive, Worthington notes, are not clear. Moreover, the impulse to forgive does not track along a predictable timeline. Some forgive quickly; others take longer. For example, two days after the massacre at the Emanuel AME Church in Charleston, South Carolina, victims gathered in the courtroom for the shooter's bond hearing. When the magistrate asked the victims and their families to come forward, they each turned toward the shooter, and, animated by their Christian beliefs, offered him forgiveness. Many were shocked, including the relatives of other victims, who had not yet buried their loved ones.[13] Sometimes, a person may say they have forgiven the offender but still harbor feelings of unforgiveness.

By contrast, *emotional forgiveness* is the shift of the negative emotions toward positive ones. Victims who experience emotional forgiveness report a reduction—not necessarily an elimination—of the feelings of unforgiveness. They describe a more emotionally neutral sense of the wrong they suffered.[14] For Dave, the decision to forgive was closely related to the emotional release he felt when the driver apologized. Dave was angry about the way his mother died, and the driver's apology enabled him also to feel compassion. For as varied as the experiences of decisional forgiveness are, emotional forgiveness offers even more texture. Given the complexity of any person's soul and psyche, the situation and personalities make each *t'shuvah* process a universe unto itself.

A victim attempting to move forward has several possible paths. A person can deny or ignore their feelings about the transgression or address the offense either intrapersonally or interpersonally. In some situations, intrapersonal interventions may be the best path forward for the victims. There, a counselor helps the victim through the experience of trauma and transformation, leaving out the direct involvement of the offender. An intrapersonal approach is reasonable when bringing victim and offender together runs the risk of re-traumatization. In the literature on interpersonal forgiveness, writers emphasize that approaches involving both victim and offender work only when it is physically and emotionally safe to do so, and when all involved freely and sincerely agree to participate.[15] Interpersonal forgiveness cannot be compelled. In fact, it may prove harmful to urge some victims toward an interpersonal forgiveness processes.

Yet, interpersonal interventions also hold a key place in the conversation. Restorative justice is a framework, a practice, and a field of study. What one means when they use the term *restorative justice* can vary, especially in approach. Yet, the common thread in restorative justice literature is the goal of addressing the harm writ large created in a transgression. To hold parties accountable, restorative justice facilitators bring people into conversation with one another, with the sole intent to address the harms that occurred. Restorative justice practitioners prepare carefully for encounters between victims and offenders. Forgiveness is not an objective of the restorative justice encounters. Yet, for those interested in how restorative justice practices may inform a *t'shuvah* process, the nature of these sort of facilitated encounters is helpful.[16] By bringing the victim and offender together when appropriate, these moments mutually honor the humanity of both the victim and offender, opening the door to an emotional transformation for all involved.[17]

The Apology Process

Returning to Dave and his family: When the driver approached Dave's family to apologize, he was sincere and remorseful. As we well know, in times of loss, sometimes the only thing to say is, "I am sorry." The driver knew he could not bring Dave's mother back, but at the memorial service, he could offer his heartfelt condolence, saying that he too wished the circumstances were otherwise. With his apology, he unlocked the powers of forgiveness and did his part to help all parties to heal.

The moment in which the offender apologizes to the victim is the keystone to an interpersonal *t'shuvah* process. Just as it was for Dave and the driver, these are vulnerable and intimate moments when a victim and offender come together. Apologies "constitute —in their most responsible authentic, and, hence, vulnerable expression—a form of self-punishment that cuts deeply because we are obliged to retell, relive, and seek forgiveness for sorrowful events that have rendered our claims to membership in a moral community suspect or defeasible,"[18] writes sociologist Nicholas Tavuchis.

When offenders apologize, they recall the offense committed which neither they nor the victim can change.[19] Yet, the interpersonal apology process presents for everyone involved the possibility of healing. Recognizing that this is easily said, the specific reality of an offense complicates the pursuit of an apology in service of repair and wholeness. As criminal legal systems demonstrate, there is a categorical difference between wronging someone accidentally and harming them deliberately.

Because an apology lives in the world of interpersonal relationships, it fits a set of paradoxical rules.[20] This is where *t'shuvah* is both clear and not so simple. Each person brings their personality, perspectives, and biases to an apology. The apology is also colored by the particularities of the wrongdoing. Thus, while one can point to the general patterns that make apologies effective, we also need to acknowledge that each transgression has aspects that make it unique.

In his study *On Apology*, the late psychiatrist Aaron Lazare identifies four key steps one takes to say "I'm sorry" effectively : 1) the acknowledgment of the offense; 2) the explanation; 3) expressions of remorse, shame, humility, and sincerity; and 4) reparations.[21]

When the victim agrees to an encounter with the offender, and the offender is moved to apologize, these four steps pave a path toward restoration. These actions are consistent with what we know from the rabbinic tradition. [22] An offender who comes to perform *t'shuvah g'murah* is to describe what they did wrong, express a sense of remorse, and show how they will not do it again.

In *acknowledging* having wronged the victim, the offender takes ownership for what happened and its effects. By acknowledging the harm and pain caused, the wrongdoer admits that they violated the social contract between the victim and themself.

With an *explanation*, the offender then offers an understanding of what happened. "An explanation relieves one of these burdens even though it does nothing to lessen the other: By hearing the offender's reason for his or her behavior, [victims] can stop endlessly speculating about what happened and can begin to grieve the loss they have suffered."[23] The way the victim receives the explanation also matters, as they are now able to assess the level of *sincerity*, *remorse, shame, humility,* and *accuracy* with which the offender has offered their explanation.[24]

Reparations are a signal made from the offender to the victim that they are taking the apology process seriously, that they fully recognize the harm and injury done, that all parties are entitled to a hopeful future, and that they are willing to *repair* what was done.[25] For, as significant as reparations are in the apology process, reparations can never undo the injury committed; thus they remain an imperfect but necessary tool. "Yet," legal scholar Martha Minow notes, "even inadequate monetary payments or an apology without any reparations can afford more opportunities for a sense of recognition and renewal for survivors, observers, and offenders than would an unsuccessful struggle for an apology, for reparations, or for the restitution of property . . . ."[26]

Maimonides also distinguishes between reparations and acknowledgement.[27] There he puts in parallel two actions a wrongdoer takes in pursuit of *t'shuvah g'murah*. To perform *t'shuvah*, the offender must *ya-chazir lo*, return to the victim. Often this is inferred or elaborated as *ya-chazir ba't'shuvah*, returning in repentance. In practice the offender is meant to make the aggrieved whole, to perform reparations for the harm committed. Reparations is an aspect of making *t'shuvah*, as much as asking for forgiveness. Moreover, the offender may also *yish-al mimeinu kaparah*, request from the victim atonement or expiation. Just as Lazar's framework shows us that there are multiple actions one must take to achieve an effective apology, Maimonides recognizes that apology, and thereby *t'shuvah*, is a multi-stepped process.

Forgiveness is the healing of the hurt caused by a transgression. It is important to note that some are affected directly by a particular transgression, and some are affected indirectly, and to varying degrees. Those differences may generate diverse desires among the aggrieved. Some may call for punitive action while others may want just to forget. Crucially, any extrajudicial apology process does not take the place of other forms of accountability or punishment. When considering the balance between restoration and retribution, the two may not be mutually exclusive, with the victims needing to surrender one for the sake of the other. "In theory, forgiveness does not and should not take the place of justice or punishment," writes Minow. "Forgiveness marks a change in how the offended feels about the person who committed the injury, not a change in the actions to be taken by a justice system."[28]

When a victim and offender come together, they co-create an opportunity that can help the aggrieved cope with the stress and harm created during the transgression. Given the particularity of these situations, we now turn to several scenarios, each with its own set of considerations.

Four Scenarios for Interpersonal *T'shuvah*

In Tavuchis's sociological study of apology, he identifies four scenarios in which apologies happen. Each scenario involves a different grouping of an individual, which he calls the One, or a collective, which he labels the Many. The Many may be any collection of people: a class of students, a synagogue community, or even larger communities. Each combination has its own dynamics.

One-to-One: The first scenario is one we know well. This is siblings reconciling, two former business partners burying the hatchet, a wrongdoer directly apologizing to the victim. It is the driver apologizing and seeking forgiveness from Dave's father, from Dave, and from his siblings, individually.

Interestingly, while the One-on-One apology is direct, it impacts others adjacent to the incident. The wrongdoing and the apology process both can have ripple effects. A third-party complicates the situation. This is the farthest thing from a reason to shy away from addressing harm that occurs in a communal context, however it is worth noting how much more communal transgressions are gordian knots when compared to a One-to-One scenario. As we turn to the three other scenarios in which harm occurs, it is important to keep in mind the increased complexity communal harm introduces.

One-to-Many: The middle two scenarios are similar but have some key differences. First, there is the One-to-Many, in which an individual offends the collective. In that case, the individual could offer an apology to the group. At the most basic level, this is the officemate who does not meet the agreed-upon deadlines for a team project, setting everyone back. It is the public figure who says something hateful about a group of people.

When these instances of wrongdoing take place, and the individual issues an apology, that then sparks other considerations: Does the person's apology and punishment go far enough? Will the community ever see that person in the same light again? As we will see with other examples of apologies that involve the Many, the answers are complicated.

Many-to-One: The Many-to-One is the collective who has wronged the individual. These are the classmates who spread malicious gossip about a peer. Tavuchis argues that this scenario makes an apology more difficult to accept. After all, when one is cast out of a collective, one may be hard-pressed to accept an apology from that group. It would hold little social value. For a meaningful apology in a Many-to-One scenario, the One must believe that the collective can speak with one voice, which is a leap of imagination. And what collective is ever of one mind?[29]

Many-to-Many: The final scenario is the most elaborate because it is a situation in which groups harm other groups. Genocide, apartheid, and mass violence all fall under this scenario. Those extreme examples raise the question that any scenario involving collective *t'shuvah* process presents: Who apologizes, and how? Can such an apology ever satisfy? These questions are present within the Reform Movement today, as well.

A proxy for the group must be designated when a collective is involved. Someone speaks for the group. It can be anyone who has the authority to use the phrase, "On behalf of . . . ". There are significant differences between an individual who personally offers an apology and someone serving as a proxy. When speaking for him or herself, one can authentically use emotional language, conveying how one feels about the transgression, the relationship, and the various parties involved. A proxy for the Many speaking in emotional terms risks sounding callous and hollow. The collective does not experience a single emotion or discrete set of feelings related to the transgression.

As a result, the risk an institution runs in conducting a communal *t'shuvah* process rests with the emotions involved. As a collective, institutions must show what they are *doing* to perform *t'shuvah*. Institutional *t'shuvah* is action-oriented. A proxy's effective apology reflects this. Perhaps the proxy can describe their personal feelings in a way that can be received as valid by others. But, at that moment, the proxy does not speak for the Many. Instead, this designee describes what policies, circumstances, or institutional attitudes will be changed, not to undo the harm already done (because this is not possible), but to assure that others do not fall victim again. In short, the proxy describes what those within the Many will do that is different from before.

In December 2020, hundreds of competitive gymnasts agreed to a $380 million legal settlement with USA Gymnastics for the role it played in enabling its former team doctor to sexually abuse the athletes. While the settlement represents a sort of retributive justice for the injury and harm committed, one survivor asserted, "No amount of money will ever repair the damage that has been done and what these women have been through."[30] When the team doctor was most active in his abuse, the coaches, trainers, and other involved adults were focused on the athletic success of these young athletes. Their commitment was to win Olympic medals. Elite athletes are often told that they must take on maximal effort and tolerate high levels of discomfort to achieve their goals; however, as law professor Amos Giuria notes, there are limits. "USA Gymnastics, under the banner of the U.S. Olympic Committee, failed to protect the children in their care and allowed them to fall prey to those seeking to benefit from their successes. No one gave a damn what it took to achieve those successes."[31]

Considering the vast harm that USA Gymnastics enabled, the CEO's statement after the settlement illustrates how a proxy's apology operates for the Many. She said:

> USA Gymnastics is deeply sorry for the trauma and pain that Survivors have endured as a result of this organization's actions and inactions. The Plan of Reorganization that we jointly filed reflects our own accountability to the past and our commitment to the future. Individually and collectively, Survivors have stepped forward with bravery to advocate for enduring change in this sport. We are committed to working with them, and with the entire gymnastics community, to ensure that we continue to prioritize the safety, health, and wellness of our athletes and community above all else.[32]

Here we have a model on how to apologize. Her apology acknowledges the harm that was done, takes ownership of the inaction of those in positions of leadership and influence, honors the survivors' actions, and identifies a Plan of Reorganization. Details on that plan are not outlined in the body of the apology; however, later communications gave more specifics.

With this critique in mind, this example shows that in instances of mass wrongdoing, apologies are an essential part of the return to wholeness, but they alone cannot bring full restoration. For an institution, it takes policy and culture shifts after the apology has been issued to evidence that change *is underway*.

Not everyone—within and outside of the Many—will be satisfied by the proxy's apology. After the official apology from the CEO of USA Gymnastics, some of those spoke of their satisfaction over the institution's apology and action steps outlined immediately after.[33] But, the range of replies on Twitter to the institution's apology illustrates just how broadly people experience institutional transformation in practice. The limitation of an apology to or from the Many is complicated because no collective is an emotional monolith, as it comprises groups of human beings, each with individual emotional responses to the transgression. When the proxy issues the apology on behalf of the institution, those individuals inside the collective react, each in their own way. They may react to the wrongdoing itself, the institution's handling of the case, or both. People will be critical of the apology mainly because these apologies usually come after decades of abuse and denial. Collectives are messy.

Here again, Maimonides can be helpful. Maimonides recognized the difficulty for an individual to achieve *t'shuvah g'murah* when having wronged a collective. There are transgressions that "make it impossible for the transgressor to make a *t'shuvah g'murah*, because they involve sins between people for which one does not know the other against whom he sinned, to whom he can make recompense, or from whom he can seek forgiveness." Maimonides offers several situations that fall under this category of transgressions for which one cannot fully repent, significantly including "one who curses the many, who did not curse an individual in order to know to whom he can ask for pardon."[34]

In this *halachah*, Maimonides writes that the curse is against ha-rabim, the many. I find the distinction between *ha-rabim* and *ha-tzibur* useful, as it helps us further distinguish the nature of the collective with which we are dealing. The rabim is a non-specific collective, literally the Many, understood as the public. Whereas the *tzibur* is the community. A community, as opposed to a public, is a collection of individuals who have established institutions. These groups have rules and policies, and they make collective statements. In any situation that involves the Many, it is useful to consider if the proxies claim to speak on behalf of *ha-tzibur* or *ha-rabim*.

What emerges out of Maimonides' insight is that in situations that involve the rabim, one cannot expect to make complete *t'shuvah*, for *t'shuvah* happens between individuals. When one transgresses a collective (*tzibur*), it is impossible to achieve a complete *t'shuvah*.

This reality highlights a challenge inherent in the phrase "institutional *t'shuvah*". If *t'shuvah* lives most effectively within the bounds of the One-to-One scenario, then describing a communal processes to restore relationships after a transgression on the part of an institution feels out of place. Yet, that does not mean that repair should not be pursued. Quite the opposite. Rather, those involved and those looking on need to manage their expectations about what end products of successful repair look like.

The independent reports commissioned by the Reform movement institutions investigating wrongdoing within our community all recommend an institutional *t'shuvah* as part of the process to heal and move forward. A close read of the recommendations shows that the steps the institution can take to repair the harm done are all tangible, related to their institutional policies and procedures. The CCAR's *T'shuvah* Task Force is examining how the Reform rabbinate might take collective repentant action. Changing how the Reform movement's institutions operate is the evidence of *t'shuvah*, not at the expense of the emotional reactions of those within our collective, but in consideration of them. When the reports came out, CCAR leadership offered sessions for members to process their initial emotional reactions to the reports. Any apology scenario that involves a collective is predicated on the maintenance of dignity for each person who counts themselves among the Many. When bringing members of the Many together, we see people coming from different places. Victims and survivors will be among the crowd. Apologists for the offenders may show up, too. The feelings inside the collectives can be fierce, and they can be directed not only toward offenders but also toward the proxy. To offer sessions for processing the findings of the investigations and how they are impacting each of us as community members is a compassionate approach to an unpleasant task. It allows those within this Many to explore and address the emotional plane of the disclosures.

As clergy, we know how ritual can transform and bring spiritual healing. People need creative ritual moments that can give space to participants to name the experience through which they have traveled, express their hopes and desires for how things can be different, perform some form of release, and essentially help one another arrive in a new sacred space that no institution can foster. The ritual held online for CCAR members prior to Yom Kippur, along with the letter issued by CCAR leadership, speaks to ritual's potential to contribute to communal healing.

Great care should be taken to understand what is happening inside the collective during a group *t'shuvah* process, as there is high risk of misunderstanding one another and doing further harm. Still, a central question remains unanswered: *T'shuvah* is traditionally understood as an internal experience played out between individuals. Can we successfully map that highly individualized construct onto the action steps organizations take to repair harm they caused?

How to Do Interpersonal *T'shuvah*

Two truths emerge regarding interpersonal *t'shuvah*--we seek to repair what the transgression damaged, and we strive to maintain the humanity of both the victim and the offender.[35]

Considering the disclosures of decades of wrongdoing within the Reform Movement, and the investigations they prompted, we are called to ask about the role that *t'shuvah* plays in holding one another accountable. The CCAR, HUC-JIR, and URJ reports propose a *t'shuvah* process as part of our collective work to heal our community. These are calls for communal *t'shuvah*—for us to be an effective Many—separate and apart from the *t'shuvah* to which any one wrongdoer is also called. For both the individual and the community, a clear set of guidelines on *t'shuvah* enables personal growth and healing for individuals and allows us as a community to work transparently to strengthen our collective moral standing.

T'shuvah is multidimensional, as the experiences, emotions, and desires involved vary broadly, which is why we need to understand how it operates. One midrash captures the many voices on accountability well:

> They asked Torah: "How is the sinner to be punished?" Torah replied, *Let them bring a sacrifice and be pardoned.*
> They asked prophecy: "How is the sinner to be punished?" And prophecy replied, "The person who sins… shall die" (Ezekiel 18:4).
> They asked David: "How is the sinner to be punished?" David replied, "May sinners disappear from the earth and the wicked be no more" (Psalm 104:35).
> They asked Wisdom: "How is the sinner to be punished?" Wisdom replied, "Misfortune pursues the sinners" (Proverbs 13:21).
> They asked the Holy One of Blessing: "How is the sinner to be punished?" God replied, "Let the sinner do repentance, and I will accept it, as it is written, 'Good and upright is the Eternal; therefore God shows sinners the way'" (Psalm 25:8).[36]

What are we to do when the wrongdoers among us come forward to apologize for their transgressions? When we wrestle collectively with injustice and harm, we hold a range of perspectives and a variety of opinions all at the same time. Just as Jonah was angry with God for showing mercy toward the Ninevites, sometimes we just want the sinners to be punished. Some will say the damages paid in court will make them whole, a contemporary *kaparah*. Some may argue that justice comes with karma, that misfortune will be an offender's punishment. Yet, the power of this midrash lies in its reminder that the work of *t'shuvah*, with all its complexities, is what God desires.

Final Thoughts

When teaching relational theology, I—like so many of us—quote Martin Buber's assertion that, "All life is encounter." Yet, I've always been troubled by what happens to that idea when our relationships sour or when we suffer harm or trauma. We do not stop being in relationship with people from whom we are estranged. A commitment to being in relationship with one another guides how we pave a path toward personal and communal restoration.

It is not an uncommon experience, especially around Yom Kippur, for congregants to come to discuss the hurt they have been holding onto, not knowing where to take it. There are those who seek us out because they do not know if they can ever offer an apology or give forgiveness. When someone shares how they did wrong, asking, "Could I ever be forgiven?" Or, when someone shares with me how they were victimized, asking, "Rabbi, can I ever forgive?" I want to both listen to and honor the pain from which these questions emerge. I need a framework by which to understand the emotional and spiritual processes in which these individuals can engage to answer their essential questions.

Part of the answer lies in *t'shuvah*'s nature as relational and action oriented. Whether the circumstances involve two people or many, the actions of interpersonal *t'shuvah* are the same. As the halachic literature teaches for the offender: take ownership of what you did wrong, give your version of the events, listen carefully to how others experienced it, and offer to do what you can to repair the situation. And from the social sciences for the victim: in processing the harm suffered, you also hold the power to forgive, which is both a decision you can make and an emotional experience to be lived.

These dynamic, relational moments, share the same goal, namely, to hold one another accountable, uphold one another's humanity, and to strive for *sh'leimut*.

Notes

1. I thank Rabbi Rachel Adler and Dr. Marilyn Armour for their valuable comments and suggestions on various versions of this article.

   I started to study accountability and *t'shuvah* in 2018 when a sometimes-Shabbat attendee at my synagogue was publicly accused of sexual assault. He continually denied the allegations and remained publicly unrepentant. When he and his wife came to Shabbat services after the disclosure, I did not know how to behave toward him. That confusion prompted this research. This pre-dated the Reform movement's investigations. While this tangential personal story connects with this research, I know that, for others, discussion of wrongdoing and repair is personal. I offer the following research and thinking with an awareness that my approach is essentially intellectual and theoretical. I have never been a victim, nor do I defend the actions of offenders. Wrongdoing and *t'shuvah* bring with them strong emotions, and I honor the experiences and feelings each person brings toward this literature. My aim is for the theoretical framework to shine a light onto an often-clouded understanding of *t'shuvah*.

2. Much of the literature on forgiveness and restorative justice discuss wrongdoing between a *victim* and *offender*. Some today caution against labeling people involved in these conflicts as *victim* and *offender*, arguing that the labels limit individuals' identities, invalidating the complexity of who they are, fighting against the very goal of a restorative justice process. With that consideration in mind, I use *victim* and *offender* as technical terms to identify, respectively, who was wronged, and who wronged another. Moreover, I use gender neutral pronouns throughout so as not to unnecessarily delimit the bounds of a person's experience in any given case of wrongdoing.

3. JT Yoma 8:7. Notably, a victim's death does not absolve the offender from seeking *t'shuvah*. The offender is to go with witnesses to the victim's grave to seek forgiveness again.

4. Ibid.; cf. JT Nedarim 5:4 regarding a declaration of *cherem*.

5. In the Mishneh Torah, *Hilchot T'shuvah* 2:3-4, Maimonides offers several paths by which one can show their change in behavior and thus his change of heart: "Among the ways of *t'shuvah* are for the repentant to continue to cry out to God in tearful supplication, to make tzedakah according to their means, to exceedingly distance themself from the sin, to change their name as if to say, 'I am different. I am not the same person who did those things,' to change the entirety of their actions for a good and straight path, and to exile themself from their place, as exile atones for iniquity and it leads one to be submissive and humble."

6. With thanks to my friend and congregant Dave, for permitting me to share his story.

7. Research has linked forgiveness with both mental and physical health benefits. In addressing the harm, one may experience the removal of the injustice, inducing a physical response. Moreover, by addressing the negative emotions, a person can reduce their physical stress by coming into a new positive emotional state. See Everett L. Worthington et al., "Forgiveness, Health, and Well-Being: A Review of Evidence for Emotional versus Decisional Forgiveness, Dispositional Forgivingness, and Reduced Unforgiveness," *Journal of Behavioral Medicine* 30, no. 4 (August 2007): 291–302, and Charlotte V.O. Witvliet et al., "Retributive Justice, Restorative Justice, and Forgiveness: An Experimental Psychophysiology Analysis," *Journal of Experimental Social Psychology* 44, no. 1 (January 2008): 10–25.

8. Vengeance is a critical element of how we respond to wrongdoing, as it honors the instinct to retaliate for the wrongs we have suffered. Yet, acting on our vengeful impulses does not satisfy on a personal level, only creating more pain in what could become a downward spiral, a tit-for-tat competition between the victim and offender. On a communal level, vengeance can propagate further hatred. See Martha Minow, *Between Vengeance and Forgiveness: Facing History after Genocide and Mass Violence* (Boston: Beacon Press, 2009), 10-14.

9. Coupled with unforgiveness is the concept of injustice. When one experiences a transgression not only as a personal violation but as an injustice, researchers describe that as an "injustice gap." Forgiveness as a coping mechanism can also address the injustice gap by (1) giving victims a sense of shared values with the offender, (2) giving the victims a sense of "moral fortitude," and (3) helping restore the power differential between the victim and offender. See Don E. Davis et al., "The Injustice Gap," *Psychology of Religion and Spirituality* 8, no. 3 (August 2016): 175–84.

10. Everett L. Worthington, *Handbook of Forgiveness* (New York: Routledge, 2020), 386.

11. Worthington's research has heavily informed restorative justice practices, which focus on mediation between the victim and offender. Significantly, just as some are beginning to question the use of victim and offender labels, researchers are also examining a variety of interventions both including and beyond victim-offender mediation, to bring about healing when harm has been done. See Mary Achilles, "Will Restorative Justice Live Up to Its Promise to Victims?," in *Critical Issues in Restorative Justice,* ed. Howard Zehr and Barb Toews (Boulder: Lynne Rienner Publishers, 2010), 65–73.

12. Worthington, 11.

13. Jennifer Hawes, *Grace Will Lead Us Home: The Charleston Church Massacre and the Hard, Inspiring Journey to Forgiveness,* first ed. (New York: St. Martin's Press, 2019), 72-79.?

14. Worthington, *Handbook of Forgiveness*, 11.

15. Ibid, 13.

16. Ibid. While forgiveness and restorative justice practices are related, many theoreticians and practitioners assert that restorative justice is not primarily concerned with forgiveness. For a comprehensive study on the relationship of forgiveness and restorative justice practices, see Marilyn Armour, *Violence, Restorative Justice and Forgiveness : Dyadic Forgiveness and Energy Shifts in Restorative Justice Dialogue* (London : Jessica Kingsley Publishers, 2018). In one UK study, researchers examined how participants in restorative justice encounters understood forgiveness. They found that, in many cases, participants felt a sense of relief at having taken part in the conference, or that they felt an increase in compassion for the others involved in the process, but they often did not use the word *forgiveness* to describe the experience. The researchers' explanation for this is the secularization of the UK and that forgiveness is perceived as a religious concept. See Joanna Shapland, "Forgiveness and Restorative Justice: Is It Necessary? Is It Helpful?" *Oxford Journal of Law and Religion* 5, no. 1 (February 2016): 94–112.

17. See, again, Armour, *Violence, Restorative Justice and Forgiveness.*

18. Nicholas Tavuchis, *Mea Culpa: A Sociology of Apology and Reconciliation* (Stanford, CA: Stanford University Press, 1993), 8.

19. Tavuchis, *Mea Culpa*, 6: "An apology does *one* thing only: it recalls ('accounts for') that which neither the offender nor the offended can change, a fait accompli."

20. Tavuchis, *Mea Culpa, 5 and Lazare, On Apology* (New York: Oxford University Press, 2007), 22-43.

21. Aaron Lazare, *On Apology*, 35.

22. *Hilchot T'shuvah* 2:4.

23. Lazare, *On Apology,* 121.

24. Lazare, *On Apology,* 105-27.

25. Lazare, *On Apology,* 127-33.

26. Minow, *Between Vengeance and Forgiveness*, 93.

27. *Hilchot T'shuvah*, 4:3.

28. Minow, *Between Vengeance and Forgiveness*, 15.

29. Tavuchis, *Mea Culpa*, 98.

30. Juliet Macur, "Nassar Abuse Survivors Reach a $380 Million Settlement," *New York Times*, December 13, 2021, https://www.nytimes.com/2021/12/13/sports/olympics/nassar-abuse-gymnasts-settlement.html.

31. Amos N. Guiora, *Armies of Enablers: Survivor Stories of Complicity and Betrayal in Sexual Assaults* (Chicago, IL: American Bar Association, 2020), 54.

32. USA Gymnastics. Twitter post. December 13, 2021, 3:50 PM. https://twitter.com/USAGym/status/1470496385640325123?s=20.

33. Dan Murphy and John Barr, "USA Gymnastics and U.S. Olympic & Paralympic Committee Agree to Pay $380 Million to Survivors of Former Olympic Team Doctor and Convicted Sexual Predator Larry Nassar," *ESPN*, December 13, 2021, https://www.espn.com/olympics/story/_/id/32859504/usa-gymnastics-us-olympic-paralympic-committee-agree-pay-380-million-survivors-former-olympic-team-doctor-convicted-sexual-predator-larry-nassar.

34. *Hilchot T'shuvah*, 4:3.

35. For a fuller understanding of the rabbinic understanding of justice, and the ways that forgiveness and restorative justice fit within that, see Aryeh Cohen, *Justice in the City: An Argument from the Sources of Rabbinic Judaism*, New Perspectives in Post-Rabbinic Judaism (Brighton, MA: Academic Studies, 2012).

36. JT Makkot 2:6, also recorded in a genizah fragment published by Shlomo Wieder, *Tarbiz* 17 (1946): 133.

Aliyat Hanefesh: How to Raise the Community's Spiritualty One Step at a Time

Rabbi Lester Polonsky

In 2006 I was diagnosed with multiple sclerosis. Multiple sclerosis (MS) is the disease in which the insulating covers of the nerve cells in the brain and spinal cord are damaged. According to WebMD, this damage means your brain can't send signals through your body correctly. Your nerves also don't work as they should to help you move and feel. While the symptoms vary and may not be consistent, it is very difficult to diagnosis MS if you are exhibiting only a few symptoms.

For many years I had problems sleeping and was told that restless legs interrupted my sleep. I took all kinds of medicine. I even went to a sleep clinic where they videotaped how restless legs kept me awake. It wasn't until the summer of 2006 on a drive to the Berkshires that I experienced nonstop leg spasms. At that point, my wife, Helene, insisted I see a neurologist.

After several MRIs, he declared that I have MS. As he shared this diagnosis, he said, "MS is very difficult to diagnosis when you experience just a few symptoms. Your experience with restless legs was not enough to bring MS into question. Now that MS has been discovered, we can prescribe the appropriate medications." This experience has taught me a very valuable lesson, the symptoms are manifestations of a greater problem. To treat the restless legs effectively, you must understand that MS is the center of the problem.

I carry this valuable lesson forward. Based on thirty-two years of the rabbinate serving five Reform congregations, I now have a new vision of how synagogues function. The synagogue is a living

RABBI LESTER POLONSKY (NY78) enjoys the peace of retirement and the blessings of grandchildren.

breathing body of Jewish life and at the heart of its being are the challenges of money and membership.

There are certain factors in these challenges that must be acknowledged as unchangeable:

1. Money is needed to operate the synagogue. In each synagogue, a financial structure has evolved to provide the level of services and programs.
2. Membership is needed to create and sustain the essence of a Jewish community.

Emanating from these challenges are the questions:

- How do we collect enough money to operate?
- How do we recruit new members?
- How do we engage the current membership?

Dr. Lawrence Hoffman, in his book *Rethinking Synagogues, A New Vocabulary for Congregational Life*, recommends a unique method as to how the synagogue can address the questions of money and membership: "Redescriptions require new sentences and new sentences need new words to string together in promising and provocative ways."[1]

The following sections "The Challenge of Money," "The Challenge of Membership: Recruitment," and "The Challenge of Membership: Engagement" will describe new methods and new terminology.

The Challenge of Money

Money is needed for the operation of the synagogue. Dedicated volunteers must monitor the flow of cash, income, and expenditures. The cost for providing an array of synagogue services must be borne by the synagogue membership. The annual budget will present the overall costs which are then divided among the membership. Even though the synagogue is a religious institution, it is guided by the business perspective to balance gains and losses. The religious values of compassion and sensitivity should be the guiding force when someone requests a dues reduction.

There are times when the collection of dues does not reach the amount set forth by the annual budget. Sometimes this situation is the result of overall societal economic downturn. The recent

COVID pandemic caused great economic stress as businesses and services shut down. Sometimes it is the membership.

Rabbi Jonathan Bernhard shares the story when his congregation moved from the traditional dues structure to the Fair Share System. Rabbi Bernhard writes, "It was completely obvious that the traditional dues model had completely broken down for us. Other congregations may be able to handle it better than we managed it, but for us, the dues model was an utter catastrophe. So why not try something new?"[2] The new approach they tried was the Fair Share System, a voluntary dues.

With the Fair Share System members are asked to pay 1 to 2.5 percent of the family income. Since family income is a private matter, the amount of their annual contribution is left to the discretion of each member. The shift to the Fair Share System presents serious concerns. Synagogue leadership fear that the amount of money collected will not satisfy the annual budget. Will members be honest?

Congregation Emanu-El in San Francisco returned to mandatory dues after thirteen years with a Fair Share System. David Goldman, Emanu-El's executive director, explains the change back: "A system that was designed to be fairer didn't seem to be that way because we had people with very similar uses of the temple and very similar means paying very dissimilar amounts."[3] For every congregation that experimented with the Fair Share System and failed, there are the congregations that successfully implemented this system.

Rabbi Dan Judson, who teaches at Hebrew College Rabbinical School and is an expert on the history of the financing of American synagogues, explains why synagogues need to adopt a new venue: "The dues system has fallen out of alignment with the zeitgeist. People want to feel that whatever they want to give to a religious community should be valued as a gift. They don't want to feel like they're giving money and still it's not good enough."[4]

The problem lies not in the financial structure. The problem lies in the terminology. When financial contribution is referred to as "dues," it projects the concept of a short-term commitment. You pay dues to the country club, JCC, and when this service is no longer a priority, you stop paying dues and terminate your membership. So too with the synagogue; when the synagogue is no longer a priority in your life, you terminate your affiliation. I had always thought of composing a *talking blue grass* song, titled, "The Synagogue Is Just Another Pit Stop on the Road of Life."

How do we encourage the membership to maintain their financial commitment for a longer period? Dr. Hoffman teaches that to change the language will change the thinking and eventually change the culture. It is time to replace the term "dues" with "investment." To refer to the financial commitment as "investment" projects the meaning of a deeper obligation. Investment invests in the synagogue, the Jewish community, and the Jewish people not only for the present but also for the future. The one who pays the investment is no longer a member, they are "investors." To promote this new concept, "stock certificates" can be presented to investors acknowledging their years of support. Together these new terms "investment" and "investors" project an entirely new focus causing the synagogue community to look upon their annual financial commitment as a promise for the future.

The Challenge of Membership: Recruitment

How to welcome the stranger who visits the synagogue on Friday evening is a challenge. It may be easy to identify a visitor standing alone at the *Oneg* but how to approach them? Dr. Ron Wolfson, in his book *Relational Judaism* speaks of his philosophy of how nurturing relationships can improve the quality of the Jewish community. Visitors are looking to connect with a community. They are interested in learning how they can become involved.

You can ask the visitor "Did you like the service?" or "What brought you to our doors?" The congregant can ask about their work and maybe connect them to a congregant in a similar profession. But, **don't discuss membership and don't mention dues!** Membership and dues are clues that the community is only interested in money, and the visitor will never return. If the visitor asks about membership and dues, the diplomatic response should be, "Its Shabbat and we don't talk temple business on Shabbat. We can discuss these issues later. Let's learn more about you."

The Challenge of Membership: Engagement

Dr. Wolfson identifies two entry portals to the congregational community, the visitor to Friday evening worship and new membership.

We have already addressed how to connect with the visitor on Friday evening. The perfect time to draw this new member into the committees and projects is when someone makes a commitment to officially join the congregation. Wolfson recommends a demographic form to elicit pertinent information about the perspective member. Wolfson describes how this demographic form should elicit information (e.g., work, interests, level of Jewish knowledge, Hebrew skills). Once again Wolfson describes a problem and suggests a remedy but leaves the reader clueless as to how to implement this remedy. His recommendation of the demographic form is a great idea, but he fails to describe how this information is to be used. Who collects this information, and once collected, who contacts the perspective member, and how to conduct an interview, as well as what questions to ask and not ask?

The membership committee should be empowered to review the new member's information. A workshop is conducted to teach people what to look for in the personal information. The next step is to create a membership profile. From the profile, the membership committee can choose which synagogue activities would interest the new member and then schedule a meeting with the new member to present activity recommendations.

At one time becoming a member meant completing a membership application accompanied by a check and by completing this task the new member will engage in synagogue activities. We have discovered that that assumption is no longer valid. People are looking to become actively engaged in a synagogue community; they just need a helping hand to reach out and guide them.

As rabbis we are involved with change, whether we are the initiators or facilitators. I find the *Maariv* prayer offers exceptional insight:

בָּרוּךְ אַתָּה יְיָ, אֱלֹהֵינוּ מֶלֶךְ הָעוֹלָם
אֲשֶׁר בִּדְבָרוֹ מַעֲרִיב עֲרָבִים
בְּחָכְמָה פּוֹתֵחַ שְׁעָרִים
וּבִתְבוּנָה מְשַׁנֶּה עִתִּי
וּמַחֲלִיף אֶת הַזְּמַנִּים

In the *Maariv* prayer there are two words for change: *mishaneh* and *machalief*. I have highlighted those words. *Mishaneh*, I believe, means "slow change." Through the magic of midrashic thinking, *mishaneh* can be Mishnah, Mishnah refers to study, and study, at least for me, is a slow process.

The verb *machalief* in modern Hebrew is used as *machalief kasef*, that is, the exchange of money, from shekels to dollars, or dollars to shekels, an immediate change.

There are two types of change, long term and immediate. The change from "dues" to "investments" and "members" to "investors" will not change the existing financial structure. It will be an immediate change as it enters normal synagogue conversation, but it will be long-term change for people to internalize the concept.

The Meet and Greet program is a long-term change. Congregants will recognize their responsibilities now include the mitzvah of welcoming the stranger. They will learn how to approach the visitor and engage in conversations. Considering the training workshops will be the beginning of the program, this will be a change that will require time.

The new approach as inspired by the redesigned membership application will also require time and patience. Congregants will learn how to interpret the information and become familiar with a follow-up procedure.

Whether the change is *mishaneh* (long term) or *machalief* (immediate), rabbis and lay leaders must practice patience and compassion as our congregants struggle with these new changes to synagogue culture. We know that these changes will improve the quality of Jewish life and enrich the life of our synagogues.

Notes

1. Rabbi Lawrence A. Hoffman, *Rethinking Synagogues: A New Vocabulary for Congregational Life* (Woodstock: Jewish Lights, 2007), 2.
2. Dr. Ron Wolfson, *Creating Sacred Communities* (Encino, CA: Kripke Institute, 2022), 55.
3. Michael Paulson, "The 'Pay What You Want' Experiment at Synagogues," *New York Times*, February 2, 2015.
4. Paulson, "The 'Pay What You Want' Experiment."

Book Reviews

From Strength to Strength: Finding Success, Happiness, and
Deep Purpose in the Second Half of Life
by Arthur C. Brooks
(New York: Portfolio/Penguin, 2022), 273 pp.

In his new work, *From Strength to Strength: Finding Success, Happiness, and Deep Purpose in the Second Half of Life*, Arthur C. Brooks reflects on his own life experience, and on popular social science around how to create meaning in the second half of life. Brooks warns that the skills that make one successful in one's younger years will eventually degrade, and that one needs a different plan for the second half of life. I think the book is best directed to those in the prime of their working years, particularly very successful middle-aged men in lucrative careers. Brooks speaks of the "striver's curse" and of the danger of allowing an addiction to work to occlude other aspects of life. He warns that structural changes in the brain make professional decline inevitable as one becomes less good at inventing ideas, solving problems quickly, and multi-tasking —what he terms "fluid intelligence." Using examples of both famous and more anonymous individuals, he describes the emotional pain some experience in their later years, feeling irrelevant, unnecessary, and lacking meaning in their lives.

But the news for rabbis is not all bad. There are other kinds of intelligence that improve with age. Brooks points to "crystallized intelligence," which allows us to become wiser rather than smarter, to teach well, and to synthesize and utilize complex ideas. This form of intelligence is probably more important in our field of work. Our work is more like that of historians who peak 39.7 years after the onset of their careers and less like those in business who tend to peak two decades after starting out. Though Brooks considers writers among those who peak on the earlier side, I can't help but think of Philip Roth and others who continue to create great, and sometimes even greater, masterpieces in their later years. In addition, those rabbis who work as part of a team can benefit from the talents of younger colleagues, while drawing on the skills that develop through experience.

Brooks has had an interesting life, having to give up his aspirations to become a concert musician, earning his academic degrees relatively later in life, and more recently, leaving behind a ten-year stint as the director of a nonprofit organization, the American Enterprise Institute, to move into teaching and writing. An added dimension of the work is the way Brooks draws from his own experience of Catholic spirituality as well as his deep interest in Indian and Hindu teachings. He includes prayers of personal meaning to him throughout the book. Developing one's spiritual life is a recommendation he makes in the strongest terms—and one that I believe rabbis would welcome for themselves and their congregants.

It was particularly interesting that Brooks, who focused much of his professional life advocating a very strong individualism in American economic life, stressed the importance of relationships and community to a good life. Using the image of the aspen and redwood trees, he stresses how interconnected we are as humans, something our Jewish communitarian tradition also stresses. Brooks suggests beginning to focus on relationships well before entering the second half of one's career, and he comments on the loneliness of many in high prestige occupations. He notes that another adjustment is to more highly value our spousal relationships. Our children grow up and lead their own lives.

While the book is so au courant that sometimes I felt that Brooks was overdoing it in talking about every contemporary social science trend, I do think those with "first world problems" will find it a convincing argument to rethink their current practices, pay more attention to their lives, and focus on building a life of meaning.

RABBI MELANIE ARON (NY81), rabbi emerita of Congregation Shir Hadash in Los Gatos, California, is currently residing in Washington DC with her husband, and regularly spending time with her grandson. She appreciates the welcome she received from the community of retired rabbis in the area and has gotten involved in environmental activism.

Power and Gender in Rabbinic Sexual Abuse
A Review Essay
Rabbi Rachel Adler, PhD

Reviewing
When Rabbis Abuse: Power, Gender, and Status in the Dynamics of Sexual Abuse in Jewish Culture
by Elana Sztokman
(Lioness Books and Media, 2022), 442 pp.

Not long ago, rabbis' sexual abuses were subjects of whispered gossip or confidential committees that often exonerated them or administered slaps on the wrist. Now, newspapers and legal notices announce perpetrators and penalties. Organizations like HUC-JIR and the CCAR have *t'shuvah* committees and Zoom sessions where survivors tell each other their stories and weep together. Dr. Elana Sztokman, an anthropologist, feminist, Jewish educator and publisher, and veteran of several Jewish organizations, has written a comprehensively researched book in which she documents rabbinic sexual abuse and analyzes its strategies and impacts not only on its victims but on Jewish institutional structures and communal life across the Jewish spectrum. Sztokman establishes conclusively that these types of abuse occur across all the movements of Judaism —from ultra-Orthodox to Jewish Renewal.

Organization of the Book

When Rabbis Abuse is meticulously researched and carefully organized. Sztokman seems aware that those readers who most need information may be reluctant to read. Consequently, she begins each chapter with an outline and ends with two pages of essential takeaways. Footnotes are immediately accessible at the bottom of the page. The book includes an extensive index of topics and names and nineteen pages of bibliography.

The book is divided into five sections, each containing two to four chapters:

- Part 1 consists of the stories of victimization.
- Part 2, titled "The Abuse Process," is the largest section. In four chapters it details the grooming tactics of abusers, abuser

profiles, settings conducive to abuse, and Gender Abuse—the discriminatory dynamic that leads to sexual abuse. Most researchers have not linked gender discrimination inherently to sexual abuse, but Sztokman argues that gender discrimination is, in fact, a form of abuse that creates inhospitable work and social environments ripe for sexual abuse. She also maintains that sexual abuse correlates with lower status and lower social power.[1] A statistical study of sexual abuse in various religions that she cites finds that over 95 percent of victims of sexual exploitation by clergy are adult women.[2] Informal as well as formal social hierarchies support abuse, Sztokman contends.[3] Women as a group are lower status community members than men, but those who have other markers of low status such as underage girls, converts, Jews of color, gay/ l lesbian, nonbinary, or trans Jews are at even great risk.[4] Chapter 3 addresses abuse by donors and other celebrities, some of them well-known predators whose behavior was tolerated or ignored because their financial or charismatic contributions to the organization were so highly prized that they were permitted to abuse with impunity the female staff or the organization's clients (such as campers, students, or members of congregations). Chapter 6 of this section analyzes profiles of some notorious abusers.

- Part 3 describes what happens when victims disclose and report, and the types of responses they receive from the community. Disclosure means the victim's divulging to someone else that they were sexually abused by someone. Reporting means informing authorities so that the complaint can be followed up. Reporting seldom results in any action to investigate, much less curb, the abuser. Most victims never report. Sztokman explains that reporting requires confronting the trauma, the possibility that they will not be believed, and that they may be blamed or face retaliation, all realistic apprehensions. Silencing the complainant is a common response to reporting.[5]

- Part 4 discusses the impacts on victims and on the Jewish community. As participants learned by listening as victims shared the impacts upon them and their careers in public meetings, the wounds can last a long time. The impacts on Jewish communities that Sztokman lists are costly: losses of Jewish connection, of able Jewish professionals and women rabbis, and of dedicated volunteers.

- Part 5 offers conclusions. Chapter 13 suggests some similarities between abuse in Jewish communal culture and that of other faith communities. Sztokman contends that a shared characteristic in all faith communities is clergy abusers tending to be narcissists who assume a godlike role.[6] In all faith communities, pastoral care is a prime setting for preying on the vulnerable. In all, institutions are protected at the expense of victims. And in all, victims experience spiritual impacts that estrange them from their faith and faith communities.

More Than Narcissism

My one concern about this otherwise excellent book is that it oversimplifies the reasons why rabbis abuse and reduces them to the single clinical diagnosis of Narcissistic Personality Disorder. There are many other possible reasons:

- Some rabbis were never taught the rules about appropriate rabbinic boundaries with congregants. The remedy for that is better rabbinic education.
- Some rabbis have a one-time transgression incident because of some traumatic circumstance in their own lives. Such rabbis can be often completely rehabilitated with professional psychological counseling and an intensive review of the rules.
- Some rabbis have other undiagnosed psychological problems, some of which could be ameliorated by therapy.

The most basic rule for rabbinic boundaries that should be impressed upon every rabbis is that *there can be no true consent to intimate relationships where one party possesses significantly more power, authority, privilege, or credibility than the other.* That is why doctors cannot have sexual relationships with their patients, or adults with children, or caregivers with developmentally disabled persons. Moreover, *when participants have simultaneously an official or professional relationship and a secret intimate relationship, the secret relationship subverts the goals of the official relationship.* The original and publicly known goal is to benefit the less powerful or knowledgeable participant: counseling, education, healing, or spiritual enlightenment. The revised, exploitative goal substituted in the secret intimate relationship benefits the more powerful and more authoritative party.[7]

Sztokman is undoubtedly correct that people with Narcissistic Personality Disorder should not become rabbis, nor should people with Borderline Personality Disorder. Personality Disorders are a category of mental illnesses that involve long-term patterns of behavior and thinking and are resistant to treatment.[8] They require expert diagnosis, and even experts at interpreting psychological tests like the MMPI, which HUC-JIR has used in addition to psychological interviews for screening applicants, sometimes fail to see problematic symptoms or behavior that manifests later. Without the judgment of a trained diagnostician, however, labeling people as narcissists is just name-calling. People who have full-blown personality disorders (as opposed to tendencies) have limited ability to differentiate between their own desires and goals and those of other people and limited ability to change their behavior.

Theologically and ethically, we would have to say that because of these deficits, persons suffering from personality disorders have impaired ability to do *t'shuvah*. In the *yeshiva shel maalah* such diagnoses should result in mercy for the offender, but *yeshivot shel matah*, such as the CCAR Ethics Committee, also have an obligation to prevent future victimizations. Given the number of perpetrators who are known to have perpetrated multiple times, perhaps when a rabbi is found to have violated the ethics code, a trained diagnostician should be asked to determine the likelihood that the violator is capable of behavioral and moral change.

Accurately identifying people with personality disorders and not admitting them to rabbinic school would be the first line of defense. Expelling them from rabbinic school when they have demonstrated that they didn't understand that this was wrong, would be the second line of defense. Expelling them from the rabbinical organization would then become the third line of defense. In every context, taking women's reporting seriously would be an essential preventative measure.

Balancing Charisma with Empowerment

Sztokman's demonization of charisma is also unnuanced. Undeniably, some people use their charisma to exploit and abuse others, but there are rabbis, teachers, leaders, and performance artists who have considerable charisma and yet have learned the discipline of *tzimtzum*, contracting ourselves so that there is room for others to grow and to shine. Expanding to fill the entire universe, metaphorically, is not charisma but rather the *abuse* of charisma. Treasuring charisma needs to be balanced by equally valuing the ability to facilitate others' growth and empowerment.

Some people have a natural gift for facilitation, but most people can learn to do it successfully. However, facilitating and empowering requires an equally invested partner: a learner willing to take risks and make efforts to master what is still unknown. Learning makes us vulnerable. We must begin by acknowledging that we don't know—yet. We must make mistakes and be unskillful at first. We must curb our frustration and learn patience. It helps a lot when the teacher/facilitator/empowerer praises our efforts, comforts us in our failures, rejoices with us in our triumphs, but only the learners themselves can put in the sweat and tears it takes to master something new. Just being an audience for someone else's charisma is far less risky and much less effort, and that is the seduction of charisma for its audiences. Of course, most audiences get bored eventually and must seek out a new source of charisma. In contrast, people who have been empowered can go on learning, can empower others, can contribute their skills to a community. Then many people can share the spotlight during services, learn from one another, or take on leadership roles. The more generous we are and the more appreciative of everyone's efforts, the more we feel competent and necessary, the more cohesive and respectful a community we can build.

Perhaps the most important area in which we have work to do to ensure congregant safety is pastoral counseling. Many of Sztokman's interviewees confirmed that pastoral counseling was the settling for their abuse, and Sztokman copiously documents additional cases from other sources. Unlike therapists who may be required by state law or the standards of their professional associations to have supervision, most rabbis who counsel have no supervision at all. When a case touches their personal issues or they experience sexual countertransference from a counselee, they have no designated person or setting to which they can bring their problem. If rabbis formed supervision groups and hired an experienced therapist to supervise them, they would not have to wrestle with tumultuous feelings all alone. Supervisor and supportive peer groups could support struggling counselors and help them maintain professional boundaries. In addition, pastoral counselors should be required to take a seminar every year to update their information and refresh their skills.

When rabbis abuse, the stakes are very high. In 1993, I wrote

> When a physics professor or a plumber is exposed as a sexual [perpetrator], physics and plumbing are not discredited. But . . . the entire enterprise of Judaism is called into question by the rabbi's infraction. Because Judaism is not a body of objectively verifiable data or technology but rather a particular way of being in the world, it has no credibility independent of its practitioners. Hence, the most convincing advocacy for the Jewish way of being in the world is the rabbi's embodiment of its transformative effects upon the rabbi's self. If, after all the rabbi's learning and observance, Judaism has failed to make the rabbi a better human being, congregants are entitled to wonder whether Judaism has any real effect upon human character and whether the synagogue's religious project is a sham and a scam.[9]

Knowing Elana Sztokman, I feel certain that this is what she would want as well. In the meantime, *When Rabbis Abuse* is a powerful analysis of what should not be happening. It is up to us to create the policy and safeguards that will ensure everyone's safety.

Notes

1. Elana Sztokman, *When Rabbis Abuse: Power, Gender, and Status in the Dynamics of Sexual Abuse in Jewish Culture* (Lioness Books and Media, 2022), 139 (hereinafter Sztokman).
2. Mark Chavez and Diana Garland, "The Prevalence of Clergy Sexual Advances toward Adults in Their Congregations," *Journal for the Scientific Study of Religion* 48, no. 4 (2009): 817–24; Sztokman, 15.
3. Sztokman, 139.
4. Sztokman, 15.
5. Sztokman, 265–66.
6. Sztokman, 336.
7. Rachel Adler, "A Stumbling Block Before the Blind: Sexual Exploitation in Pastoral Counseling," *CCAR Journal* 60 (Spring 1993): 15–16.
8. American Psychiatric Association, *Diagnostic and Statistical Manual of Mental Disorders*, 5th ed. (DSM-5), https://psychiatry.org/psychiatrists/practice/dsm.
9. Adler, "A Stumbling Block," 25.

RABBI RACHEL ADLER, PhD (LA12) is professor emerita of Modern Jewish Thought at HUC-JIR/LA and author of *Engendering Judaism*. Her article on rabbinic sexual misconduct appeared in the *CCAR Journal* (Spring 1993).

The Beauty of Dusk: On Vision Lost and Found
by Frank Bruni
(New York: Avid Reader, 2022), 307 pp.

One morning, in 2017, award-winning *New York Times* columnist Frank Bruni awoke to a new reality. Overnight he had experienced a stroke in one of his optical nerves; one eye was permanently and seriously compromised. "I went to bed believing that I was more or less in control of my life—that the unfinished business, unrealized dreams and other disappointments were essentially failures of industry and imagination and could probably be redeemed with a fierce enough effort. I woke up to the realization of how ludicrous that was" (p. 1).

Well, not quite. The "realization of how ludicrous that was" would take months and years. In this work Bruni takes us on his personal journey in his sixth decade of life as he learns to cope with the real, and increasingly realized, facts of aging and diminishing ability. The book, published in 2022, takes note of the COVID-19 pandemic and how the blend between enforced and voluntary social distancing has seemingly irrevocably changed how we see ourselves, how we see and interact with others and how they see and interact with us. Plus, there is the indisputable fact of our aging. He writes, "To what extent do I accept it, recognizing that there comes a time definitely as we grow older, where we can't do what we once did and must say goodbye to certain aspirations and feats? Defiance or resignation?" (p. 16). He remembers the essence of what a professor had said when Bruni was in college, "Life . . . is about adjusting to loss" (p. 38).

As the subtitle of this work indicates, this book is about vision lost and found. Vision, of course, in the double sense, literally seeing, and then seeing conceptually. A cup-half full can be an image that is "workable and totally plausible . . . It has a moral: While we have minimal control over events that befall us, we have the final say over how we regard and react to them" (p. 86). As a successful journalist, Bruni interviewed hundreds, possibly thousands of people; numerous of them are household names. Many of them populate these pages, and after a while there is a sense of name-dropping. Still, in many cases he focuses on people who are facing life-threatening or certainly potentially life-limiting circumstances through illness or accident. Unsurprisingly, many are vision-compromise-related. In one way or another, the message that keeps repeating in various forms throughout the book is what was just mentioned, "While we have minimal control over events that befall us, we have the final say over how we regard and react to them."

In terms of medical care, Bruni reminds us that "Doctors are flawed. They're human. We want them to be gods, because we want that certainty, that salvation. We want clear roles: The doctor commands; the patient obeys. But, at times, in their imperfection and arrogance and haste, they make assumptions and mistakes. So, it's crucial to approach a relationship with a doctor, any doctor, as a partnership and to consider yourself an equal partner, respectful but not obsequious, receptive but skeptical" (p. 59).

A bit further in the book Bruni observes, "To feel sorry for yourself is to ignore that *everyone* is vulnerable to intense pain and that almost everyone has worked or is working through some version of it." He then goes on to write, "'Why me?' There's a better question, of course: 'Why *not* me?'" (pp. 106–7, emphases in original).

When faced with life-threatening or life-diminishing circumstances, Bruni observes that "there comes a fork. A decision . . . [One either gives in to one's] sadness and scaredness or [one takes] . . . deliberate, concrete steps to move beyond them . . . Let me amend that: There can be a few such make-or-break passages. A series of forks. They can be the products of unusual hardship, physical or psychological; they can be the wages of normal aging. When they happen, you're tested, and you can either determine that as long as you're alive, you have to keep moving, or you can be so thrown by how much less easily you move that you go nowhere at all" (pp. 136–37). Bruni does not reference Deuteronomy 30:19, "Choose life," but that is his message. We do have choices. He learns anew his "fresh appreciation of the bounty in [his] life" and how his life is fuller when he tries to be "unhurried about [them]— 'mindful' would be the more fashionable word" (pp. 214–15).

There is wisdom in this book, yet there is much that can be skimmed over. One might quibble over the question if we need to know that he enjoys the company of his dog, or that he made an effort to see his niece in a high school production. Likewise, that he has been on numerous cruises, had assignments in exotic places, and that he was, for a period of time, the *NYT* restaurant critic. Yet if these are the examples that address the bounty in his life, then so be it.

There are important lessons for us in this work. They apply to our own lives, and oftentimes they will be applicable to the lives of those whom we counsel. To sum up the message of the book: "Life . . . is about adjusting to loss." "While we have minimal control over events that befall us, we have the final say over how we regard and react to them." "To feel sorry for yourself is to ignore that *everyone* is vulnerable to intense pain and that almost everyone has worked or is working through some version of it." As Bruni observes, "'Why me?' There's a better question, of course: 'Why *not* me?'"

RABBI DAVID J. ZUCKER, PhD (C70) retired in 2011 as director of Chaplaincy Care at Shalom Cares in Aurora, Colorado. His book *American Rabbis: Facts and Fiction*, 2nd ed. (Wipf and Stock, 2019) considers the real American rabbinate and how it is reflected in fiction. He is the author with Moshe Reiss, z"l, of *The Matriarchs of Genesis: Seven Women, Five Views* (Wipf and Stock, 2015).

A God We Can Believe In
edited by Richard Agler and Rifat Soncino
(Eugene, OR: Wipf and Stock Books, 2022), 222 pp.

Over the extended course of the long "SCOTUS wars," a common trope has been that presidents need to appoint "the most qualified candidate" to the high court. I once asked my congregant, a substantial legal mind who himself has presented before the Supreme Court, what he thought. He responded thusly, "There are hundreds of jurists who fit in that category but almost by definition, they are all in their seventies. And what president wants to appoint a justice who will serve for little more than a decade?"

I thought of this conversation while reading *A God We Can Believe In*. Noting that of the twenty-eight contributors, no less than sixteen self-identify as "emeritus/emerita" rabbis, scholars, or professors, I realized this speaks to both the consistently high caliber of the contributions, but also to the limitations of this anthology. But first, the contents.

Our colleague Rifat Soncino proposes a definition of "religious naturalism," mostly in a time-honored Jewish way, by saying what it is not. I understand his definition, but to paraphrase another justice, I still can't fully define religious naturalism, though I know when I see it. To me, (I'm about to mix metaphors) it looks like a banyan tree—it has many visible supporting roots. In this book we encounter those roots: Kaplan's and Gittlesohn's transnaturalism, Slonimsky's and Kushner's limited God theology, Fromm's religious humanism, Schulweiss's predicate theology, and even some process theology. The two authorities most cited, however, are Maimonides and the creator of Polydoxy, my teacher Alvin Reines. Perhaps the most surprising authority cited is A. J. Heschel. Certainly, despite his grand-glorious rhetoric about the Divine, Heschel was a limited-God theologian. He was also a passionate advocate of divine pathos. He was constantly running toward, rather than retreating from, God as person (or personality).

Plucking pieces from these intersecting, sometime competing, roots, the book prepares for us a rich repast. This stew is, not surprisingly, theology-heavy. The editors, for example, add again to their earlier thoughtful and useful interpretations of Judaism from an anti-supernatural perspective. I particular appreciated Sandy Sasso's foray into process theology, embedded in her career-long project of expressing theology through children's literature

The frequent discussion of, and appeal to, Maimonides also draws attention to some tension over how to create a Judaism that better reflects naturalism. A particular preoccupation of some contributors is the often-problematic language of our siddur. There are several appeals to further reform our prayers to better reflect a modern naturalistic understanding of the cosmos. This is understandable. Our people's prayer book was largely composed when our relationship to deity was not only perceived as personal, but also transactional (see *The Gift* by Marcel Mauss and *On Sacrifice* by Moshe Haberstal). Supplication and petition were, for most of human religion, the norm. But this same critique applies to our Torah. Yet it is clear that the essays focused on text study celebrate the authority to read our sacred scriptures intact, yet as analogy, allegory, and myth (the title of my essay on sacred study in *The Sacred Encounter*). This is in keeping with the spirit of Maimonides, who despite his discomfort with the more human and transactional aspects of our *mesorah* regarding God, to my knowledge, he never proposed rewriting our prayers.

Truly, our inherited metaphor of God as king is a broken metaphor, for how many of us have any experience with actually royalty? At the same time, substitute metaphors proposed, like "energy" and "force," are every bit as problematic. We experience energy, but we are not obligated to venerate it, nor do we even think to do so. We are familiar with force, but that does not inspire us to worship it. If even familiar personalist metaphors like "father/mother" "judge/friend" are also irredeemably misleading, this calls into question the very rubric of prayer, not simply its rhetoric. Conversely, if we can metaphorize our Torah (I read no proposal to discard it, or even revise it), why is changing the words of our liturgy imperative?

I would be remiss if I did not note the sparsity of women contributors. By my count, there are only four. This is a problem in itself, but brings me, indirectly, back to my opening remarks. The chief limitation I see in this otherwise worthy anthology is that it overwhelmingly represents thinking and reasoning from a relatively narrow slice of time in the intellectual history of American Jewry. It is by and large rooted in the last quarter of the twentieth century, when over half of the contributors received their religious training and engaged in their active rabbinate or were employed in their scholarly positions. Women rabbis and philosophers were rare, if they existed at all, and their impact was only beginning to be felt. I was pleased to see Ralph Mecklenburger incorporated more recent neurological research into why people are religious. Other than that, we read only smatterings of postmodern religious thought, embodied or engendered theology, or other more current ways of framing the religious experience from the younger contributors. Not at all to suggest that the earlier greats are not still great. They have not changed, in that regard. It's just that we have.

Still, despite these reservations, I recommend this work. If not entirely a framework, certainly a fertile ground on which future Jewish religious naturalism can grow and flourish.

RABBI GEOFFREY DENNIS (C96) is rabbi of Congregation Kol Ami in Flower Mound, Texas, adjunct instructor in Jewish Studies at the University of North Texas, and the author of two books. His most recent article, "Avenged Seven-Fold: Monster Theory and the Golem in European Cinema," is awaiting publication.

Search: A Novel
by Michelle Huneven
(New York: Penguin Press, 2022), 400 pp.

The departure of a senior clergy leader from their pulpit is sure to rouse ripples of change throughout the community. Many rabbis in our ranks have witnessed this transition or experienced it personally when making a professional change. In this novel, the task of calling a new spiritual leader is presented from the particular point of view of a lay search committee at a midsized Unitarian Universalist Church, but readers with congregational experience will find in it the universal feelings of frustration and humor faced when shouldering the future of a beloved institution. This work of autobiographical fiction is told through the eyes of Dana Potowski, a restaurant food critic, disaffected churchgoer, and onetime seminarian. In hopes of finding her next book, Dana applies to join the search committee for a new minister while secretly taking notes for a memoir (with recipes!) about the experience. Thus, this meta-book provides a description of the yearlong process of discernment, surveys, applications, and interviews in real-time through the lenses of committee meetings, retreats, and congregational votes. The narrator moves from a blasé opinion of religious organizations to a fervent hope that she alone can protect the fate of her community. At its heart, this novel calls into question who is qualified to guide a diverse communal institution and who is responsible for putting said guide at the helm.

The fictional plights of Huneven's UU Church will feel familiar to congregational leaders of all faith backgrounds. Issues faced include sectarian divisions in their ranks, significant questions of theology, the relative emphases on preaching and pastoral care, the use of technology in ritual, the place of innovation versus tradition, and most of all, who will cater the next meeting? As a food writer, Huneven and her alter ego narrator devote a portion of the text to covering the meals and mixology that sustain the search committee during their crusade. (Look out for a shoutout to matzah!) This combination of passions highlights the committee's dual yearning for spiritual and earthly sustenance.

Rabbinic readers will benefit from a vicarious view from the pews, even in a religious tradition other than Reform Judaism. While many of us have endured a placement process replete with occasional turbulence, this novelization from the other side of the interview table provides fertile grounds for clerical self-reflection. Some of the candidates portrayed here defy belief with their respective egotistical charades, but behind the humor is an earnest hope for integrity and humility among religious leaders. Abuse of power, fiscal irresponsibility, and plagiarism are all showcased among the vices of the clergy applicants.

The committee members are also not without fault—the meetings reveal their individual pettiness and an age-based division over "wokeness." Even after taking a course on bias awareness, the committee squabbles over the right "vibe" for their congregation. Questions emerge over "How Things Must Be" and whether it is necessary to change for the sake of change. Though ostensibly burdened with holy purpose, the committee's progress is challenged by mundane inanities and underhanded machinations. Each of the search committee members must question whether they individually represent the collective.

It doesn't take much imagination to see that this "Search" is for more than a new clergy leader. Potowski contends with what she calls "midlife spiritual drift" and pins her own hopes for the future of religious life on the pursuit of a new minister. Her ploy seems doomed by the unpredictability of communal shifts despite strenuous planning processes. The outgoing minister warns Potowski that "not everyone survives prolonged exposure to all the behind-the-scenes and inner workings of an institution" (p. 14). Can earnest optimism endure the absurdity and lack of control promised by a congregational search? Readers of Stephen Fried's *The New Rabbi* will recognize a glimpse of a seldom publicly revealed but regularly experienced episode for institutions of American religious life.

RABBI BENJAMIN ALTSHULER (C20) serves the Jewish communities of the Northwoods at Mt. Sinai Congregation in Wausau, Wisconsin. He also serves on the rabbinic council for Avodah, of which he is an alumnus.

The Third Temple
by Abraham B. Yehoshua
(Hakibbutz Hameuchad Publishing, 2022), 64 pp. In Hebrew.

The Third Temple is the last book by Abraham B. Yehoshua (1936–2022), on the short list of Israel's premier authors as well as peace activists such as Amos Oz and David Grossman, known for their center-left political and social orientation. Yehoshua ended advocating for a binational Jewish and Palestinian state while giving up on his long-held two-state solution. He asserted that only Israel should be the Jewish people's home. The *New York Times* dubbed him, "The Israeli Faulkner."

Just as his previous book, *The Only Daughter*, based in Italy, delved into the inevitable complexities and contradictions of

Jewish identity in postmodern times, so does Yehoshua's final intricate and colorful novel, which is light in size but profound in issues. His literary, as it were, last will and testament is treated through the author's trademark of highly critical and sarcastic lenses and lessons, aimed at the Orthodox religious establishment as well as controversial aspects of rigid halachah.

Labeled as a "dialogical novel," there are only a few participants in the book's lively interaction that would befit a dramatic theatrical play. Esther Azulai is the French daughter of a secular French Jewish father originally from Algiers and her French mother who gave up her Catholic faith to get married. Sephardic Rabbi Nisim Shoshani who officiates at Tel Aviv's Rabbinic Court, *Agunot* Department, is handling Esther's case at the request of Rabbi Yisrael Chalfon, Tel Aviv's Head of Rabbinic Court. Curiously, Yehoshua's grandfather, a rabbi, who was Head of Jerusalem's Sephardic Court, taught young Yehoshua, a fifth-generation Jerusalemite, religious studies. In time, the author eschewed a sectarian identity, regarding himself as a proud secular Israeli and "free Jew." Rabbi Shoshani's secretary, Yechiel Berkovitz, is an Ashkenazi *chozer b't'shuvah* engaging on the side as a mohel for Sudanese and Filipino migrant families in South Tel Aviv, wishing for their sons to be accepted in Israeli society. Moriah Shoshani, the rabbi's wife, has the practical concern of maintaining a home kitchen of fresh produce, items she directs her husband to buy near his office.

Esther's case dilemma involved a Rabbi Eliyahu Modiano who came to Paris from Israel and befriended her father at the Sorbonne while exerting Jewish influence on him: "The bond between my father and Rabbi Eliyahu Modiano was interesting, for seemingly two worlds met here—the religious and the secular— finding a common language that expressed beneath the intellectual tension both curiosity and hope to dwell together, moving toward a peaceful solution" (p. 25). It reflects Yehoshua's leading drive to seek compromise between opposing views. Rabbi Modiano referred to Professor Leibovitz of the Hebrew University whom Esther's father appreciated given their mutual unorthodox Jewish approach.

Rabbi Modiano taught Esther Hebrew—with her father's permission since he only embraced the State of Israel as a secular entity —prompting her to move to the Jewish State. However, it was

Rabbi Modiano who complicated matters, suggesting converting Esther since arguing that her mother's *giur* was blemished. All that served the rabbi's unholy goal to attract Esther, who was destined to fall in love with David Mashiach, a Persian Jew who as a *kohein* could not marry a *giyoret*. Mashiach's successful carpet business took him to Iran on his French passport. Just as Queen Esther disrupted Haman's evil plot so did Esther in an act of revenge scheme to deprive Rabbi Modiano—though she initially liked him as a father figure following her father's death—of the desired post as head of the wealthy Parisian Jewish community's rabbinic court. Thus, she planned for Rabbi Chalfon to win the prestigious position, reminiscent of the Scroll of Easter's plotting and counter-plotting in the ancient Persian spirit. Perhaps it was Esther's intent to be released by grateful Rabbi Chalfon from Rabbi's Modiano's erected obstacle of her need for *giur,* that she may marry after all her beloved David Mashiach.

Esther reminds Rabbi Shoshani of a case when prime minister Ariel Sharon directed an Orthodox rabbi to approve the marriage of a war hero amputee who was a *kohein* to a *giyoret* from the Soviet Union, "Here, Mr. Rabbi, when the Rabbanut is threatened it bows before a prime minister demanding to honor a wounded soldier's love" (p. 55). Upon Rabbi Shoshani lightly responding that should we have a war so that David Mashiach gets wounded, Esther continues with a heartful testimonial, "True, your honored rabbi, David is not war-wounded, but I myself am wounded of a war in this people since receiving the Torah, thus a permit should be found to allow a *kohein* who thought he was only a Mashiach, to marry his beloved instead of threatening his father through his synagogue not to receive an *aliyah* to the Torah" (pp. 55, 56).

To Rabbi Shoshani's puzzled inquiry into Rabbi Chalfon's preference of Paris with its hundred thousand Jews over Tel Aviv with almost a million Jews, Rabbi Chalfon does not mince words concerning how secular Tel Aviv disdains him, "What this *Chareidi*, parasite who lives off us, dares to severely treat us, to rob us of our freedom that we deserve just like the French and the English; after all we came here to be a nation like all other nations, and this dark one plots to damage our deserved normalcy" (p. 38). Whereas in Paris "when a Jew identifies me in the street he is filled with joy and honor that I, a Jew prior to Jesus, a Jew whose Temple was destroyed as his Jerusalem holy city, returned to his land and to control his destiny and he is still alive, walking around the world, faithful to his Torah and proud and with God's help will yet build the Third Temple" (pp. 38, 39).

The surname Mashiach, common among Persian Jews, turns into a bridge of discussion between Esther and Rabbi Shoshani—who too is enamored with her—on the building of a Third Temple in Jerusalem, though the Orthodox rabbi shockingly doubts it while Esther is in full support. What a moving example of the author's playful twist! But Esther's idea of a Third Temple is not the traditional one on the Temple Mount with the offering of animal sacrifices. Rather, she envisions a modest structure outside the Old City with choirs singing "hymns of revival and hope and not supplications for sins' forgiveness accompanied by the blood of innocent animals cruelly slaughtered" (p. 59). This kind of uplifting and bloodless service will awaken dead multitudes on Mount of Olives and worldwide with the Messiah's personal involvement. To Rabbi Shoshani's chagrin Esther brings up Jesus —a suggested reminder of her Christian-born mom—whose millions of followers are included in the anticipated universal redemption.

Abraham B. Yehoshua concludes his inspiring literary career and dedicated life of service with valuable insights through a somewhat eccentric protagonist whose complicated and conflicted Jewish identity is no barrier and even a key asset, unlocking in a contemporary courageous Esther spiritual audacity and personal integrity lacking in beleaguered rabbis as expressed by an irate author with both sharp indignation and soothing humor.

RABBI DR. ISRAEL BOBROV ZOBERMAN (C74) is founder and spiritual leader of Temple Lev Tikvah and Honorary Senior Rabbi Scholar at Eastern Shore Chapel Episcopal Church, both in Virginia Beach, Virginia. He is a past member of the *Journal*'s editorial board. He translated all the quotes from the original Hebrew.

The Arc of Our History: A Social and Political Narrative of Family and Nation
by Stanley Ringler
(Jerusalem and Ashland, OH: Geffen, 2022), 837 pp.

Those of us who have been privileged to know Stanley Ringler, our Jerusalem-based (really Mevasseret Zion–based) colleague can recall that over the past several years whenever we asked Stanley what he was up to, he would reply that he was deeply involved in "the book." Well, now the book has been produced, and what a remarkable production it is. Almost as long as *War and Peace*, it similarly contains everything. The book, *The Arc of Our History*, gives us a broad overview of the history of Western Europe; a glimpse into the particular history of Jews within that sphere; an account of the lives of Ringler's ancestors (along with the ancestors of his remarkable wife, Marlene); his own autobiographical memoirs; a vivid presentation of the recent history of the State of Israel; the struggle for the recognition of non-Orthodox religious streams in Israel; and his insightful observations about Israeli politics and policies

Beginning with Ringler's most distant ancestors in Galicia, it places their personal experiences in the context of the great world historical events that shaped those experiences. How many of us would think to put our great grandparents and Napoleon in the same paragraph? Significantly this book offers the readers the challenge of rethinking their understanding of their own lineage: who "their people" were and what historical factors determined their lots in life. Most significantly, the volume offers a remarkable methodology for presenting Jewish history. Ringler looks at Jewish history with both a telescopic lens and a microscopic lens. He gives panoramic presentations of significant moments in world history and beautifully detailed descriptions of the lives of members of his family who were affected by them. His accounts of the lives of his ancestors, especially those of his relatives who escaped from the maelstrom of 1930s Europe, are bracing and moving. As he will in his discussion of his own life, Ringler directs us to see the individual lives of his protagonists as part of the great historic moments in which they lived.

As the book enters the mid-twentieth century, Ringler moves to an autobiographical mode. He shares memories of his own childhood, and his professional career, including his significant achievements as a Hillel Director in Florida, as a member of the national staff of Hillel in Washington DC, and, after his *aliyah*, his various roles in the Israeli Labor Party, the World Labor Zionist Movement, and other progressive programs in Israel. Especially moving is his description of his second *aliyah* to Israel and the challenges he encountered in the process of absorption and acculturation into Israeli life.

For many of the readers of this journal, Ringler's presentation of events now fifty years in the past will resonate with many of their experiences that paralleled his own. Reading *The Arc of Our History*, many of Ringler's contemporaries might be moved to essay their own memoirs, though they would likely lack the breadth and erudition of his. He describes his own involvement in and reaction to historical events in the United States and in Israel that may seem like yesterday to many readers and evoke their own personal reminiscences: the internal battles in the Jewish community about the propriety of criticizing Israeli policy, the movement to free Soviet Jews, and the struggle to reconcile the realpolitik of Israel as a normal nation with the prophetic ideals at the heart of Ringler's and our values as Reform Jews. Ringler writes movingly about his involvement in various efforts on behalf of shaping Israel as a just and inclusive society.

Perhaps the most compelling parts of the book are Ringler's trenchant and insightful description of numbers of the significant events that constitute the history of Israel since his *aliyah* and his insightful and illuminating discussion of many of the issues that have confronted Israel during those years and which continue to bedevil it. Here Ringler shares the deep understanding with which many of us have been familiar from his writing in this journal and in countless other venues. His is a voice both analytic and prophetic —one that continues to demand our attention.

In the process of his autobiographical memoir, Ringler sheds new light on many of the significant events of his lifetime and introduces information that may be unfamiliar even to readers who had themselves participated in these events or considered themselves knowledgeable about them. Ringler's interweaving of his own involvement in these significant historical moments with extensive informative presentations about the moments themselves, evokes the extent to which his life, and the lives of many of his contemporaries, really can be understood as threads in a larger, truly momentous, tapestry. Ringler writes that before his first *aliyah*, he explained his motivation for moving to Israel as follows: "Modern Jewish history was being written in Israel, and I wanted to be a part of this drama" (p. 159). The book is a testimony to the fact that in that aspiration he has succeeded. It is a reminder to many of the readers of his generation that they, in their own ways, were part of the drama of history as well and made their own contributions to it. The book invites us to see the arc of Jewish history, and the historical moments in which we have participated, in a dramatic new light. For that we can be grateful to Ringler for this remarkable labor of love.

RABBI DANIEL POLISH (C68) is the recently emeritized rabbi of Congregation Shir Chadash of the Hudson Valley, LaGrange, New York.

Headstone
by Mark Elber
(Baltimore, MD: Passager Books, 2022), 112 pp.

Post High Holy Days I dove into Rabbi Mark Elber's collection of poems in his latest compilation, *Headstone*. The themes of the season—returning, remembering, and renewing ourselves and our people—remain with me a month after the holy days. Perhaps not intended, Elber's collection helps to keep those themes fresh. In particular, "Headstone," pulled me back into the holy day season with its images of Elber's father's last day at synagogue on Yom Kippur. The importance of that day for him and his family ripples off the pages.

Full of alliteration, secret metaphors, and revealing imagery, Elber describes different parts of his life. He begins with his birth in Astoria, Queens, aligning his birth with the wrestling of Jacob, resulting in a new life for Jacob. Throughout his collection, Elber connects with the words of the *Tanach*, especially the well-known lines from Exodus—"I am that I am" (Exodus 3:7–8, 13–14). He aligns this phrase with Descartes's words, "I think, therefore I am," showing how he has been inspired by both these phrases.

He continues to use unique words to convey his love and awe for his father and their connection. Elber invites us to learn about their relationship through the transportation system of New York. In "Further Notes from the Underground," one sees the city through Elber's young eyes as he rides with his father on the subway. The reader learns more about his father in the poem, "Red Hair," where his father yearns to stay young as he realizes parts of his life are foreshadowing his death. The collection's title poem, "Headstone," describes his father's experience with World War II and his time in concentration camps. In this poem, the reader learns Elber's life history through his father's life. It is effectively a eulogy to his father.

Because so many of the poems include scriptural references, it is easy to see how they could be utilized in our rabbinic work. For example, as a Pittsburgh native, I am inspired to use Elber's poem "Pittsburgh" in the coming years as we observe the anniversaries of that horrific attack. Aside from this personal connection, I hope to use his poems about his wedding and his relationship with his family in upcoming life-cycle ceremonies. "Your Small Hands" would be a great poem for a baby naming or a bris with its images of a "five pound, small lipped, and cheerios."

Rabbi Elber was ordained by ALEPH in 2012 and is the rabbi of Temple Beth El, a Conservative synagogue in Fall River, Massachusetts. He is a certified Jewish meditation teacher. Elber has been writing poetry since he was a teenager, yet this is his first book of poems to be published. I can see his expertise and am in awe of this work. Readers will be able to get a glimpse into Rabbi Elber's life through reading his poetry. More than that, his work offers us the following lesson using High Holy Day themes—to remember is to return to our past. Returning to our past allows us to feel renewed in the new year.

RABBI NATALIE LOUISE SHRIBMAN (C20) is a hospital chaplain at the Marshfield Clinic and a rabbi at Temple Sholom in Eau Claire, Wisconsin. She lives in Wausau, Wisconsin, with her rabbi partner and cat.

Poetry

Homeless No More

I saw a homeless person resting
On a glittering patch of dew-covered grass,
Whose face was turned heavenward
Like Biblical Jacob on the run
Seeking a ladder to escape
Pursuing brother and/or perhaps
Searching for Elijah's fiery chariot
To show the way
In the dark of night,
Safely to return home some day
To yearning mother – earth accompanied
By guiding angels dancing- dangling
On a rope of life -support,
To build a haven-shelter for
The wayward of the world,
Resembling the open tent of Abraham
And Sarah in the wilderness of yore,
Ever ready to absorb today's lost souls
That their dreams too would
Merge heaven and earth!

RABBI DR. ISRAEL BOBROV ZOBERMAN (C74) is founder and spiritual leader of Temple Lev Tikvah and Honorary Senior Rabbi Scholar at Eastern Shore Chapel Episcopal Church, both in Virginia Beach, Virginia. He is a past member of the *Journal*'s editorial board.

The Night Before
My Doctor's Appointment

Richard Fein

I dreamed I was in Israel
and everybody was friendly,
everybody was considerate,
though not towards me
because I had learned Yiddish
and had not learned Hebrew.
I asked my closest friends
if I had made a mistake
and should have learned Hebrew,
the living language of a country.
The alarm clock went off,
sounding at first as if
it was coming from my dream.
Then I lay in bed thinking,
and I decided "No, no,
I should have learned Hebrew."
Then it came to me, "No, no,
no language could save you,
not even Yiddish, not even Yiddish,
nisht afileh Yiddish, nisht afileh Yiddish."

RICHARD FEIN has published twelve books of poetry and three books of translations of Yiddish poetry. He has also published a critical study, *Robert Lowell*; a memoir of Yiddish, *The Dance of Leah*; and a book of personal essays, *Yiddish Genesis*. His latest book of poems is *Losing It.*

Call for Papers: *Maayanot*

The *CCAR Journal: The Reform Jewish Quarterly* is committed to serving its readers' professional, intellectual, and spiritual needs. In pursuit of that objective, the *Journal* created a new section known as *Maayanot* (Primary Sources), which made its debut in the Spring 2012 issue.

We continue to welcome proposals for *Maayanot* —translations of significant Jewish texts, accompanied by an introduction as well as annotations and/or commentary. *Maayanot* aims to present fresh approaches to materials from any period of Jewish life, including but not confined to the biblical or Rabbinic periods. When appropriate, it is possible to include the original document in the published presentation.

Please submit proposals, inquiries, and questions to *Maayanot* editor Rabbi Daniel F. Polish, dpolish@optonline.net.

Along with submissions for *Maayanot*, the *Journal* encourages the submission of scholarly articles in fields of Jewish studies, as well as other articles that fit within our Statement of Purpose.

The *CCAR Journal: The Reform Jewish Quarterly*
Published quarterly by the Central Conference of American Rabbis

Volume LXX No. 1 Issue Number: Two hundred seventy-three
Winter 2023

STATEMENT OF PURPOSE

The *CCAR Journal: The Reform Jewish Quarterly* seeks to explore ideas and issues of Judaism and Jewish life, primarily—but not exclusively—from a Reform Jewish perspective. To fulfill this objective, the *Journal* is designed to:

1. provide a forum to reflect the thinking of informed and concerned individuals—especially Reform rabbis—on issues of consequence to the Jewish people and the Reform movement;

2. increase awareness of developments taking place in fields of Jewish scholarship and the practical rabbinate, and to make additional contributions to these areas of study;

3. encourage creative and innovative approaches to Jewish thought and practice, based upon a thorough understanding of the traditional sources.

The views expressed in the *Journal* do not necessarily reflect the position of the Editorial Board or the Central Conference of American Rabbis.

The *CCAR Journal: The Reform Jewish Quarterly* (ISSN 1058-8760) is published quarterly by the Central Conference of American Rabbis, 355 Lexington Avenue, 8th Floor, New York, NY 10017.

Subscriptions should be sent to CCAR Executive Offices, 355 Lexington Avenue, 8th Floor, New York, NY 10017. Subscription rate as set by the Conference is $140 for a one-year subscription, $250 for a two-year subscription. Overseas subscribers should add $36 per year for postage. POSTMASTER: Please send address changes to *CCAR Journal: The Reform Jewish Quarterly,* c/o Central Conference of American Rabbis, 355 Lexington Avenue, 8th Floor, New York, NY 10017.

Typesetting and publishing services provided by Publishing Synthesis, Ltd., 39 Crosby Street, New York, NY 10013.

Copyediting services provided by Michael Isralewitz.

The *CCAR Journal: The Reform Jewish Quarterly* is indexed in the *Index to Jewish Periodicals.* Articles appearing in it are listed in the *Index of Articles on Jewish Studies* (of *Kirjath Sepher*) and in *Religious and Theological Abstracts.*

GUIDELINES FOR SUBMITTING MATERIAL

1. The *CCAR Journal* welcomes submissions that fulfill its Statement of Purpose whatever the author's background or identification. Inquiries regarding publishing in the *CCAR Journal* and submissions for possible publication (including poetry) should be sent to the editor, Rabbi Edwin Goldberg, at journaleditor@ccarnet.org.

2. Other than commissioned articles, submissions to the *CCAR Journal* are sent out to a member of the editorial board for anonymous peer review. Thus submitted articles and poems should be sent to the editor with the author's name omitted. Please use MS Word format for the attachment. The message itself should contain the author's name, phone number, and e-mail address, as well as the submission's title and a brief author biography.

3. Books for review and inquiries regarding submitting a review should be sent directly to the book review editor, Rabbi Ari Lorge, at alorge6@gmail.com.

4. Inquiries concerning or submissions for poetry should be directed to the editor, Rabbi Edwin Goldberg, at journaleditor@ccarnet.org.

5. Inquiries concerning or submissions for *Maayanot* (Primary Sources) should be directed to the *Maayanot* editor, Rabbi Daniel F. Polish, at dpolish@optonline.net.

6. Based on Reform Judaism's commitment to egalitarianism, we request that articles be written in gender-inclusive language.

7. The *Journal* publishes reference notes at the end of articles, but submissions are easier to review when notes come at the bottom of each page. If possible, keep this in mind when submitting an article. Notes should conform to the following style:

a. Rachel Adler, *Engendering Judaism: An Inclusive Theology and Ethics* (Philadelphia: Jewish Publication Society, 1999), 101–6. [**book**]

b. Lawrence A. Hoffman, "The Liturgical Message," in *Gates of Understanding*, ed. Lawrence A.Hoffman (New York: CCAR Press, 1977), 147–48, 162–63. [**chapter in a book**]

c. Richard Levy, "The God Puzzle," *Reform Judaism* 28 (Spring 2000): 18–22. [**article in a periodical**]

d. Adler, *Engendering*, 102. [**short form for subsequent reference**]

e. Levy, "God Puzzle," 20. [**short form for subsequent reference**]

f. Ibid., 21. [**short form for subsequent reference**]

8. If Hebrew script is used, please include an English translation. If transliteration is used, follow the guidelines in the **Master Style Sheet**, available on the CCAR website at www.ccarnet.org.